Foundation Physics

For Class X

Part-2 of 2

NOTION PRESS

NOTION PRESS

India. Singapore. Malaysia.

ISBN xxx-x-xxxxx-xx-x

Dedicated to our Beloved Prime Minister Shree Narendra Modi ji, whose life gives the Inspiration to every Individual

*If a Man **Decides** to achieve something in his life nothing is Impossible*

कर्मण्येवाधिकारस्ते मा फलेषु कदाचन।

मा कर्मफलहेतुर्भूर्मा ते सङ्गोऽस्त्वकर्मणि॥ २-४७

Karmanye vadhikaraste Ma Phaleshu Kadachana,

Ma Karmaphalaheturbhurma Te Sangostvakarmani

You have the right to work only but never to its fruits.

Let not the fruits of action be your motive, nor let your attachment be to inaction.

CONTENT

TOPIC NAME **PAGE NO.**

4. LIGHT REFLECTION AND REFRACTION

5. HUMAN EYE AND THE COLOURFUL WORLD

4 LIGHT REFLECTION AND REFRACTION

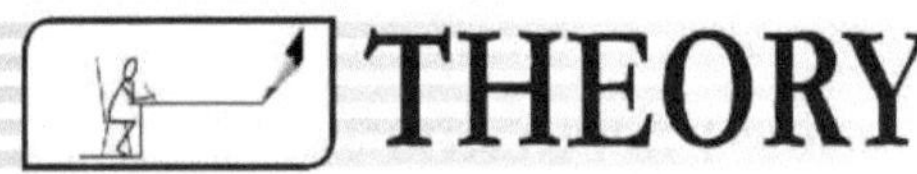

THEORY

4.1 INTRODUCTION

A thought always comes to our mind that how the various things (objects) become visible to us? Which phenomenon is the cause for it? Actually it is the light that helps us in visualizing the objects.

Light is an electromagnetic waves within a small range of wavelength of about 400×10^{-9} m to 750×10^{-9} m.

When the light reflected from an object excites the retina of our eye then the object becomes visible to us. In this chapter, first of all, we will study about the nature of light and will try to understand in what form the light is emitted from a source and it propagates from one place to another place?

After this, we will consider the phenomenon of reflection and refraction, using the ray picture of light. Using the basic laws of reflection and refraction, we shall study the image formation by plane and spherical reflecting and refracting surfaces.

Light is electromagnetic radiation, such as that emitted by the Sun, which acts like a wave in frequency range that the human eye can perceive. At the same time, light also acts like a stream of particles, which are called photons (hence the expression "beam of light"). Electrons emitted from atoms and molecules can split, simply by the impact of photon striking them. A film in a camera is exposed in this way; the light splits the silver bromide into silver and bromine. The silver darkens the film and a negative is created. Light is a combination of electric and magnetic oscillations in mutually perpendicular directions as shown in Figure. But the light wave itself propagates in a direction perpendicular to both the oscillation.

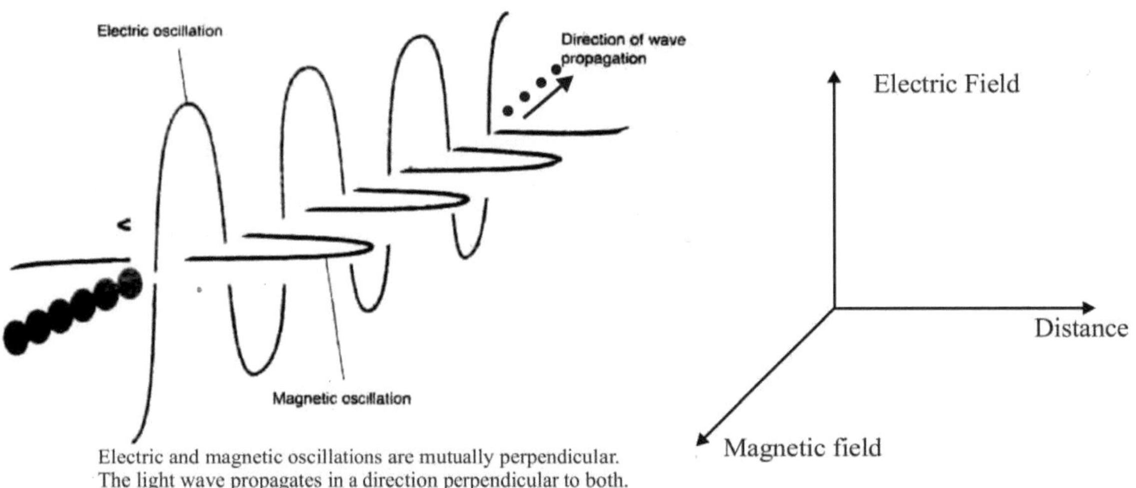

Electric and magnetic oscillations are mutually perpendicular. The light wave propagates in a direction perpendicular to both.

Different theories on nature of light

The different theories proposed by different scientists are as follows.

1. **Electromagnetic theory :** Electromagnetic theory was proposed by Sir, Maxwell. According to him, light is an electromagnetic wave consisting of time-varying electric and magnetic fields. Both the fields are perpendicular to each other and also perpendicular to the direction of propagation of light.

2. **Wave theory :** In 17th century Huygens gave the wave theory, according to which light is a wave, rather than a stream of particles.

3. **Quantum theory :** This theory was proposed by Einstein. According to this theory, light is a bunch of energy, packet of energy or bundle of energy. Each bundle or each packet or each bunch is called a photon. Energy of each photon is

$$E = h\nu$$

where, E = Energy of photon; h = Planck's constant; ν = Frequency of light

4. **Corpuscular theory :** This theory was first proposed by Isaac Newton. According to this theory, light is emitted by a luminous source as a stream of weightless particles called corpuscles. These particles move in straight line with very high speed.

5. **Dual nature of light :** According to de-Broglie, light exhibits both the wave nature as well as the particle nature. In some phenomenon like reflection, refraction, polarization light exhibits its wave nature and can be explained by wave theory. In some phenomenon like photoelectric effect, Raman effect, light exhibits its particle nature and can be explained on the basis of the quantum theory. But de-Broglie proposed that light has a dual nature. The wavelength (λ) associated with any moving particle of momentum 'p' is given by

$$\lambda = \frac{h}{p}$$

where, λ = shows the wave nature, h = plank's constant , $p = mv$ shows the particle nature

4.2 PROPERTIES OF LIGHT

Light is an electromagnetic wave within a small range of wavelength of about 400×10^{-9} m to 750×10^{-10} m. In some phenomena light behaves as particle and in some other phenomena it behaves as wave.

Since wavelength of light is very small compared to the size of ordinary objects that we encounter commonly. So, it can be considered to travel from one point to another along a straight line joining them. The path is called a ray of light, and the bundle of such rays constitutes a beam of light.

The light has the following properties:

(i) Light travels in a straight line

(ii) Medium is not required for the propagation of this wave.

(iii) Velocity of light is maximum in vacuum and is equal to 3×10^8 m/s.

(iv) These waves are transverse in nature and the properties of the medium through which these waves propagate remain unaffected.

Ray of Light

Let us consider a source of light(s). Also consider the light which passes from the point A to the point B in medium.

Actually, the light passes through all the points of the straight line AB. Such a straight line path is called a ray of light, generally represented by a directed arrow (→).

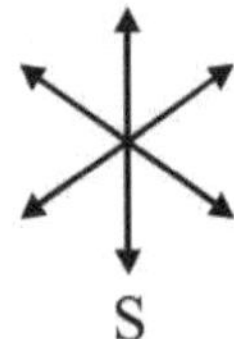

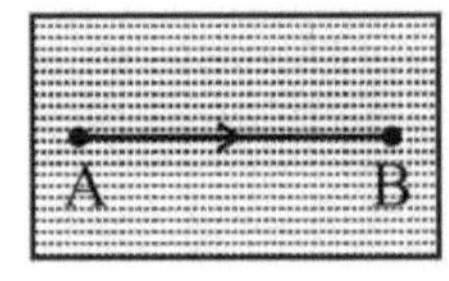

AB is a ray of light in a medium

Beam of Light

A bundle of light ray is called a beam of light. The following figure shows a parallel beam of light.

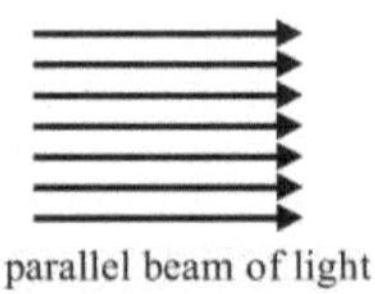

A parallel beam of light

Illustration 1

A person in a dark room looking through a window can clearly see a person outside in the daylight, whereas the person outside cannot see the person inside. Explain.

Solution

When a person inside a darkroom is looking through a window to another person outside in broad daylight, then enough reflected rays come inside to the eye of the observer from the person outside. So he can be seen clearly. But if the person in daylight, looks through the same window to the person inside the dark room, there is hardly any reflected rays coming from the body of person inside the dark room to the eye of the observer outside. So the outside observer can't see the person inside the room.

4.3 REFLECTION OF LIGHT

When a ray of light falls upon any smooth surface, it is sent back into the same medium from which it came. This phenomenon is called reflection of light.

OR

The process of returning (or coming back) the light to the same medium after striking a surface is called reflection of light.

Silver is the best reflector.

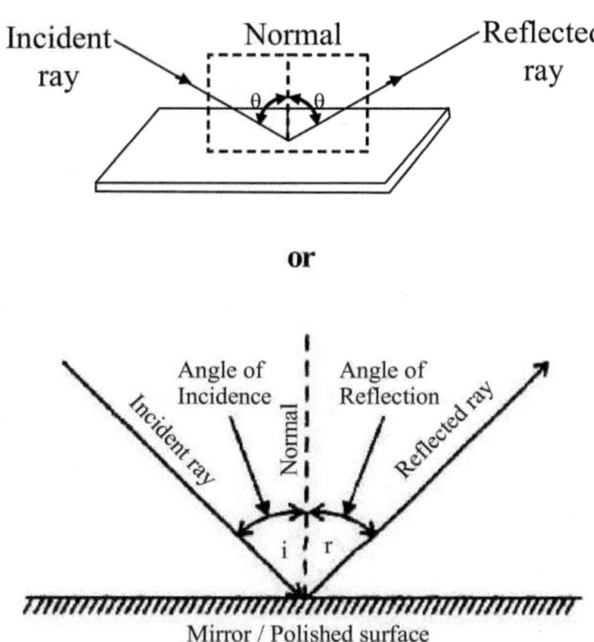

According to the law of reflection ∠i = ∠r.

The incident ray, the reflected ray, and the normal all lie in the same plane.

Laws of reflection

(i) **The angle of incidence is equal to the angle of reflection (∠i = ∠r).**

(ii) **The incident ray, the reflected ray and the normal at the point of incidence, all lie in the same plane.**

Knowledge Enhancer

1. Laws of reflection are applicable for plane surface as well as curved surfaces.

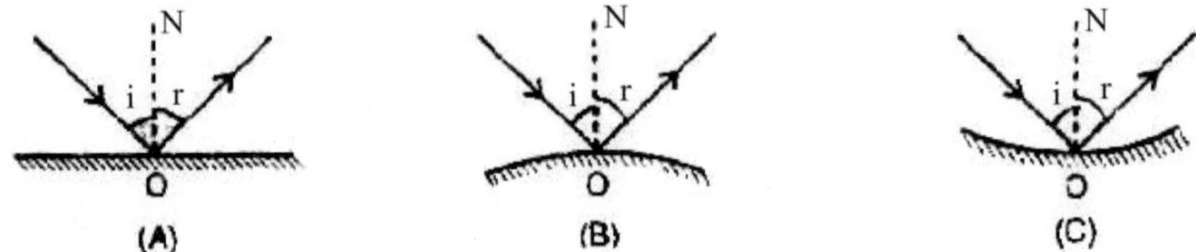

2. Most people are surprised by the fact that light can be reflected back from a denser medium. For instance, if you are diving and you look up at the surface of the water, you will see a reflection of yourself.

Important Information

1. **A ray of light striking the surface normally retraces its path.**

   Explanation : When a ray of light strikes a surface normally, then angle of incidence is zero, i.e. $\angle i = 0$. According to the law of reflection, $\angle r = \angle i = 0$ i.e. the reflected ray is also perpendicular to the surface. Thus, an incident ray normal to the surface (i.e. perpendicular to the surface) retraces its path as shown in figure.

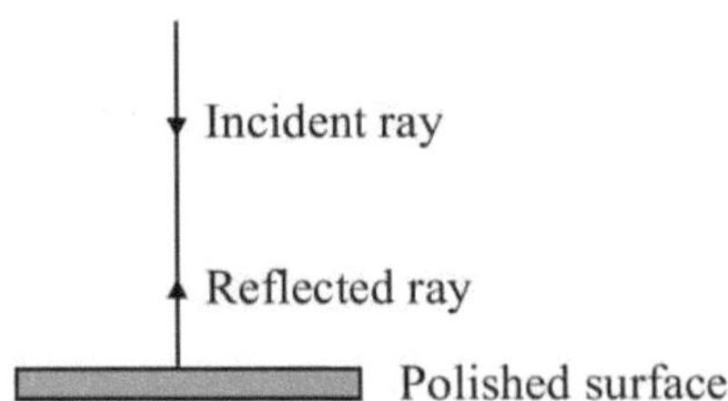

2. Laws of reflection are also obeyed when light is reflected from the spherical or curved surface as shown in figure. **In other words, laws of reflection hold good for all types of mirrors**.

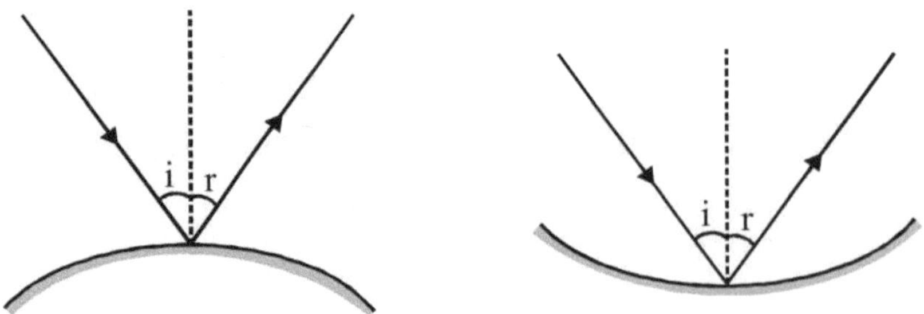

Illustration 2

A mirror is inclined at an angle of θ° with the horizontal. If a ray of light is incident on mirror making an angle θ° with the mirror, then the reflected ray makes the following angle with the horizontal.

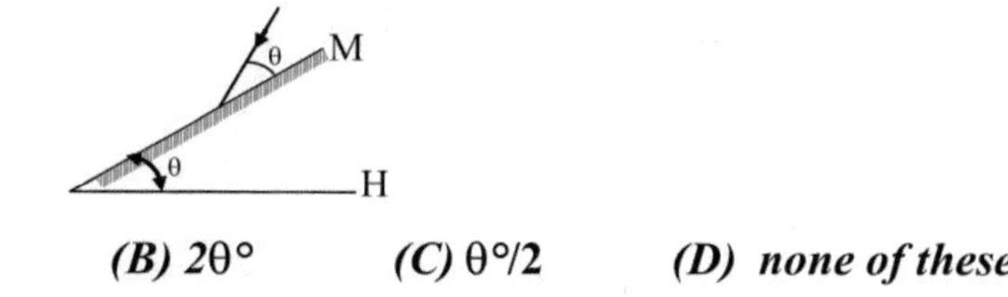

(A) θ° *(B)* 2θ° *(C)* θ°/2 *(D) none of these*

Solution

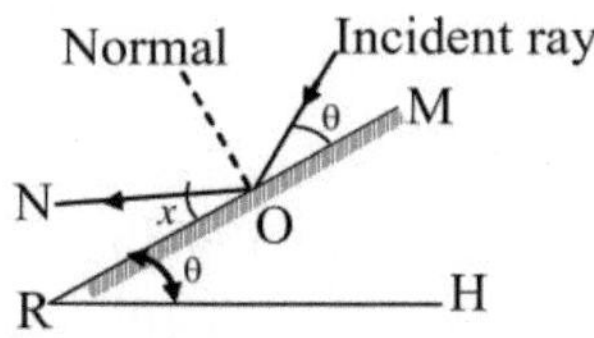

Angle of incidence $= (90 - \theta)$

Angle of reflection = Angle of incidence

$= (90 - \theta)$

But angle of reflection $+ x = 90°$

or $90° - \theta + x = 90°$

or $x = \theta$

or $\angle NOR = \angle ORH$ (but these are alternate angles)

or NO || RH

or Reflected ray is parallel to horizontal

or Angle between reflected ray and horizontal = 0° $\therefore$ **(D)**

4.4 TYPES OF REFLECTION

Regular reflection (or Specular reflection) : When a parallel beam of light falls on a smooth and highly polished surface, then the reflected beam is also parallel and directed in a fixed direction. Such reflection of light is called regular reflection.

The glare of regular reflected light beam is dazzling **Search light** and **Automobile head light** are the examples of regular reflection of light.

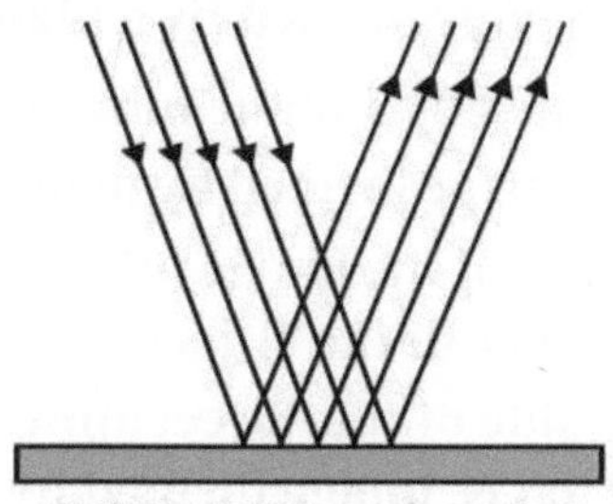

Irregular reflection (Diffused reflection): When a parallel beam of light falls on a rough surface, then the reflected light is not parallel but spreads over a wide area. Such reflection of light is called **irregular** or **diffused reflection**. This type of reflection of light is shown in figure.

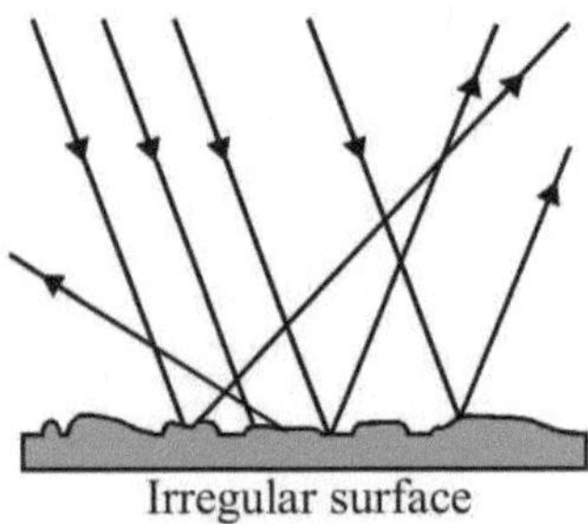

Light reflected from the wooden table, newspaper etc. is the example of diffused reflection of light.

Try yourself

1. A ray of light making an angle 10° with the horizontal is incident on a plane mirror making an angle θ with the horizontal. What should be the value of θ. So that the reflected ray goes vertically upwards?

(A) 20° (B) 30° (C) 40° (D) 45°

4.5 IMAGE

When we stand in front of a looking mirror, we see our face. The picture of our face in the mirror is known as the image of our face. Image are of two types(1) Real image and (2) Virtual image.

(1) **Real Image :** When a beam of light from an object actually meets at a point after reflection, then the image of the object formed at that point is known as real image.

(2) **Virtual image :** When a beam of light from an object does not meet at a point but appears to diverge from it after reflection, then the image of the object at that point is known as virtual image.

S.No.	Real Image	Virtual Image
1	When Rays of light after reflection meet at a point, real image is formed.	When rays of light do not meet at a point but appears to meet at a point, virtual image is formed.
2	Real image can be obtained on a screen.	Virtual image cannot be obtained on a screen.
3	Real image is formed in front of a mirror.	Virtual image is formed behind the mirror.
4	Real image is always inverted.	Virtual image is always erect (i.e. upright).

Properties of the image formed by a plane mirror

(i) Image formed by a plane mirror is virtual and erect.

(ii) Size of the image formed by plane mirror is equal to the size of the object.

(iii) The distance of the image (of an object) behind the plane mirror is equal to the distance of the object from the mirror.

(iv) The right side of the object appears as the left side of its image and vice - versa. That is, image formed by plane mirror laterally inverted.

4.6 REFLECTION FROM PLANE SURFACE

Let's apply ray-diagram methods to the case of an object in front of a plane mirror in order to determine the position of the image of that object. Here's the configuration.

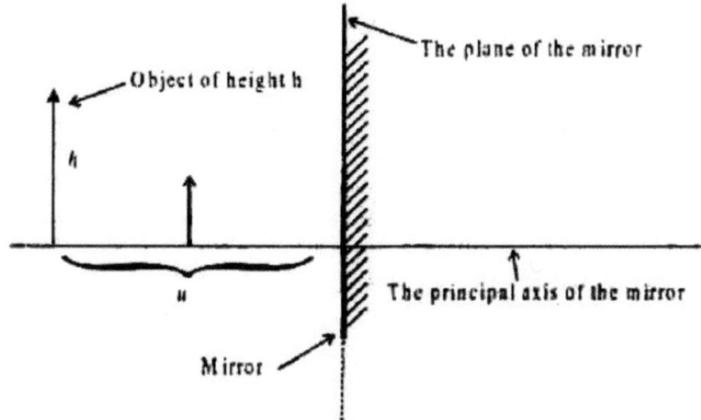

We have an object of height h, at distance u from the plane of the mirror. Our object is represented by an arrow. The tail of the arrow is on a reference line that is perpendicular to the plane of the mirror i.e. the reference line "the principal axis of the mirror." The plane of the mirror is the infinite plane that contains the surface of the mirror.

We use the method of principal rays to determine the position of the image of the object. *In the method of principal rays, we consider only a few incident rays for which the reflected rays are particularly easy to determine.* Experimentally, we find that the position of the image is independent of the size of the mirror, so we consider the mirror to be as large as it needs to be for the principal rays to hit it. In particular, if a principal ray appears to miss the mirror in our diagram, we show the ray as reflecting off the plane of the mirror nevertheless. Our Principal Ray 'I' for the case at hand is one that approaches the plane of the mirror along a line that is parallel to the principal axis of the mirror.

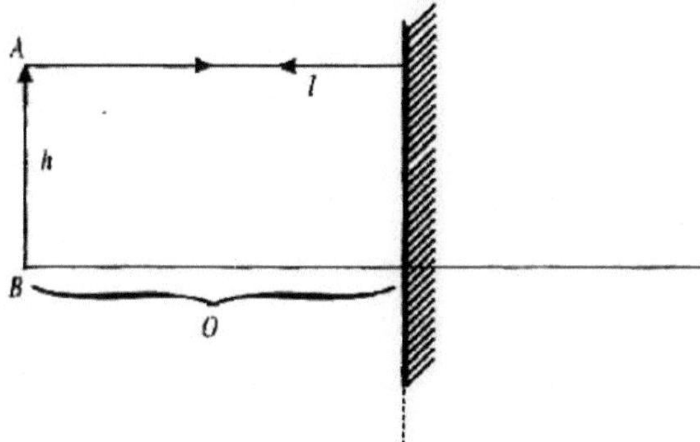

According to the law of reflection, principal ray I is reflected straight back on itself as depicted in the following diagram.

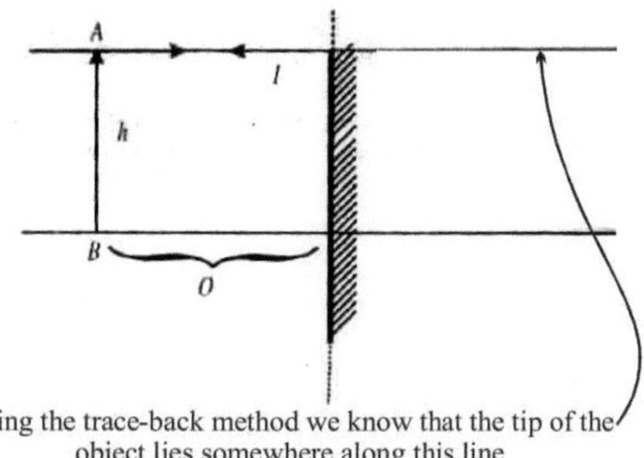

Using the trace-back method we know that the tip of the object lies somewhere along this line

Principle ray II hits the mirror right where the principal axis of the mirror intersects the mirror. In accordance with the Law of Reflection, with, for the ray in question, the principal axis of the mirror being the normal, the reflected ray makes the same angle with the principal axis of the mirror as the incident rays does.

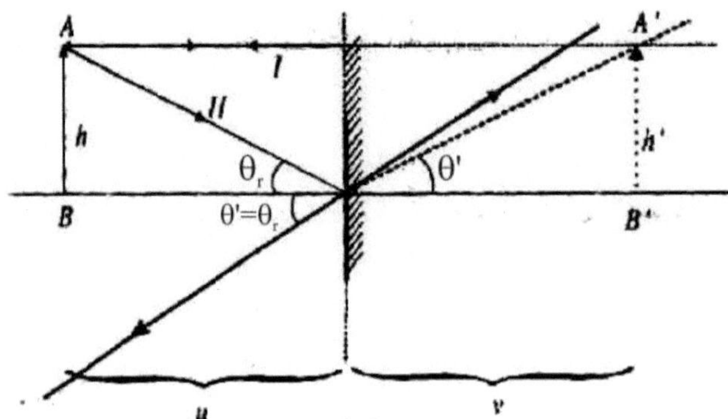

Tracing back the second reflected ray, to the point where it intersects the first reflected ray traceback line, yields the position of the image of the tip of the arrow. The image height h' is the distance between the same two parallel lines that the object height h is the distance between. So h' = h. Since vertical angles are equal, we have θ' in the diagram above being equal to θ_R which we know to be equal to θ_1 from the law of reflection.

Thus the right triangle of side h' and angle θ' is congruent to the triangle of height h and angle θ_1.

Hence, since corresponding sides of congruent triangles are equal, we have v = u. That is to say that the image distance, from the plane of the mirror, is equal to the object distance.

Characteristics of image formed by plane mirror :

1. Distance of object from mirror = Distance of image from mirror.
2. The image is laterally inverted.
3. The line joining the object point with its image is normal to the reflecting surface.
4. The size of the image is the same as that of the object.

(i) For a real object the image is virtual and for a virtual object the image is real.

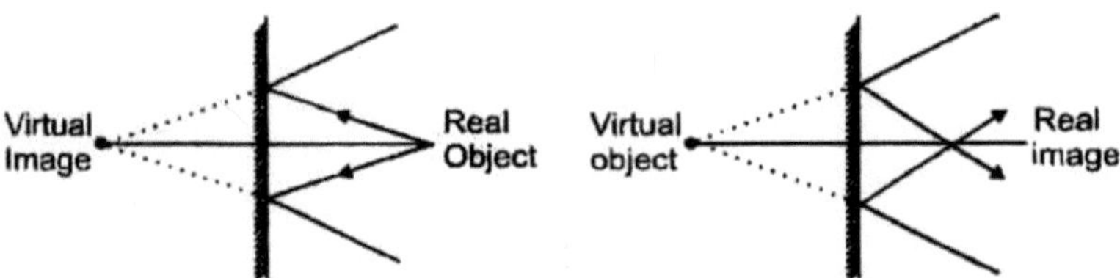

(ii) If keeping the incident ray fixed, the mirror is rotated by an angle θ, about an axis in the plane of mirror, the reflected ray is rotated through an angle 2θ.

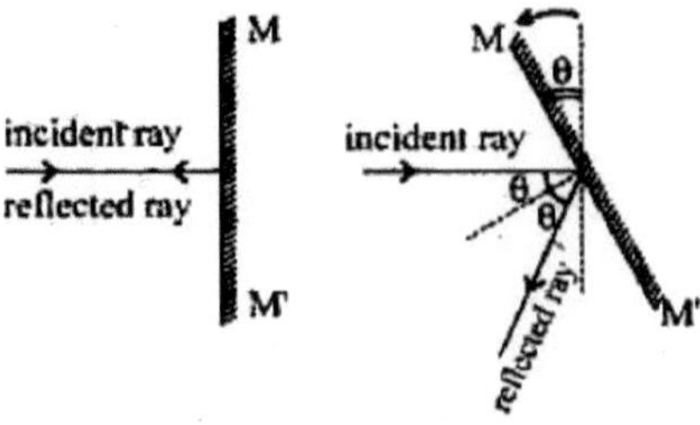

Knowledge Enhancer

1. If two plane mirrors are kept inclined to each other at angle θ with their reflecting surfaces facing each other, multiple reflection takes place and more than one images are formed. Number of images (n) for $\theta \leq 180°$ are given by :

$$n = \begin{cases} \dfrac{360°}{\theta} - 1 \text{ if } \dfrac{360°}{\theta} \text{ is even (object may be placed symmetrically or asymmetrically)} \\ \dfrac{360°}{\theta} - 1 \text{ if } \dfrac{360°}{\theta} \text{ is odd, the object is kept symmetrically (on bisector) w.r.t. the mirrors.} \\ \dfrac{360°}{\theta} \text{ if } \dfrac{360°}{\theta} \text{ is odd, the object is kept asymmetrically (not on bisector) w.r.t. the mirrors.} \\ \dfrac{360°}{\theta} \text{ if } \dfrac{360°}{\theta} \text{ is not an integer.} \end{cases}$$

All this is given below in a tabular form.

S.No.	θ in degress	m = (360/θ)	No. of images formed if object is placed	
			asymmetrically	symmetrically
1	0	∞	∞	∞
2	30	12	11	11
3	45	8	7	7
4	60	6	5	5
5	72	5	5	4
6	75	4.8	4	4
7	90	4	3	3
8	112.5	3.2	3	3
9	120	3	3	2

(a) If an object is placed between two parallel mirrors ($\theta = 0°$), the number of images formed will be $\dfrac{360}{0} = \infty$ but of decreasing intensity in accordance with $I \propto \dfrac{1}{r^2}$.

(b) The number of images formed by two mutually perpendicular mirrors ($\theta = 90°$) will be 3. All these three images will lie on a circle with centre at C – the point of intersection of mirrors M_1 and M_2 and whose radius is equal to the distance between C and object O.

(c) Two mirrors inclined to each other at different angles may provide same number of images, e.g. for any value of θ between 90° and 120° the number of maximum images formed (n) is 3. This in turn implies that if θ is given, n is unique but if n is given, θ is not unique.

(d) The number of images seen may be different from the number of images formed and depends on the position of observer relative to object and mirrors – e.g., if $\theta = 120°$ maximum number of images formed will be 3 (object not on bisector) but no. of images seen can only be 1, 2, or 3 depending on the position of observer.

2. **If an object moves towards (or away from) a plane mirror at speed v, the image will also approach (or recede) at same speed v, i.e., the speed of image relative to object will be $v-(-v)=2v$. Similarly if the mirror is moved towards (or away from) the object with a speed v the image will move towards (or away from) the object with a speed 2v.**

3. To locate the image of an object from an inclined mirror, see the perpendicular distance of the object from the mirror.

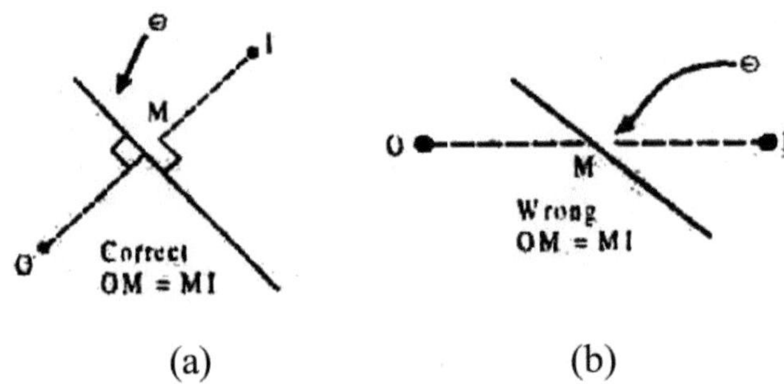

(a) (b)

4. If angle between two mirrors is θ after consecutive reflection total deviation $d=\delta_1+\delta_2=2\pi-2\theta$.

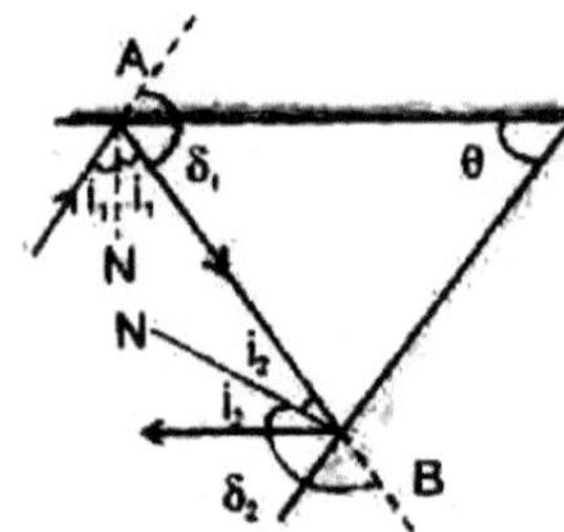

4.7 REFLECTION FROM SPHERICAL SURFACE

CURVED OR SPHERICAL MIRRORS

A curved or spherical mirror is the reflecting part of a spherical surface.

Types of (polished) spherical mirrors. There are two types of spherical mirrors:

1. Concave Mirror 2. Convex Mirror

1. **Concave mirror**: Concave mirror is the part of a hollow sphere whose outer surface (i.e. bulging surface) is silvered and the inner surface (i.e. depressed surface) acts as reflecting surface (polished) (As shown in the figure below).

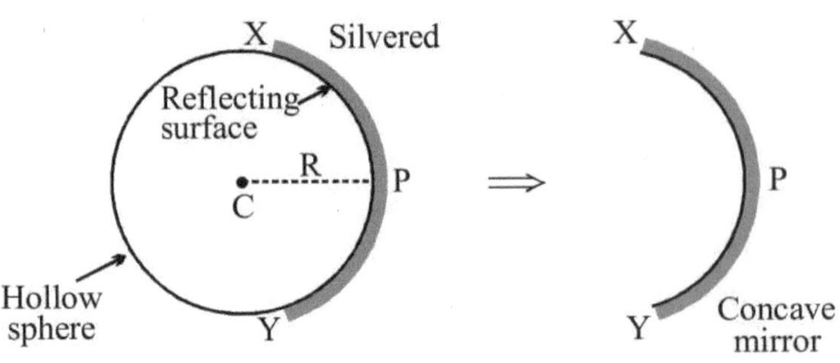

2. **Convex mirror:** Convex mirror is the part of a hollow sphere whose outer surface (i.e. bulging surface) acts as a reflecting surface (polished) and the inner surface (i.e. depressed surface) is silvered (As shown in the figure below).

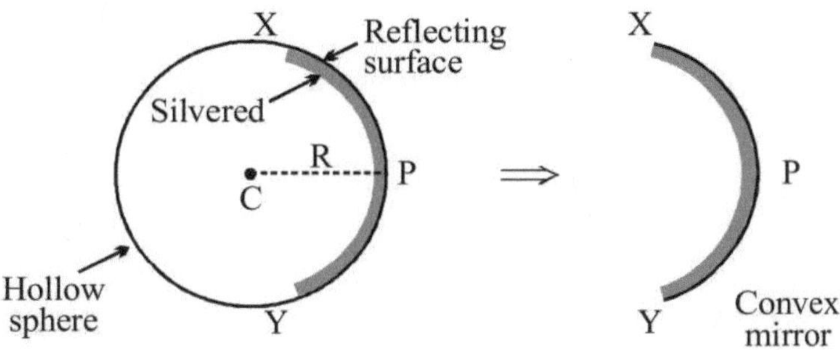

Convergence and divergence of light

Convergence of light: If a parallel beam of light after reflection meets at a point, then the process is known as convergence of light.

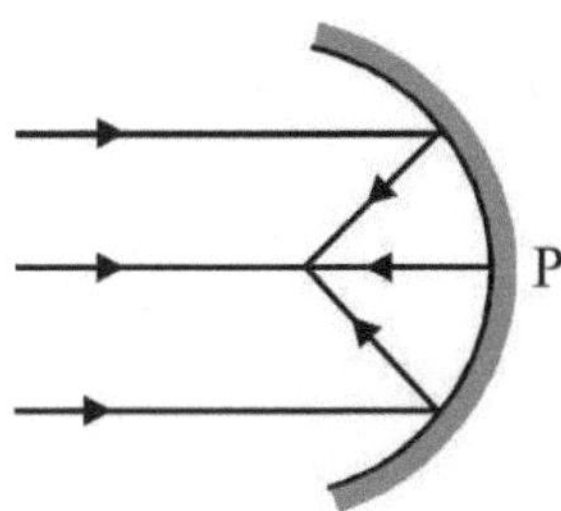

Concave Mirror

Divergence of light: If a parallel beam of light after reflection diverges (i.e. spreads out) and appears to come from a point, then the process is known as divergence of light.

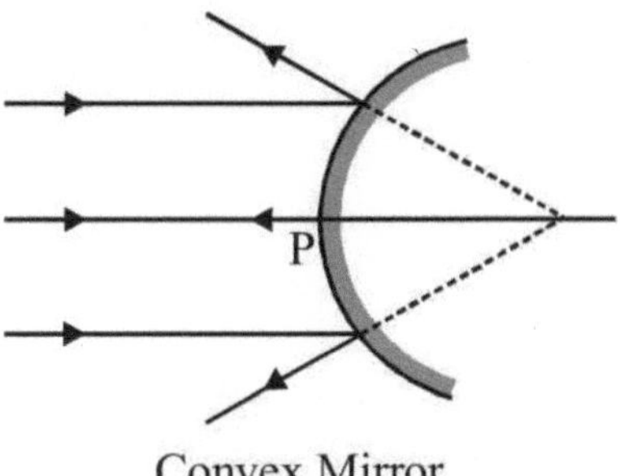

Convex Mirror

(i) Concave mirror converges a parallel beam of light falling on it, so concave mirror is also known as **convergent mirror.**

(ii) Convex mirror diverges a parallel beam of light falling on it, so convex mirror is also known as **divergent mirror**.

4.8 IMPORTANT TERMS WITH RESPECT TO SPHERICAL MIRRORS

1. **Centre of curvature:** The center of a hollow sphere of which the curved or spherical mirror forms a part is called centre of curvature. It is denoted by C.

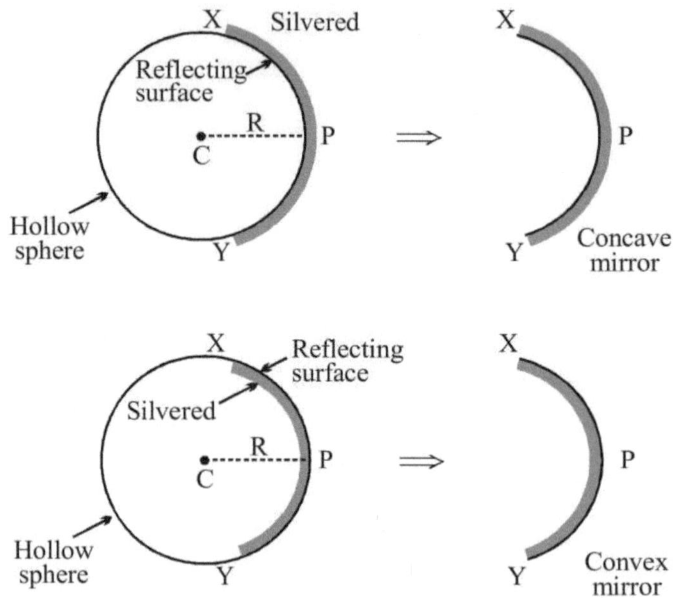

2. **Radius of curvature:** The radius of a hollow sphere of which the spherical mirror forms a part is called radius of curvature. It is denoted by R.
3. **Pole:** The mid point of a spherical mirror is called its pole. It is denoted by P.
4. **Aperture:** The part of a spherical mirror exposed to the incident light is called the aperture of the spherical mirror. In other words, diameter of a spherical mirror is known as its aperture. The apertures of a concave mirror and a convex mirror are represented by XY as shown in figure.

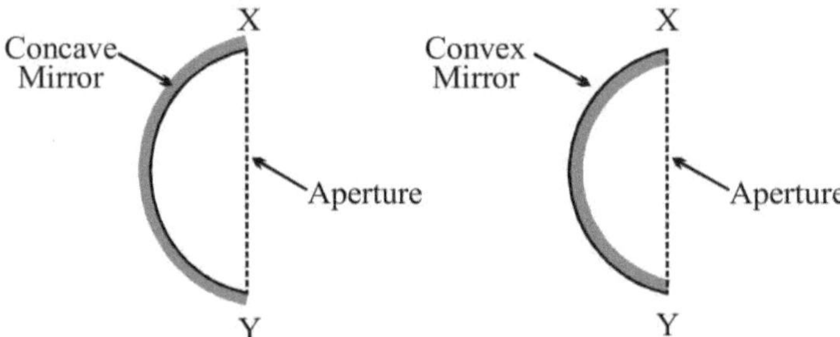

5. **Principal Axis:** A line joining the centre of curvature (C) and pole (P) of a spherical mirror and extended on either side is called principal axis .
6. **Principal Focus:** A point on the principal axis of a spherical mirror where the rays of light parallel to the principal axis meet or appear to meet after reflection from the spherical mirror is called principal focus. It is denoted by F.
7. **Focal Plane:** A plane normal or perpendicular to the principal axis and passing through the principal focus (F) of a spherical mirror is called focal plane of the spherical mirror.
8. **Focal length:** The distance between the pole (P) and the principal focus (F) of a spherical mirror is called the focal length of the mirror. It is denoted by f. Focal length of a mirror is given by f = PF

Important Terms

(i) **Pole :** The centre of the spherical mirror.

(ii) **Centre of Curvature :** Centre of the sphere of which the mirror forms a part.

(iii) **Radius of curvature :** The radius of the spherical surface of which the mirror is a part.

(iv) **Linear aperture :** Distance between two extreme points on the periphery of the spherical mirror.

(v) **Angular aperture :** The angle which the periphery of spherical mirror subtends at the centre of curvature.

(vi) **Principal axis :** The line joining the pole and the centre of curvature.

(vii) **Principal focus (F) :** The point on the principal axis at which all the light rays parallel to the principal axis after reflection from the spherical mirror converge (concave mirror) or appear to diverge from (convex mirror).

(viii) **Focal length (f):** The distance between the pole and principal focus denoted by f.

(ix) **Paraxial rays :** The rays parallel and close to the principal axis.

(x) **Marginal or Peripheral rays :** The rays parallel and away from the principal axis and strike the mirror near its boundary.

(xi) **Focal Plane :** Plane passing through the principal focus and at right angles to the principal axis.

4.8.1 Rules for constructing the images formed by spherical mirrors

To construct the ray diagram, in order to locate the image of an object, it is convenient to consider only two rays.

The intersection of at least two reflected rays give the position of image of the point object. Any two of the following rays can be considered for locating the image.

(i) A ray parallel to the principal axis after reflection passes through (concave) or appear to come from the principal focus (convex).

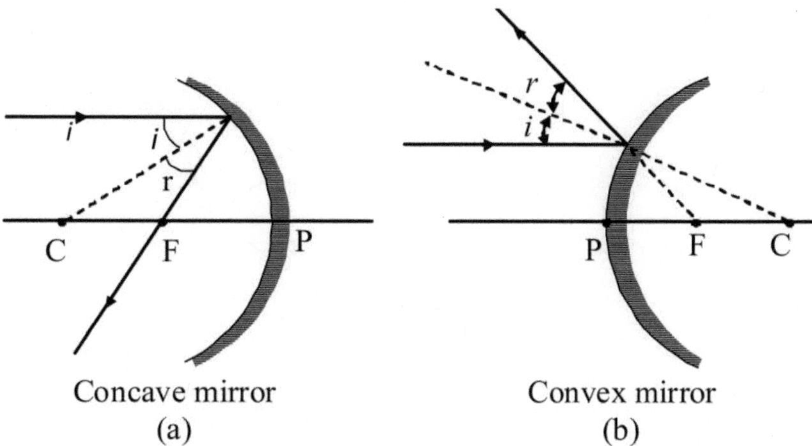

Concave mirror
(a)

Convex mirror
(b)

(ii) A ray which passes through (concave) or directed towards (convex) the principal focus after reflection becomes parallel to the principal axis.

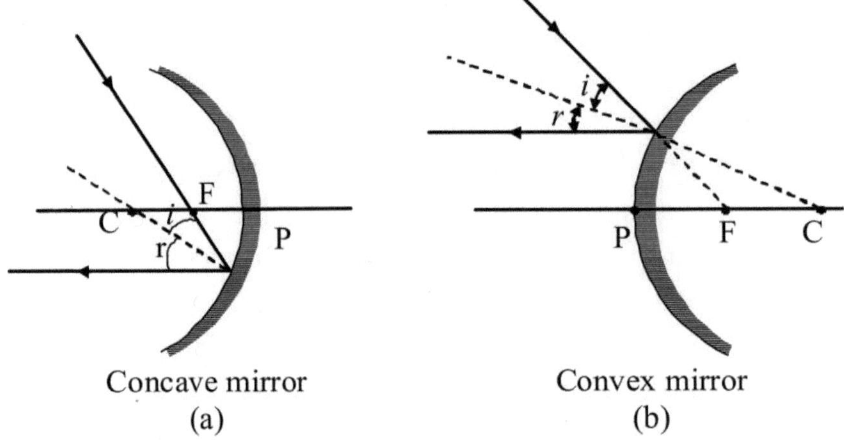

Concave mirror
(a)

Convex mirror
(b)

(iii) A ray which passes through the centre of curvature after reflection retraces its path back.

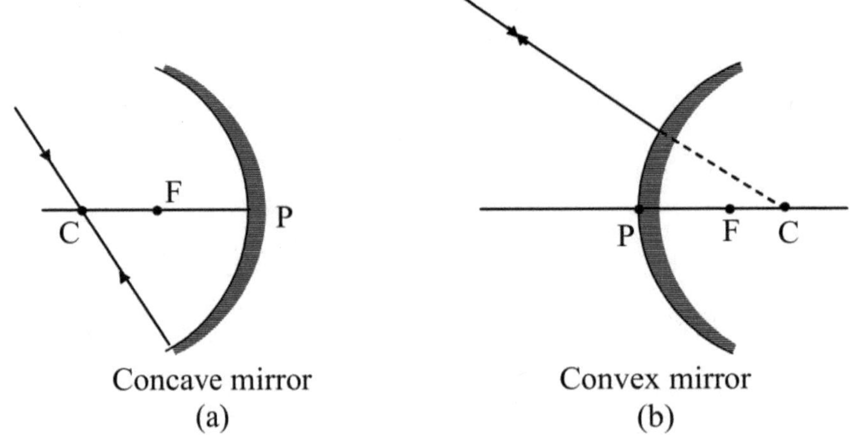

Concave mirror
(a)

Convex mirror
(b)

(iv) A ray of light incident at the pole and making an angle with the principal axis, after reflection goes on the other side of the principal axis making the same angle with it.

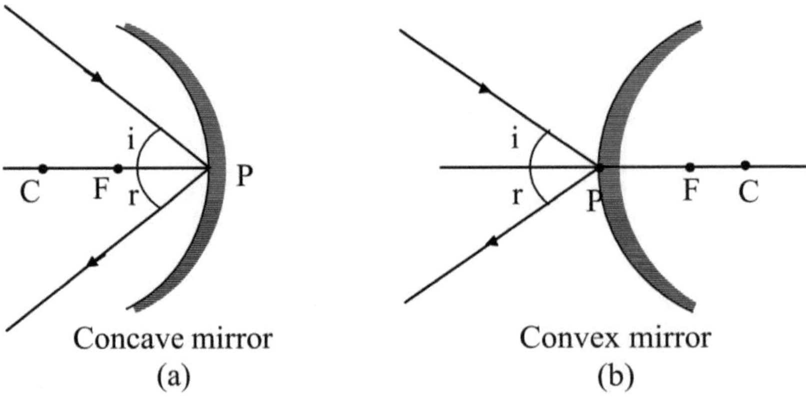

Concave mirror
(a)

Convex mirror
(b)

4.8.2 Sign convention for reflection by spherical mirrors

While studying the reflection of light by spherical mirrors and formation of image by spherical mirrors, we use some sign conventions as given below:

1. All distance are measured **from the pole** of a spherical mirror.
2. Distance measured **in the direction of incident light** are taken as **positive** while distance measured **in a direction opposite to the direction of the incident light are taken as negative.** (As shown in the figure below).
3. The **upward distance** perpendicular to the principal axis are taken as **positive**, while the **downward distance** perpendicular to the principal axis are taken as **negative**.

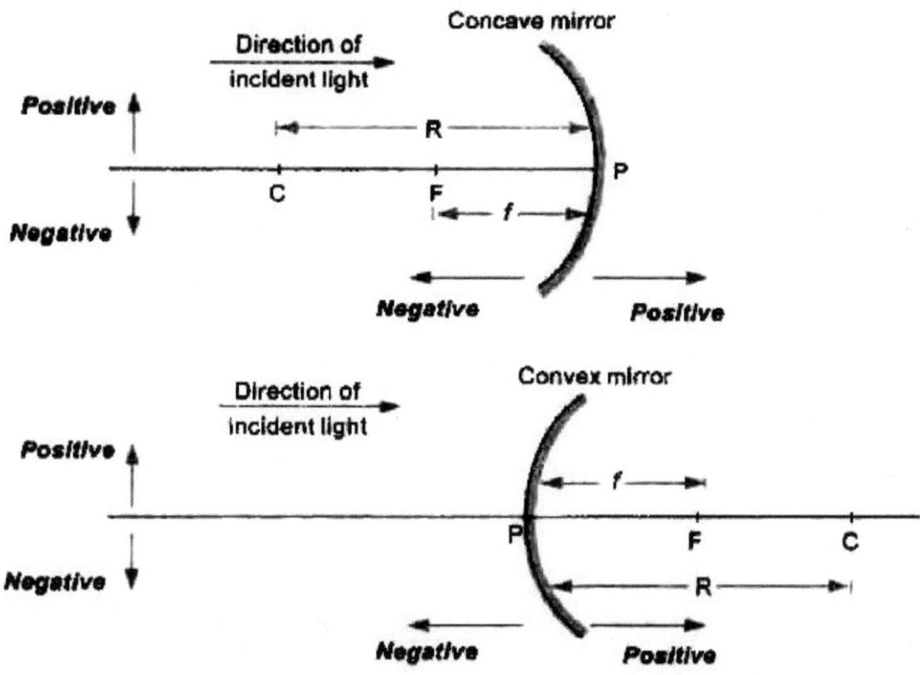

1. **Focal length and radius of a curvature of a concave mirror are taken as *negative*.**
2. **Focal length and radius of curvature of a convex mirror are taken as *positive*.**

4.8.3 Image formation in case of spherical mirrors

(i) As the object gradually moves from infinity towards the focus of a concave mirror, the image moves from focus to infinity. The image formed is real, inverted and its size increases gradually.

(ii) As the object comes at the focus of the concave mirror, its real inverted and highly magnified image is formed at infinity.

(iii) As the object come between the focus and pole of the concave mirror, its virtual, erect and magnified image is formed behind the mirror.

(iv) As the object gradually moves from infinity towards the pole of a convex mirror, then irrespective of the placement of the object in front of the mirror, the image formed is always virtual, erect and diminished and is formed behind the mirror. The size of the image goes on increasing as the object is moved closer to the mirror.

Image formed by the concave mirror

Position of object	Position of image	Nature	Figure
At infinity	At the focus	Real, inverted & diminished	
Between infinity & centre of curvature	Between focus & centre of curvature	Real, inverted & small in size	
At centre of curvature	At centre of curvature	Real, inverted and of the same size	
Between Focus & centre of curvature	Between centre of curvature and infinity	Real, inverted and enlarged	
At Focus	At infinity	Real, inverted and very large	
Between Focus & Pole	Behind the mirror	Erect, virtual & enlarged	

4.8.4 Applications / uses of a concave mirror

1. **Reflector :** Concave mirrors are used in motor head lights, search lights and torches etc., to produce an intense parallel beam of light. A bulb is placed at the focus of a concave mirror. The beam of light from the bulb after reflection from the concave mirror goes as a parallel beam (figure).

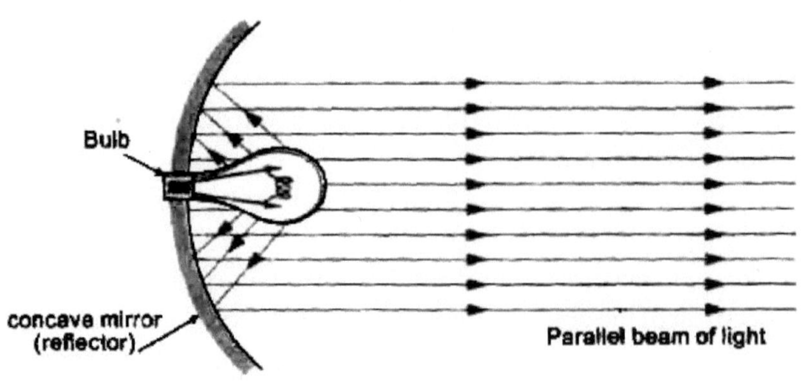

2. **Shaving and make up mirror:** When an object is placed close to a concave mirror (i.e. between the pole and focus of the concave mirror), an erect and enlarged (large in size) image is formed. Because of this fact, concave mirror is used by men to see their enlarged face while shaving. Similarly, a lady can see her face better with the help of a concave mirror while doing makeup.

3. **Solar Cooker:** When a parallel beam of sun light falls on a concave mirror, this beam is brought to the focus of the concave mirror, as a result of this, the temperature of an object (say a container containing un - cooked food) placed at this focus increase considerably. Hence the food in the container is cooked (The arrangement as shown in figure given below).

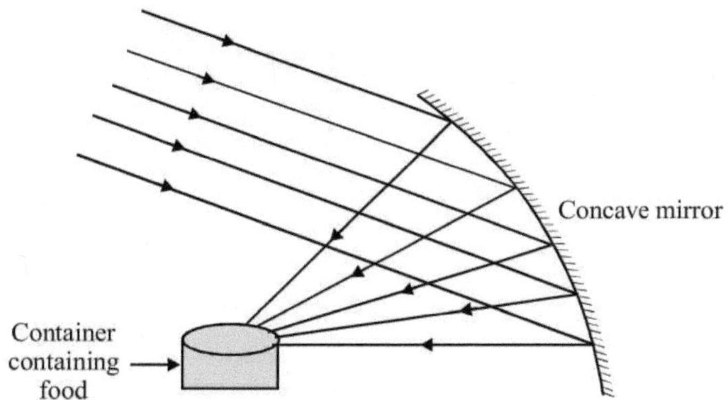

4. **Hospitals :** Concave mirrors are used by dentists and ENT specialists to focus light on teeth, nose, eye and throat to examine these organs.

Image formation by convex mirror

Position of the object	Position of the image	Size of the image	Nature of the image
At infinity (figure a)	At the focus F, behind the mirror	Highly diminished, point-sized	Virtual and erect
Between infinity and the pole P of the mirror (figure b)	Between P and F, behind the mirror	Diminished	Virtual and erect

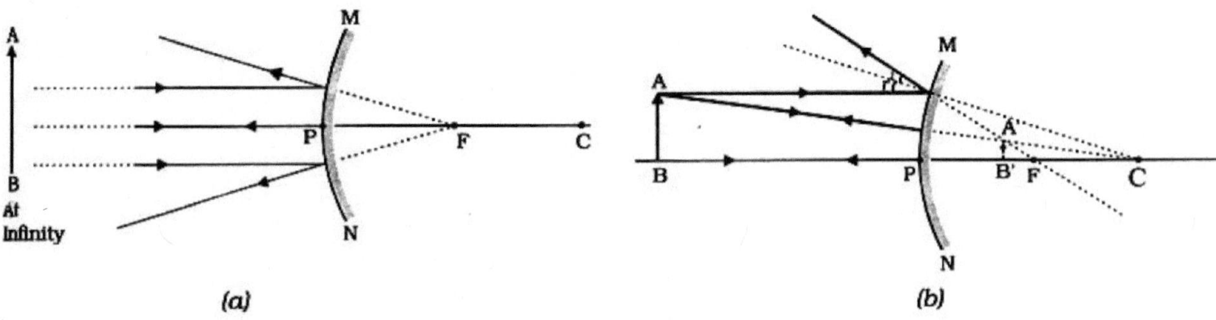

Important Information :

(1) Concave mirror produces **real** as well as **virtual image** depending upon the position of the object.

(2) A concave mirror produces **virtual image** when object lies between the pole (P) and focus (F) of the mirror.

(3) A convex mirror always produces **virtual** and diminished image irrespective of the position of the object in front of the mirror.

(4) A real image is **inverted** while virtual image **erect**.

4.8.5 Applications / uses of a convex mirror

1. **Rear view or driver's mirror:** Convex mirror is used as a rear view mirror because this mirror produces an effect and diminished image of an object behind the vehicle. Since the image of the object formed is small in size, so the field of view is increased. It means, the driver of a vehicle can see the traffic over large area behind his vehicle. **This mirror is also known as driver's mirror.**
2. **In street lights:** Convex mirror is used in street lights to diverge light over a large area (As shown in the figure given below).

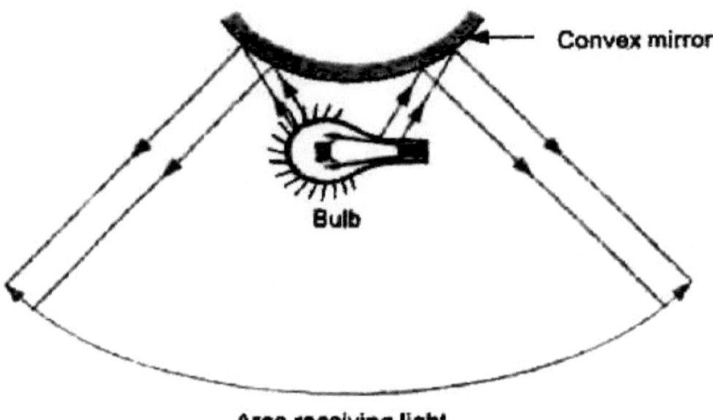

3. **In big shopping stores:** Convex mirror are used in big shopping stores to watch the activities of the customers. This is because field of view of a convex mirror is large and even a single convex mirror can monitor the activities of customers in large area of the store.

1. Convex mirror definitely forms a full length image of a distant tall building or a tall tree.
2. A small **convex mirror** fitted on the wall of **Agra Fort** is used to see the full length **image of Taj Mahal**.
3. The field of view of a plane mirror is smaller than the field of view of a convex mirror as shown in figure.

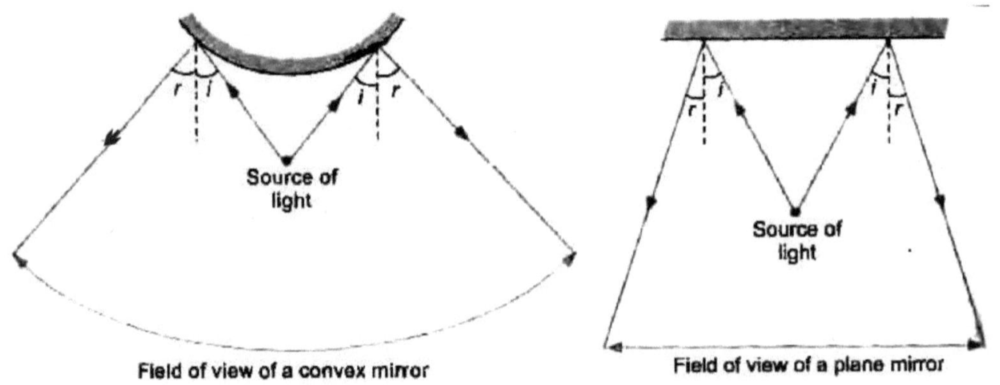

Field of view of a convex mirror

Field of view of a plane mirror

4. To form the full length image of an object in a plane mirror, the size of the plane mirror should be half the size of the object.
5. Full length image of an object is formed by a concave mirror, only when the object is far away from the mirror.

4.9 MIRROR FORMULA

The distance of the position of an object on the principal axis from the pole of a spherical mirror is known as **object distance**. It is denoted by u.

The distance of the position of the image of an object on the principal axis from the pole of a spherical mirror is known as **image distance**. It is denoted by v.

The relation among, u, v, **and focal length (f) of a spherical mirror is known as mirror formula.**

It is given by $\boxed{\frac{1}{u}+\frac{1}{v}=\frac{1}{f}}$

or $$\frac{1}{\text{Object distance}}+\frac{1}{\text{Image distance}}=\frac{1}{\text{focal length}}$$

Note: (i) Mirror formula holds good for both concave and convex mirrors.

(ii) While solving Numerical Problems, sign conventions are used when values of u, v and f substituted.

4.10 MAGNIFICATION (OR LINEAR MAGNIFICATION)

4.10.1 Linear Magnification produced by a mirror is defined as the ratio of the size (or height) of the image to the size (or height) of the object. It is denoted by m.

If h_i = Size (or height) of the image produced by the mirror

and h_o = Size (or height) of the object.

Then, linear magnification, $\boxed{m=\frac{h_i}{h_o}=-\frac{v}{u}}$

Linear magnification has **no unit**.

4.10.2 Magnification produced by a concave mirror

Let AB be an object placed perpendicular to the principal axis in front of a concave mirror. A ray BD parallel to the principal axis passes through the focus (F) after reflection from the mirror (as shown in the figure & a ray BP incoming to pole passes as PB' after reflection). These two reflected rays intersect each other at B'. So A' B' is the real, inverted and diminished image of the object AB.

Δ's APB and A'PB' are similar.

$$\therefore \quad \frac{A'B'}{AB}=\frac{PA'}{PA} \qquad .....(1)$$

Applying sign conventions, we have

A'B' = –h' (Size of image)

AB = +h (Size of object)

PA' = –v (Distance of image from the pole)

and PA = –u (Distance of object from the pole)

Hence equation (1) becomes

$$\frac{-h_i}{h_o} = \frac{-v}{-u} \quad \text{or} \quad \frac{h_i}{h_o} = -\frac{v}{u}$$

Since $\frac{h_i}{h_o} = m$ $\therefore$ $\boxed{m = \frac{h_i}{h_o} = -\frac{v}{u}}$

4.10.3 Magnification

(i) The transverse or **linear magnification**

$$m = \frac{\text{size of image}}{\text{size of object}} = \frac{I}{O} = -\frac{v}{u} = \frac{f}{f-u} = \frac{f-v}{f}$$

If $|m| > 1$ the image is enlarged

If $|m| = 1$ the image is of same size

If $|m| < 1$ the image is reduced

If $m > 0$ the image is erect

If $m < 0$ the image is inverted

(ii) If an object lies along the axis, then its magnification is called the **longitudinal magnification**. It is given by $m = -\frac{v^2}{u^2}$

(iii) For a convex mirror, the magnification is positive and less than one. That means, the image is virtual erect and diminished in size, for all positive of the object.

(iv) For concave mirror, if object lies between the pole and focus, then, image is virtual, erect and enlarged.

4.10.4 Newton's Formula

This formula provides a relationship among the focal length (f), the distance of the object from focus (x) and the distance of the image from the focus (y)

This can be expressed as

$$xy = f^2$$

Note that here the object distance and the image distance are measured from the focus of the mirror not from the pole.

Illustration 3

An object is placed at (i) 10 cm, (ii) 5 cm in front of a concave mirror of radius of curvature 15 cm. Find the position, nature and magnification of the image in each case.

Solution

The focal length $f = -15/2$ cm, $= -7.5$ cm

(i) The object distance, $u = -10$ cm

$$\frac{1}{v} + \frac{1}{-10} = \frac{1}{-7.5} \quad \text{or} \quad \frac{1}{v} = -\frac{1}{7.5} + \frac{1}{10}$$

$$\text{or} \quad \frac{1}{v} = \frac{-10+7.5}{7.5\times 10} \quad \text{or} \quad v = \frac{7.5\times 10}{-2.5}$$

or $v = -30$ cm

The image is 30 cm from the mirror on the same side as the object.

Also, magnification, $m = -\frac{v}{u} = -\left(\frac{-30}{-10}\right) = -3$

The image is magnified, real and inverted.

(ii) The object distance, $u = -5$ cm. Then $\frac{1}{v} + \frac{1}{-5} = \frac{1}{-7.5}$

$$\text{or} \quad \frac{1}{v} = -\frac{1}{7.5} + \frac{1}{5} \quad \text{or} \quad \frac{1}{v} = \frac{-5+7.5}{7.5\times 5}$$

$$\text{or} \quad v = \frac{7.5\times 5}{2.5} \quad \text{or} \quad v = 15 \text{ cm}$$

This image is formed at 15 cm behind the mirror. It is a virtual image.

Magnification, $m = -\frac{v}{u} = -\frac{15}{(-5)} = 3$

The image is magnified, virtual and erect.

Try Yourself

2. The radius of curvature of a convex mirror used on a moving automobile is 2 m. A truck is coming behind it at a distance of 3.5 m. Calculate (i) the position and (ii) the size of the image relative to the size of the truck. What will be the nature of the image?

4.10.5 Relation between 'f' and 'R'

Let two incident rays AB (parallel to the principal axis) and CP (coinciding with the principal axis) fall on the concave mirror MM′. BT and PC are corresponding reflected rays.

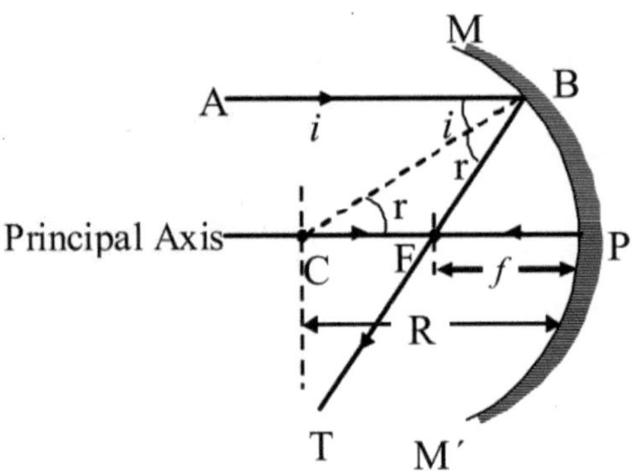

$\angle ABC = \angle CBF$ .....(i) (since $\angle i = \angle r$)

Also $\angle ABC = \angle BCF$ .....(ii) (Alternate angels)

From equation (i) and (ii), we have

$\angle CBF = \angle BCF$

$\therefore$ BF = CF .....(iii) (sides opposite to equal angels)

For the mirror of small aperture, the point B is very near to the point P, then

BF = PF .....(iv) (nearly equal)

From equation (iii) and (iv),

CF = PF .....(v)

Now, CP = CF + PF = PF + PF (from equation (v))

CP = 2PF

$\Rightarrow$ PF = CP/2

But PF = f and CP = R

$$\Rightarrow \boxed{f = \frac{R}{2}}$$

The same relation is also true for a convex mirror.

Sign convention for reflection by spherical mirror

In this convention, the pole (P) of the mirror is taken as the origin. The principal axis of the mirror is taken as the x-axis (X′X) of the coordinate system. The conventions are as follows

(i) The object is always placed to the left of the mirror. This implies that the light from the object falls on the mirror from the left-hand side.

(ii) All distances parallel to the principal axis are measured from the pole of the mirror.

(iii) All the **distances** measured to the **right of the origin** (along + x-axis) are taken as **positive** while those measured to the **left** of the origin (along -x-axis) are taken as **negative**.

(iv) **Distances** measured perpendicular to and **above the principal axis** (along +y-axis) are taken as **positive**.

(v) **Distances** measured perpendicular to and **below the principal axis** (along -y-axis) are taken as **negative**.

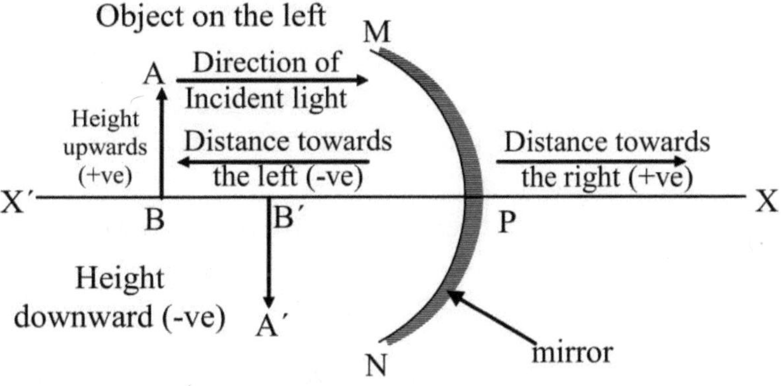

4.10.6 Spherical Aberration

The rays of light after reflection from a concave mirror meet at a single point only if a narrow beam of light falls on the mirror. In case of a wide beam, it is found that the marginal rays get focussed relatively close to the pole in comparison to the paraxial rays.

The reflected lines form a pattern and this has an envelope known as the **caustic curve**. Because of this the image is distorted. This defect is called **spherical aberration**. The spherical aberration is not present in **parabolic mirrors**.

4.10.7 Identification of Mirrors

(a) By Touching :

(i) Plane, it is a plane mirror.

(ii) Depressed inwards at the middle, it is a concave mirror.

(iii) Projected outwards at the middle, it is a convex mirror.

(b) By Seeing the Image :

(i) If the image formed is always erect and of the same size, it is a plane mirror.

(ii) If the image formed is always erect and smaller in size, it is a convex mirror.

(iii) If the image formed is erect and magnified when mirror is close to the face and the size and nature (virtual to real) of the image change on moving the mirror, it is concave mirror.

Uses of Mirror

(a) Concave Mirror :

(i) As reflectors in the headlights of cars, searchlights, etc.

(ii) Dentists (as the dentist's mirror) to focus light on the tooth to be examined.

(iii) Shaving mirrors and as make-up mirrors to see the enlarged erect image of the face. For this to happen, face must be placed closer to the mirror.

(iv) Concave mirror (or parabolic mirrors) are used as radiation collector in solar heating devices.

(b) Convex Mirror :

(i) Rear-view mirrors or side-mirror (also called driver's mirror) on automobiles, such as cars, trucks and buses to see the traffic coming from behind.

(ii) Staircase-mirrors on the double-decker buses.

(iii) Vigilance-mirrors in big shops and stores.

Illustration 4

A concave mirror produces two times magnified real image of an object placed at 10 cm in front of it. Find the position of the image?

Solution

Here, $u = -10$ cm (Sign convention)

$m = -2$ (∵ Image is real) But $m = -\frac{v}{u}$

$-2 = -\frac{v}{u}$ ∴ $v = 2u = 2(-10 \text{ cm}) = -20$ cm

Illustration 5

An object of 5.0 cm in size is placed at a distance of 20.0 cm from a concave mirror of focal length 15.0 cm. At what distance from the mirror, should a screen be placed to get the sharp image? Also calculate size of the image.

Solution

Here, $h = +5.0$ cm,

$f = -15.0$ cm (sign convention)

$u = -20.0$ cm (sign convention)

Step 1. Determination of the position of the image

Using $\frac{1}{u} + \frac{1}{v} = \frac{1}{f}$, we get $\frac{1}{v} = \frac{1}{f} - \frac{1}{u} = \frac{1}{-15} - \frac{1}{(-20)}$

or $\frac{1}{v} = -\frac{1}{15} + \frac{1}{20} = -\frac{1}{60}$

or $v = -60$ cm

So the screen must be placed at a distance of 60 cm in front of the concave mirror.

Step 2. Determination of size and its nature.

Using. $$m = \frac{h'}{h} = \frac{-v}{u}$$

or $$h' = \frac{-v}{u}h = -\frac{-(-60)\times 5.0}{-20.0} = -15.0\,\text{cm}$$

Thus, size of image = 15.0 cm

Negative sign with h' shows that the image is inverted

Illustration 6

An object 4 cm high is placed at a distance of 6 cm in front of a concave mirror of focal length 12 cm. Find the position, nature and size of the image formed.

Solution:

Here, size of the objects: $h = 4$ cm

$u = -6$ cm (sign convention)

$f = -12$ cm (sign convention)

Step 1: Using $\frac{1}{u} + \frac{1}{v} = \frac{1}{f}$,

we get $$-\frac{1}{6} + \frac{1}{v} = \frac{1}{-12}$$

or $$\frac{1}{v} = -\frac{1}{12} + \frac{1}{6} = \frac{1}{12}$$ or $v = 12$ cm

Thus, image is formed at a distance of 12 cm behind the concave mirror as v is positive. Therefore image is virtual (nature).

Step 2. Using $\frac{h'}{h} = \frac{-v}{u}$, we get

$$h' = \frac{-v}{u} \times h = \frac{-12\text{ cm}}{-6\text{ cm}} \times 4\text{ cm} = 8\text{ cm}.$$

So image is 8 cm tall. Since h' is positive, so image is erect.

Knowledge Enhancer

Power of mirror :

The power of a mirror is defined as its capacity to converge or diverge. Mathematically, it is defined as inverse of focal length. For **concave mirror** power is **positive** as it is a **converging mirror** and for **convex** it is **negative** as it is a **diverging mirror**

$$P = -\frac{1}{f(\text{in m})} = -\frac{100}{f(\text{in cm})}$$

The unit of power is diopter.

In sign convention, **f (or R) is negative for concave** or converging mirror and **positive for convex** or diverging mirror.

Identification of the mirror by the size and nature of the image:

(i) If object and image are of the same nature (i.e. both on the same side of the mirror) then they will be inverted.

(ii) If the object and image are on the opposite sides of the mirror then image is erect relative to object.

For real extended object, if the image formed by a single mirror is erect, it is always vertical (i.e. m is +ve) and in this situation if the size of image is

Smaller than object, the mirror is convex	Equal to object, the mirror is plane	Larger than object, the mirror is concave
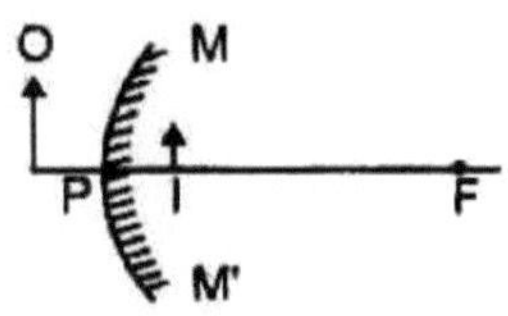 O, M, P, I, F, M' $m < +1$	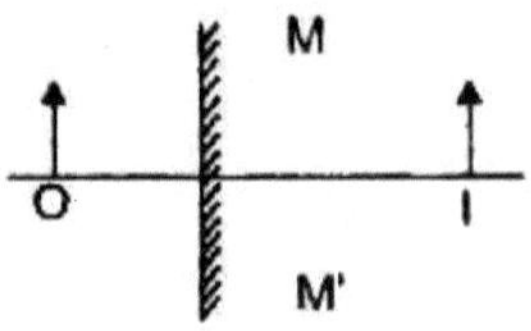 M, O, I, M' $m = +1$	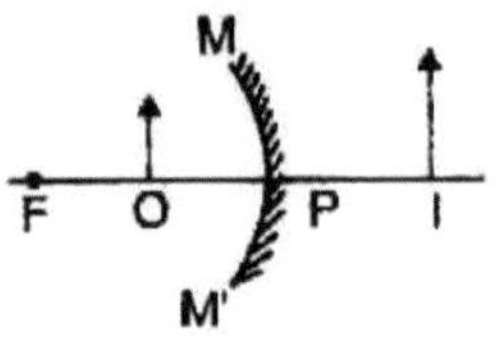 M, F, O, P, I, M' $m > +1$

So by observing the size of erect image in a mirror, we can decide the nature of the mirror i.e. whether it is convex, concave or plane. For a real extended object if the image formed by a single mirror is inverted it is always real (i.e. m is –ve) and the mirror is concave. In this situation if the size of the image is

Smaller than object, object is placed between ∞ and C and then image is formed between F and C.	Equal to object, if object is at C and then image is also at C.	Larger than object, object is placed between C and F and then image is formed between C and ∞.
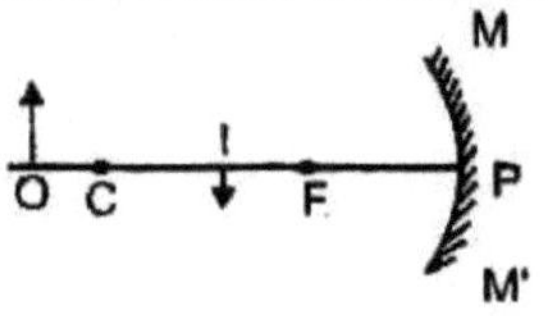 M, O, C, I, F, P, M' $m < -1$	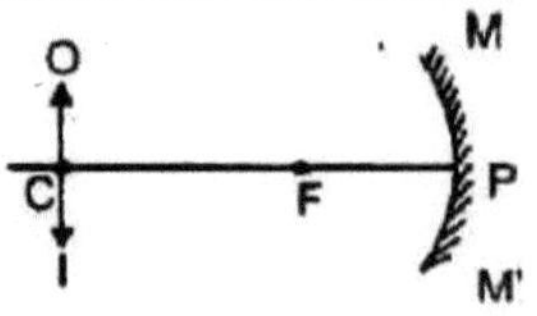 O, M, C, F, P, I, M' $m = -1$	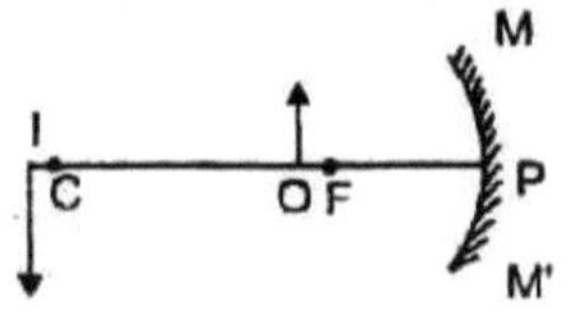 M, I, C, O, F, P, M' $m > -1$

As every part of the mirror forms complete image, if a part of mirror (say half) is obstructed (say covered with black paper) full image will be formed but intensity will be reduced.

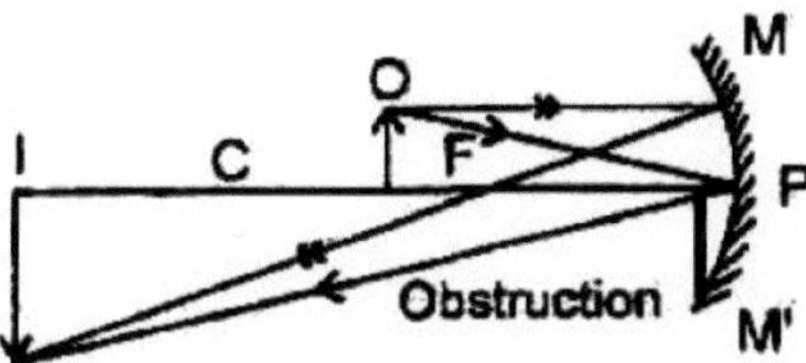

4.11 REFRACTION

When light goes from air to glass, it bends towards the normal to the interface separating these two media (Figure (a)). On the other hand, when light goes from glass to air, it bends away from the normal to the interface separating these two media (Figure (b)). This phenomenon of bending light is known as refraction of light.

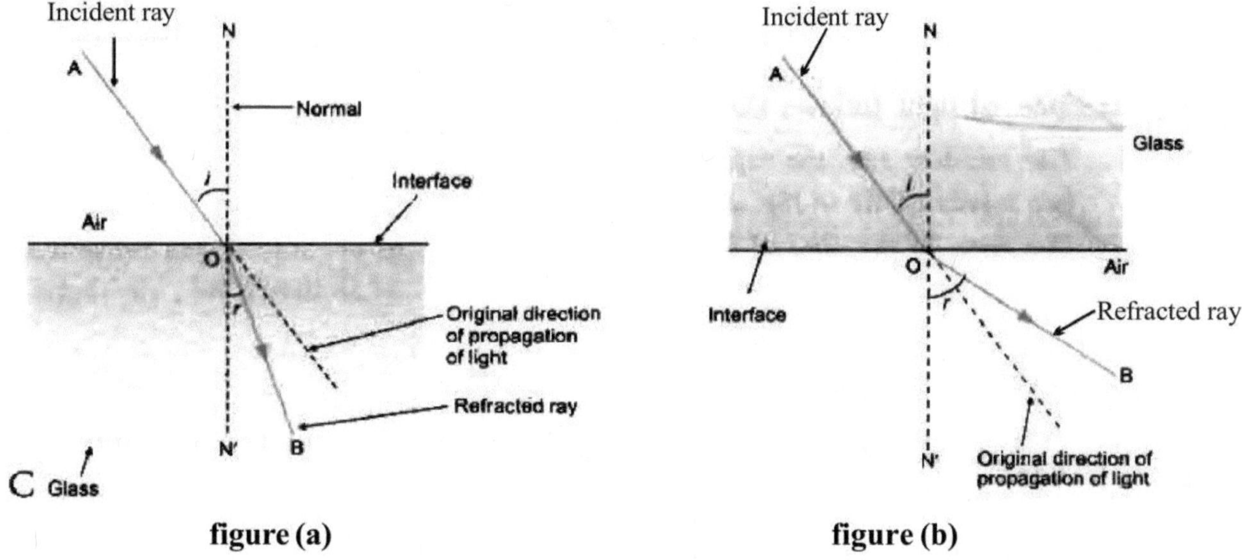

figure (a) figure (b)

Definition : The bending of light rays when they pass obliquely from one medium to another medium is called refraction of light.

The ray AO is figure (a) and (b) are called incident rays. The rays OB in figure (a) and (b) are called refracted rays. NON' is normal to the interface separating two media.

$\angle$AON is called incident angle $\angle$i and $\angle$BON' is called refracted angle $\angle$r.

Interface : A boundary or surface separating two media is called interface.

4.11.1 Cause of Refraction of light

We come across many media like air, glass, water etc. **A medium is a transparent material through which light is transmitted**. Every transparent medium has a property known as optical density. The optical density of a transparent medium is closely related to the speed of light in the medium. If the optical density of a transparent medium is low, then the speed of light in that medium is high. Such a medium is known as **optically rarer medium.** Thus, **optically rarer medium is that medium through which light travels fast**.

One the other hand, if the optical density of a transparent medium is high, then the speed of light in that medium is low. Such a medium is known as optically denser medium. Thus, **optically denser medium is that medium through which light travels slow**.

Speed of light in air is more than the speed of light in water, so air is optically rarer medium as compared to the water. In other words, water is optically denser medium as compared to air. Similarly, speed of light in water is more than the speed of light in glass, so water is optically rarer medium as compared to the glass. In words, glass is optically denser medium as compared to water.

When light ray goes from air (optically rarer medium) to glass (optically denser medium) such that the light ray in air makes an angle with the normal to the interface separating air and glass, then it bends from its original direction of propagation. Similarly, if light ray goes from glass to air, again it bends from its original direction of propagation. The phenomena of bending of light ray from its path is known as refraction. We have seen that the speed of light in different media is different, so we can say that refraction of light takes place because the speed of light is different in different media. Thus, the cause of refraction can be summarised as follows:

"The refraction of light takes place because speed of light changes when light goes from one medium to another medium."

4.11.2 Laws of Refraction

Refraction of light follows the following two laws:

(1) The incident ray, the refracted ray and the normal to the surface separating the two media all lie in the same plane.

(2) The ratio of the sine of the incident angle ($\angle i$) to the sine of the refracted angle ($\angle r$) is constant for a pair of two media.

i.e. $$\frac{\sin i}{\sin r} = \frac{n_2}{n_1} \textbf{ constant} \qquad .....(1)$$

This constant is known as the **refractive index** of the medium in which refracted ray travels with respect to the medium in which incident ray travels. **Refractive index is denoted by n. Refractive index of second medium with respect to the first medium is denoted by n_{21}.** Thus, equation (1) can be written as

$$n_{21} = \frac{\sin i}{\sin r} = \frac{n_2}{n_1} \qquad .....(2)$$

This law is also known as **Snell's law** as it was stated by **Prof. Willebrord Snell** (Dutch mathematician and astronomer).

4.11.3 Refractive index

Speed of light in vacuum is maximum and is equal to 3×10^8 ms^{-1}. In air, speed of light is little smaller than in vacuum. But for all practical purposes, we consider the speed of light in air equal to the speed of light in vacuum. However speed of light decreases in denser media like water, glass, its speed decreases. **The amount of change in the speed of light in a medium. This property is known as refractive index of the medium. Refractive index is a measure of how much the speed of light changes when it enters the medium from air.**

Refractometer is a device used to measure the refractive index of a substance.

(a) Absolute Refractive Index : Absolute refractive index of a medium is defined as the ratio of the speed of light in vacuum or air to the speed of light in the medium. **It is denoted by n.**

i.e. **Refractive index,** $$\mathbf{n = \frac{Speed of light in air or vacuum (c)}{Speed of light in medium (v)}}$$

or $$n = \frac{c}{v}, \text{ where } c = 3 \times 10^8 \text{ ms}^{-1}$$

Refractive index is a pure number. It has no unit.

(b) Relative Refractive Index

Consider a material medium 2 surrounded by another material medium 1 as shown in figure. Let the light goes from medium 1 to the medium 2, then the refractive index of medium 2 with respect to medium 1 is known as the relative refractive index of medium 2. It is given by

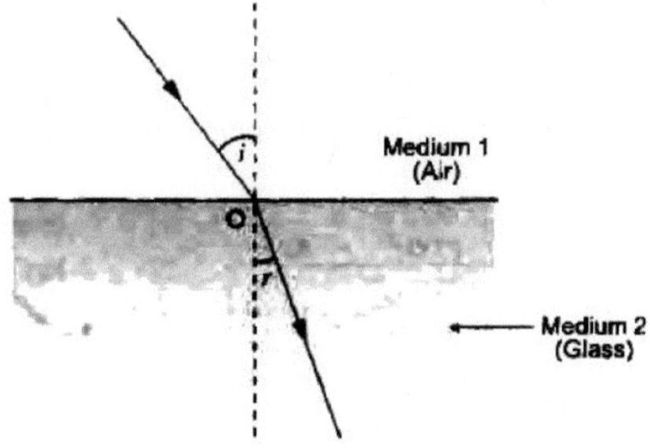

$$\mathbf{n_{21} = \frac{Speed\ of\ light\ in\ medium\ 1\ (v_1)}{Speed\ of\ light\ in\ medium\ 2\ (v_2)}}$$

i.e. $$n_{21} = \frac{v_1}{v_2} \qquad .....(1)$$

Multiply and divide R.H.S. of equation (1) by c (speed of light in air), we get

$$n_{21} = \frac{cv_1}{cv_2} = \left(\frac{c}{v_2}\right)\times\left(\frac{v_1}{c}\right) = \left(\frac{\frac{c}{v_2}}{\frac{c}{v_1}}\right) \quad .....(2)$$

Hence equation (2) can be written as

$$n_{21} = \frac{n_2}{n_1} \quad .....(3)$$

Thus, relative refractive index of medium 2 with respect to medium 1 is defined as the ratio of absolute refractive index of medium 2 to the absolute refractive index of medium 1.

Also, $$n_{21} = \frac{\sin i}{\sin r} \quad .....(4)$$

Comparing equation (3) and (4), we get

$$\frac{\sin i}{\sin r} = \frac{n_2}{n_1}$$

or $$n_1 \sin i = n_2 \sin r \quad .....(5)$$

Explanation of bending of light when it travels from one medium to another medium.

(i) When light goes from rarer medium of refractive index n_1 to a denser medium of refractive index $n_2 (n_2 > n_1)$.

According to Snell's law : $\frac{\sin i}{\sin r} = \frac{n_2}{n_1} > 1$ or $\sin i > \sin r$

$\therefore$ $\angle i > \angle r$ or $\angle r < \angle i$

Since, $\angle r < \angle i$, so the refracted ray makes less angle with the normal as compared to the angle made by incidence ray with the normal. Hence, refracted ray bends towards the normal.

(ii) When light goes from denser medium of refractive index n_2 to a rarer medium of refractive index n_1 $(n_1 < n_2)$.

According to Snell's law : $\frac{\sin i}{\sin r} = \frac{n_1}{n_2} < 1$ or $\sin i < \sin r$

or $\angle i < \angle r$ or $\angle r > \angle i$

Since, $\angle r > \angle i$, so the refracted ray makes greater angle with the normal as compared to the angle made by incidence ray with the normal. Hence, refracted ray bends away from the normal.

(iii) When incident light falls perpendicular to the interface separating two media of refractive indices n_1 and n_2.

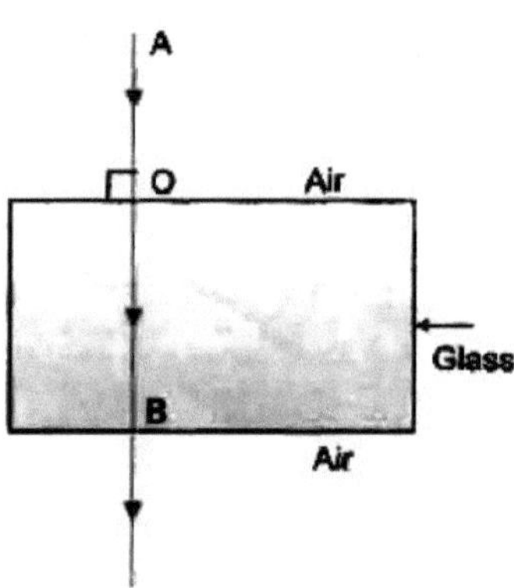

According to Snell's law : $\frac{\sin i}{\sin r} = \frac{n_2}{n_1}$, or $\sin r = \frac{n_1}{n_2} \sin i$

Since $\angle i = 0$, so $\sin r = \frac{n_1}{n_2} \sin 0° = 0$ or $\angle r = 0$

Therefore, the refracted light travels along the normal and hence, there is no bending of light (or no refraction of light as shown in figure.

(iv) When light goes from one medium to another medium of same refractive index (i.e. $n_1 = n_2$)

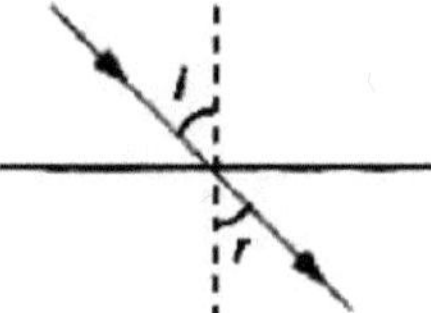

According to Snell's law : $\frac{\sin i}{\sin r} = \frac{n_2}{n_1} = 1$ or $\sin i = \sin r$ or $\angle i = \angle r$

Thus, no refraction of light takes place as shown in figure.

4.11.4 Factors on which the refractive index of medium depends

Refractive index of a medium depends upon:

(i) Nature of the material of the medium.

(ii) Density of the medium.

(iii) Colour or wavelength of the light.

4.11.5 Refractive index of medium 2 w.r.t. medium 1 is reciprocal of the refractive index of medium 1 w.r.t. medium 2.

We know, refractive index of medium 2 w.r.t. medium 1 is given by,

$$n_{21} = \frac{\text{Speed of light in medium 1 } (v_1)}{\text{Speed of light in medium 2 } (v_2)}$$

or $$n_{21} = \frac{v_1}{v_2} \quad .....(1)$$

Similarly, refractive index of medium 1 w.r.t. medium 2 is given by,

$$n_{12} = \frac{v_2}{v_1} \quad .....(2)$$

Multiplying equation (1) and (2),

we get, $$n_{21} \times n_{12} = \frac{v_1}{v_2} \times \frac{v_2}{v_1} = 1 \quad \text{or} \quad \boxed{n_{21} = \frac{1}{n_{12}}}$$

Knowledge Enhancer

1. When light travels from one medium to another medium, the speed of light and its wavelength (λ) change but **frequency (ν) of light remains the same.**

2. Since $c = f\lambda$ and $v = f\lambda_m$

$$n = \frac{c}{v} = \frac{\lambda}{\lambda_m}$$

Thus, refractive index of a medium or material depends upon the wavelength of the light falling on it. **Refractive index of a medium is minimum for red light and maximum for violet light**.
Wavelength of light in medium,

$$\lambda_m = \frac{\lambda}{n} = \frac{\text{wavelength of light in air}}{\text{refractive index of medium}}$$

3. As $n > 1$, so $\lambda_m < \lambda$. Thus, **wavelength of light decreases when it travels from air to another medium like water, glass** etc.
4. When a ray of light falls normally on a medium, $\angle i = 0$ and hence $\angle r = 0$. Then refraction of light does not take place.

5. $n = \frac{c}{v}$ or $v = \frac{c}{n}$. More is the refractive index of a medium, less is the speed of light in that medium and vice versa.

Refractive index of few substances with respect to vacuum for yellow light (sodium light of wave length 5.89×10^{-7} m or 589 nm) are given in table.

S.No.	Name of Substance	Refractive Index
1	Air	1.0003
2	Hydrogen	1.00013
3	Carbon dioxide	1.00045
4	Ice	1.31
5	Water	1.333
6	Alcohol	1.36
7	Kerosene	1.44
8	Carbon tetrachloride	1.46
9	Turpentine oil	1.47
10	Glycerine	1.47
11	Benzene	1.501
12	Crown glass	1.52
13	Rock salt	1.54
14	Carbon disulphide	1.63
15	Flint glass	1.66
16	Ruby	1.71
17	Diamond	2.42

Optical density and **mass density** of a medium are two different entities. **Optical density of a medium determines the ability of the medium to refract light. However mass density is defined as the mass** per unit volume of the substance. Optical density of a medium is directly proportional to the refractive index of the medium. For example, **refractive index of kerosene oil is 1.44 and that of water is 1.33. Therefore, the optical density of kerosene oil is more than the optical density of water. However, mass density of kerosene is less than the mass density of water.**

Illustration 7

If, while standing on the bank of a stream, you wished to spear a fish swimming in the water out in from of you, would you aim above, below, or directly at the observed fish to make a direct hit? If you decided instead to zap the fish with a laser, would you aim above, below, or directly at the observed fish? Defend your answer.

Solution

When you try to hit the fish with a spear, you need to aim below as the fish is actually at a lower depth than that observed by you from outside the water due to refraction of light.

When you aim with a laser light then also you should aim much below as the path of laser will change as it enters in water. Since it is going from rarer to denser medium, it bends towards the normal and deviates from the original path.

Illustration 8

The refractive index of water is $\frac{4}{3}$ and of glass is $\frac{3}{2}$. Calculate the refractive index of glass with respect to water.

Solution

Let the 3 media be 1, 2 and 3, 1 for air, 2 for water, 3 for glass in that order.

Given: ${}_1\mu_2 = \frac{4}{3}$, ${}_2\mu_3 = ?$, ${}_3\mu_1 = \frac{1}{\frac{3}{2}}$,

$[\because\ {}_1\mu_3 = \frac{3}{2}$ and $\therefore\ {}_3\mu_1$ is the reciprocal of ${}_1\mu_3]$

Now using the formula, ${}_1\mu_2 \times {}_2\mu_3 \times {}_3\mu_1 = 1$ and substituting values, we have

$$\frac{4}{3} \times {}_2\mu_3 \times \frac{2}{3}$$

$${}_2\mu_3 = \frac{1\times3\times3}{4\times2} = \frac{9}{8}$$

$\therefore$ The refractive index of glass with respect to water is $\frac{9}{8}$.

If ${}_1\mu_2$, ${}_2\mu_3$ and ${}_3\mu_1$ be refractive index of medium 2 w.r.t. medium 1, refractive index of medium 3 w.r.t. medium 2 and refractive index of 1 w.r.t. 3 respectively then ${}_1\mu_2 \times {}_2\mu_3 \times {}_3\mu_1 = 1$.

Knowledge Enhancer

Cauchy's relation

It gives relation between refractive index (μ) and wavelength (λ) of light. The Cauchy's relation is given by where A and B are constants.

Thus, $\lambda_{red} > \lambda_{violet} \quad \Rightarrow \quad \mu_{red} < \mu_{violet}$

If the speed of light were the same in all media refraction would not occur when light passes from one medium to another.

Illustration 9

Light reflected from a fish strikes the surface of the water at an angle of 38° to the normal. What is the angle of refraction of the light into the air? (Given : sin 38° = 0.61 and sin 55° = 0.81)

Solution

Snell' law gives, $n_w \sin\theta_1 = n_a \sin\theta_2$

$\sin\theta_2 = (1.33)\sin 38°$

$\theta_2 = 55°$

Illustration 10

Light strikes an interface between two materials of refractive indices n_1 and n_2, at an angle θ_1 to the normal to the surface. Show that a ray of the light is bent towards the normal if $n_1 < n_2$ and that a ray is bent away from the normal if $n_1 > n_2$.

Solution

Snell's law gives from any light ray

$$\sin\theta_2 = \frac{n_1}{n_2}\sin\theta_1$$

If $n_1 < n_2$, then $\sin\theta_2 < \sin\theta_1$ and $\theta_2 < \theta_1$. This means that the ray is bent toward the normal.

If $n_1 > n_2$, then $\sin\theta_2 > \sin\theta_1$ and $\theta_2 > \theta_1$. This means that the ray is bent away from the normal.

Conditions of no refraction : If light is incident normally on a boundary i.e. $\angle i = 0°$.

Then for Snell's law

$\mu_1 \sin 0 = \mu_2 \sin r$

$\Rightarrow \quad \sin r = 0 \quad$ i.e., $\quad \angle r = 0$

i.e. light passes undeviated from the boundary.

(so boundary will be invisible)

If the refractive indices of two media are equal i.e., if

$\mu_1 = \mu_2 = \mu$

Then from Snell's law

$\mu_1 \sin i = \mu \sin r$

$\Rightarrow \quad \angle i = \angle r$

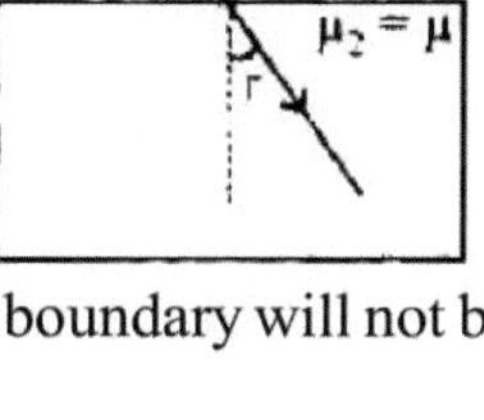

i.e., ray passes undeviated from the boundary with $\angle i = \angle r \neq 0$ and boundary will not be visible.

This is also why a transparent solid is invisible in a liquid if $\mu_s = \mu_L$.

Illustration 11

The speed of light in air is 3×10^8 m/s. What will be its speed in diamond whose refractive index is 2.4?

(A) 3×10^8 m/s (B) 1.25×10^8 m/s (C) 7.2×10^8 m/s (D) 332 m/s

Solution

Speed of light in air = 3×10^8 m/s

Refractive index of diamond = 2.4

Let the speed of light in diamond = v m/s

Then, n = c/v

or $\quad v = \dfrac{c}{n} = \dfrac{3\times10^8}{2.4} = 1.25 \times 10^8$ m/s $\quad \therefore \quad$ **(B)**

Illustration 12

A beam of monochromatic blue light of wavelength 420 nm in air travels in water (n = 4/3). Its wavelength in water will be

Solution

Wavelength of blue light in air = 420×10^{-9} m

Refractive index of water = 4/3

Let the wavelength of blue light in water be 'λ'

Then, $\quad n = \dfrac{c}{v} = \dfrac{\lambda_{air}}{\lambda_{medium}} \quad$ or $\quad \dfrac{4}{3} = \dfrac{420\times10^{-9}}{\lambda}$

or $\quad \lambda = \dfrac{420\times10^{-9}}{4} \times 3 = 315 \times 10^{-9}$ m = 315 nm

---

Try Yourself

3. The velocity of light in glass is 2×10^8 ms^{-1}, while in vacuum it is 3×10^8 ms^{-1}. What is the absolute refractive index of glass?

4.11.6 Refraction through a Glass Slab

When a ray of light falls on a glass slab obliquely (i.e. by making a certain angle with the normal), it emerges out of the glass slab parallel to its original direction of propagation. However, **there is a shift in the path of the incident ray. This shift is known as lateral shift or lateral displacement of the ray of light.**

Consider a rectangular glass slab LMNP of thickness 't'. Let incident ray AO travelling in air strikes the glass slab at an angle of incidence $\angle i$ (as shown in the given figure). After refraction, the ray bends towards the normal N_1N_1'. Let the reflected ray OB makes $\angle r_1$ with the normal N_1N_1'

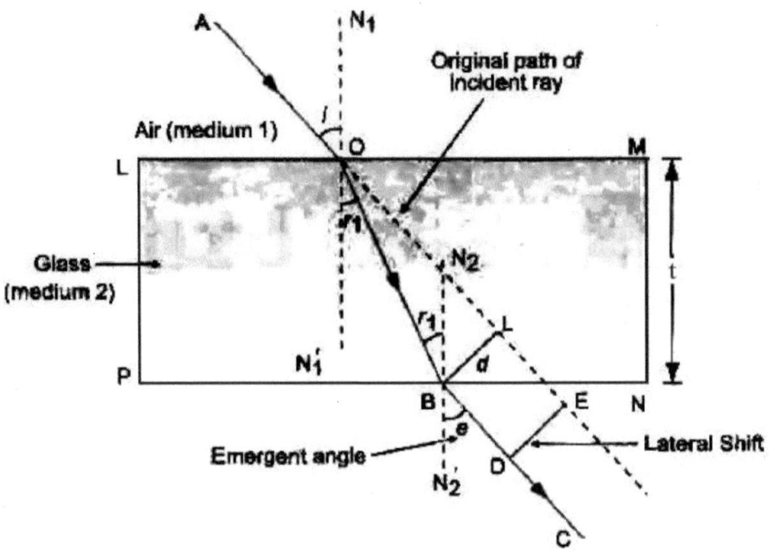

According to Snell's law of refraction

$$n_{21} = \frac{\sin i}{\sin r_1} \qquad .....(1)$$

The ray OB suffers refraction at B and emerges out of the glass slab into the air.
Let the emergent ray BC makes an angle e with the normal N_2N_2
According to Snell's law of refraction,

$$n_{12} = \frac{\sin r_1}{\sin e} \qquad .....(2)$$

We know $$n_{21} = \frac{1}{n_{12}} \qquad .....(3)$$

Substituting the values of equation (1) and (2) in equation (3), we get

$$\frac{\sin 1}{\sin r_1} = \frac{1}{\frac{\sin r_1}{\sin e}} = \frac{\sin e}{\sin r_1}$$

or $\sin i = \sin e$ or $\angle i = \angle e$

This shows that in refraction through a rectangular slab the incident ray and emergent ray of light are parallel to each other.

Lateral Shift (or displacement): The perpendicular distance between the original path of incident ray and the emergent ray coming out of a glass slab is called lateral shift or lateral displacement of the emergent ray of light .

Factors on which Lateral Shift depends

(i) Lateral shift varies directly proportional to the thickness of glass slab.

(ii) Lateral shift varies directly proportional to the incident angle.

(iii) Lateral shift varies directly proportional to the refractive index of glass slab

(iv) Lateral shift varies inversly proportional to the wavelength of incident light

Lateral displacement depends on the following factors.

(i) Refractive index of the medium (n), $x \propto n$

(ii) Thickness of the medium (t), $x \propto t$

(iii) Angle of incidence (i), $x \propto i$

(iv) Wavelength of light (λ), $x \propto \frac{1}{\lambda}$

PRACTICAL LEARNING

1. Perform an activity to show that light bends from its path, when it falls obliquely on the surface of a glass slab. Also show that angle of incidence is about equal to the emergent angle.

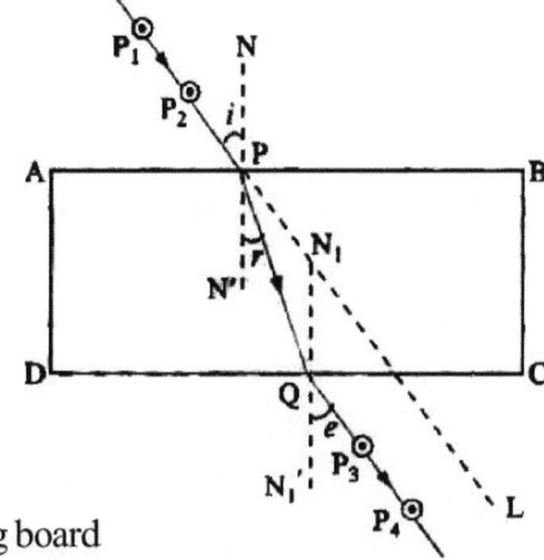

(i) Take a glass slab and place it on a white sheet of paper fixed on a drawing board.

(ii) Mark the boundary ABCD of the glass slab.

(iii) Fix two pins P_1 and P_2, vertically on the drawing board such that line joining the pins is inclined to the edge AB of the glass slab.

(iv) Now, look through the glass slab from opposite side so that the images of pins P_1 and P_2 are seen exactly in line. Fix two P_3 and P_4, vertically on the drawing board such that pins P_3, P_4 and image of P_1 and P_2 are exactly in one line.

(v) Remove the glass slab and all pins. Join the points P_1 and P_2 with a line and extend this line to touch the edge AB at P. Similarly join the points P_3 and P_4 with a line and extend the line to touch the edge DC at Q.

(vi) Join points P and Q with a straight line.

(vii) Draw normal NN' at P on the edge AB and a normal N_1N_1' at Q on the edge DC.

(viii) Measure $\angle P_2PN$ and $\angle P_3QN_1'$.

This activity shows that when light falls obliquely on a glass slab, it bends along PQ from its original path along PL.

Also $\angle P_2PN \simeq \angle P_3PN_1'$. That is, angle of incidence is about equal to the emergent angle.

2. Describe an activity to show that the apparent depth of a coin at the bottom of a bucket filled with water is less than the real depth of the coin in the water.

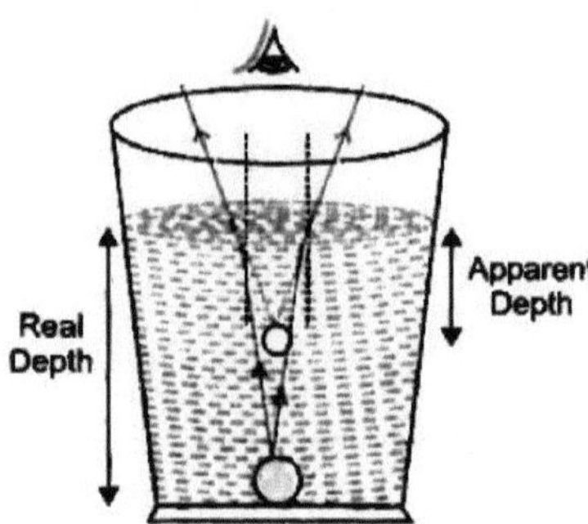

(i) Place a fifty paisa coin at the bottom of a bucket filled with water.

(ii) Look at the coin through water and try to pick up the coin at one go. It is observed that the coin is not picked up at one go.

This is because, the coin appears to be raised from its actual position due to refraction of light (as shown in the figure given above). When we try to pick up the coin in the water, we think that the coin is somewhere above the bottom of the bucket.

This activity shows that the apparent depth of the coin in water is less than its real depth in water.

Now, $\frac{\text{Real Depth}}{\text{Apparent Depth}} = n$ (refractive index of the medium)

3. Describe an activity to make a coin visible at the bottom of a bucket half filled with water, which was not visible when you look at the coin from one side above the water.

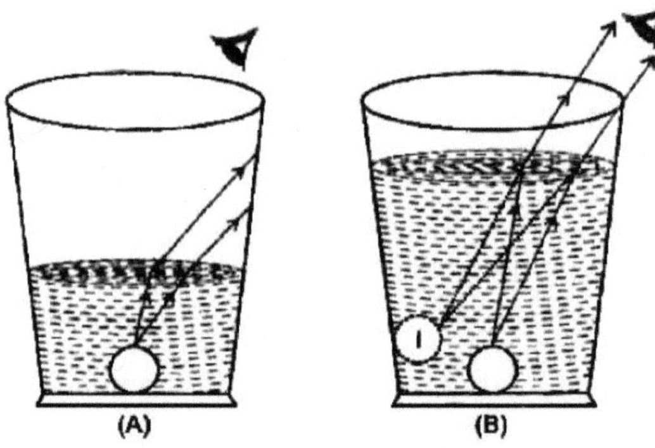

(i) Place fifty paisa coin at the bottom of a bucket half filled with water.

(ii) Place your eye at one side of the bucket and look at the water in the bucket as shown in figure A. You will not see the coin in water.

(iii) Now keep your eye at the same position and ask your friend to pour more water in the bucket.

(iv) You will see the coin in water at I when the bucket is almost filled with water (as shown in the figure above).

Conclusion : This activity shows that the distance through which an object (say coin) appears to be raised in water increases with the increase in the real depth of the object.

4.11.7 Real and apparent depths

When an object is seen from other medium, we don't see its actual depth or height. **The depth we see is called apparent depth and the actual depth is called the real depth.**

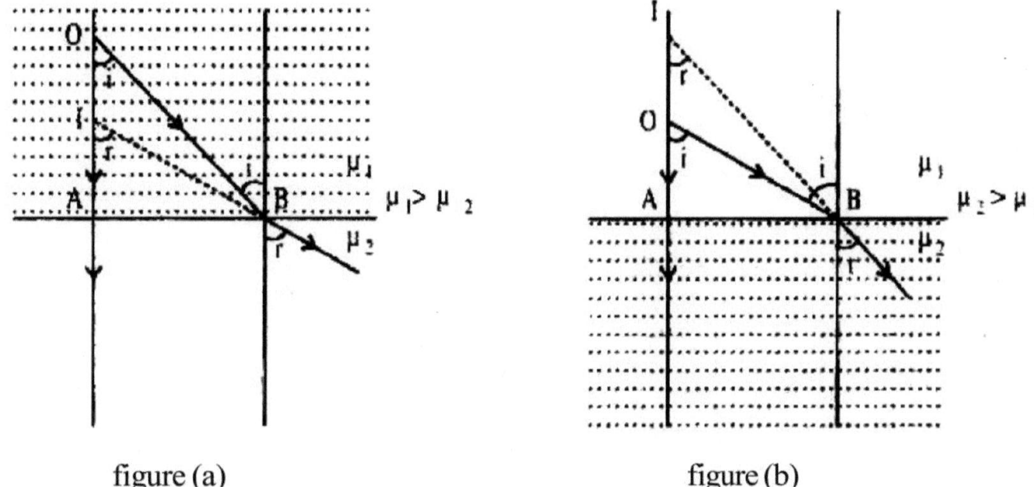

figure (a) figure (b)

Let us consider an object O placed in a medium of refractive index μ_1. It is being observed by an observer in other medium of refractive index μ_2.

Two rays OA and OP are made incident on the interface separating the two media where they get refracted. OA passes through second medium individuate as it falls normally. When the refracted rays are produced backward, they meet at I producing virtual image of O there. If $\mu_1 > \mu_2$ (fig.a) i.e. observer is in rarer medium, the image is formed at a distance less than the object from the observer. In other words the image shifts towards the observer.

If $\mu_1 < \mu_2$ (Fig.b), i.e. observer is in denser medium, the image is formed at a distance greater than the distance of the object from the observer. That is, the image shifts away from the observer.

Let us now calculate the shift OI (= Δt)

If i and r are small,

$$\sin i = \tan i = \frac{AB}{OA} \qquad \text{and} \qquad \sin r = \tan r = \frac{AB}{IA}$$

By Snell's law,

$$\frac{\sin i}{\sin r} = \frac{\mu_2}{\mu_1} \Rightarrow \frac{AB}{OA} \times \frac{IA}{AB} = \frac{\mu_2}{\mu_1} \Rightarrow \frac{IA}{OA} = \frac{\mu_2}{\mu_1}$$

Clearly, IA = Apparent depth of an object

OA = Real depth of object

$$\therefore \quad \frac{\text{Apparent depth}}{\text{Real Depth}} = \frac{\mu_2}{\mu_1}$$

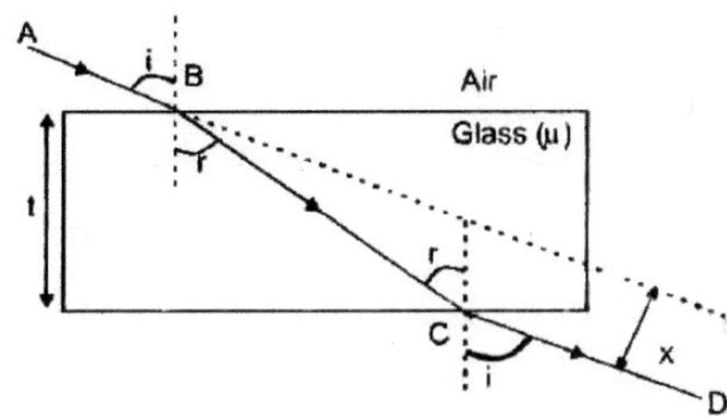

Case I: If $\mu_1 = \mu$ and $\mu_2 = 1$ (for air), then fig. (a)

$$\frac{AI}{AO} = \frac{\text{Apparent depth}}{\text{Real Depth}} = \frac{\mu_2}{\mu_1} \quad .....(1)$$

$$\Rightarrow \quad \mu = \frac{\text{Real Depth}}{\text{Apparent Depth}}$$

Now, Shift in image $(\Delta t) = OI = AO - AI = \left[\frac{AO - AI}{AO}\right] AO = \left[1 - \frac{AI}{AO}\right] AO$

or $\quad \Delta t = \left[1 - \frac{1}{\mu}\right] t$, From equation (1)

Where r = AO = thickness of the medium in which object is placed

Note: If the object is placed in the medium which consists of a number of media of refractive indices μ_1, μ_2, μ_3 ....and the thickness t_1, t_2, t_3 .... respectively, then

Virtual depth (A1) $= \frac{t_1}{\mu_1} + \frac{t_2}{\mu_2} + \frac{t_3}{\mu_3} + ...$

Virtual displacement (OI) =

$$t_1\left[1 - \frac{1}{\mu_1}\right] + t_2\left[1 - \frac{1}{\mu_2}\right] + t_3\left[1 - \frac{1}{\mu_3}\right] + ...$$

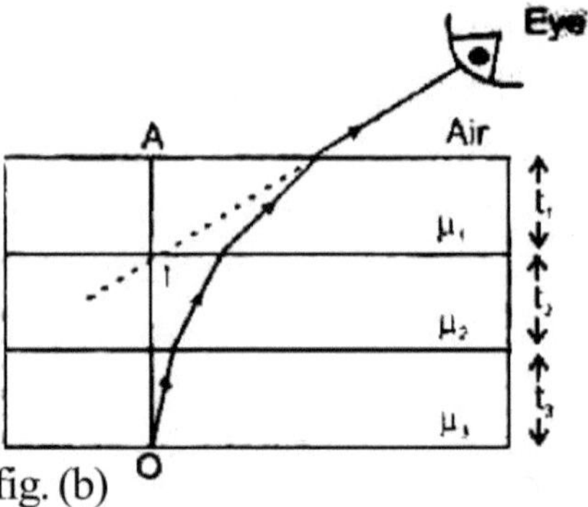

fig. (b)

Case II : If $\mu_1 = 1$ (for air) and $\mu_2 = \mu$ then

$$\frac{AI}{AO} = \frac{\text{Apparent Depth}}{\text{Real Depth}} = \frac{\mu_2}{\mu_1} = \frac{\mu}{1} \quad .....(2)$$

$$\therefore \text{ shift in image} = OI = AI - AO = \left[\frac{AI - AO}{AO}\right] AO = \left[\frac{AI}{AO} - 1\right] AO$$

$$\Rightarrow \quad \Delta t = (\mu - 1)t$$

Case III : When object and observer both are in rarer medium.

Let observer is in air & object is at a point O in air, as shown in figure, A glass is there in between observer & object. Image form at point I. Refractive index of glass is μ

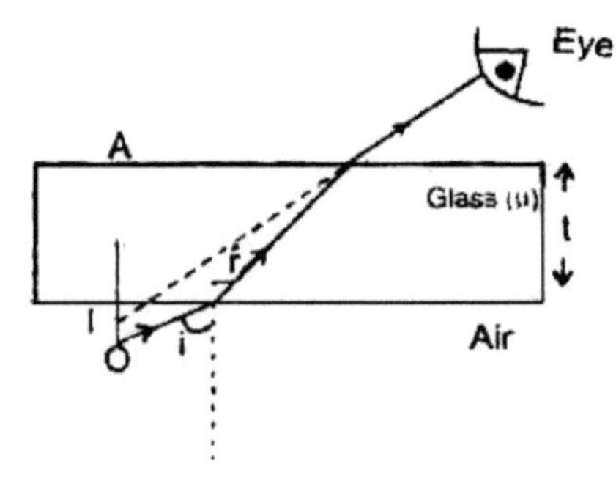

Virtual displacement $= OI = \left[t - \frac{1}{\mu}\right]$

Illustration 13

When a glass slab is placed on a dot on a paper, it appears displaced by 4 cm, viewed normally. What is the thickness of slab if the refractive index is 1.5.

Solution:

We know that Displacement $= t\left[1-\frac{1}{\mu}\right]$ So $4 = t\left[1-\frac{1}{\mu}\right]$

$$t = \frac{\mu\times 4}{\mu-1} = \frac{1.5\times 4}{1.5-1} = 12\text{cm}$$

Consider a rectangular glass slab of refractive index n_{21} and thickness t.

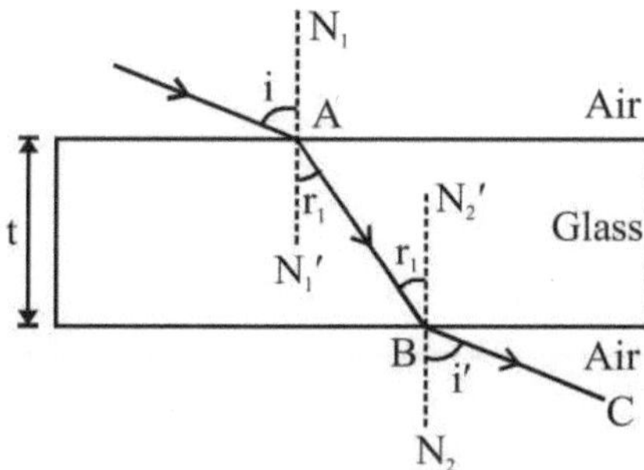

where n_{21} is refractive index of glass slab with respect to air.

At point A,

$$n_{21} = \frac{\sin i}{\sin r_1} \quad .....(i)$$

At point B, the refractive index of air w.r.t. glass slab.

$$n_{12} = \frac{\sin r_1}{\sin i'} \quad .....(ii)$$

We know that,

$$n_{21} = \frac{1}{n_{12}} \quad .....(iii)$$

From equations (i), (ii) and (iii), we get

$$\frac{\sin i}{\sin r_1} = \frac{\sin i'}{\sin r_1} \quad \text{or} \quad i = i'$$

This shows that a ray of light incident obliquely on the parallel sided glass slab emerges out parallel to the incident ray. However, the incident ray is laterally displaced.

4.11.8 Lateral shift (d):

The perpendicular distance between the direction of incident ray and the emergent ray is known as lateral shift.

From right angled ΔBOL,

$$\sin(i - r_1) = \frac{BL}{OB} = \frac{d}{OB}$$

or $$d = OB\sin(i - r_1) \quad .....(iv)$$

From right angled ΔBOD,

$$\cos r_1 = \frac{OD}{OB} = \frac{t}{OB}$$

or $$OB = \frac{t}{\cos r_1} \quad .....(v)$$

From equations (iv) and (v), we get

Lateral shift $d = \dfrac{t\sin(i - r_1)}{\cos r_1}$

Illustration 14

A ray of light refracted through a glass slab of thickness $2\sqrt{3}$ cm and refractive index $\sqrt{3}$. If angle of incidence is 60° then find the lateral shift?

Solution

$$n = \frac{\sin i}{\sin r} \quad \text{or} \quad \sqrt{3} = \frac{\sin 60^\circ}{\sin r}$$

or $$\sin r = \frac{\sqrt{3}}{2} \times \frac{1}{\sqrt{3}} = \frac{1}{2} = \sin 30^\circ$$

or $r = 30^\circ$, $t = 2\sqrt{3}$ cm

$$d = \frac{t\sin(i - r)}{\cos r} = \frac{2\sqrt{3}\sin(60^o - 30^o)}{\cos r} = \frac{2\sqrt{3}\sin 30^o}{\cos 30^\circ}$$

or $$d = \frac{2\sqrt{3} \times 1/2}{\sqrt{3}/2} = 2 \text{ cm}$$

Illustration 15

A fish in the pond of a water appears at a depth of 6 cm. What is the actual depth of the fish if refractive index of water is 4/3 ?

Solution

$n_{21} = 4/3$; Apparent depth = 6 cm

Real depth = Apparent depth × $n_{21} = 6 \times \frac{4}{3} = 8$ cm

---

Try yourself

4. A container is filled with water 12.5 cm deep. The depth of a needle lying on the bottom of the container appears to be 9.4 cm. Find the refractive index of water.

REFRACTION THROUGH MULTIPLE REFRACTING MEDIA

A compound slab made up of water and glass bounded by parallel faces and placed in air.

At point O,

$$n_{wa} = \frac{\sin i}{\sin r_1} \quad .....(i)$$

At point B,

$$n_{gw} = \frac{\sin r_1}{\sin r_2} \quad .....(ii)$$

At point C,

$$n_{ag} = \frac{\sin r_2}{\sin i} \quad .....(iii)$$

Multiplying equations (i), (ii) and (iii), we get

$$n_{wa} \times n_{gw} \times n_{ag} = \frac{\sin i}{\sin r_1} \times \frac{\sin r_1}{\sin r_2} \times \frac{\sin r_2}{\sin i}$$

or $n_{wa} \times n_{gw} \times n_{ag} = 1$ or $n_{wa} \times n_{gw} = \frac{1}{n_{ag}}$ or $n_{wa} \times n_{gw} = n_{ga}$

Illustration 16

If refractive index of glass w.r.t. air is 3/2 and refractive index of water w.r.t. air is 4/3. Find the refractive index of glass w.r.t. water.

Solution

$n_{ga} = 3/2$, $n_{wa} = 4/3$, $n_{gw} = ?$

$\therefore$ $n_{wa} \times n_{gw} = n_{ga}$ or $\frac{4}{3} \times n_{gw} = \frac{3}{2}$ or $n_{gw} = \frac{9}{8}$

Try yourself

5. The refractive index of air w.r.t. glass is 2/3. The refractive index of the diamond w.r.t. air is 12/5. What is the refractive index of glass w.r.t. the diamond?

4.12 REFRACTION BY SPHERICAL LENSES

4.12.1 Lens

A piece of a transparent medium bounded by at least one spherical surface.

4.12.2 Types of Lens

LENS

(A piece of a transparent medium bounded by at least one spherical surface)

- Convex or converging (thick in the middle and thin at the edges)
  - Double convex
  - Plano convex
  - Concavo convex
- Concave or diverging (Thin in the middle and thick at the edges)
  - Double concave
  - Plano concave
  - Convexo concave

4.12.3 Terms related to thin spherical Lenses

(a) **Optical centre (O) :** O is a point for a given lens through which any ray passes undeviated.

(b) **Principal Axis(C_1C_2) :** C_1C_2 is a line passing through optical centre and perpendicular to the lens. The centre of curvature of curved surface always lie on the principal axis (as in a sphere is always perpendicular to surface).

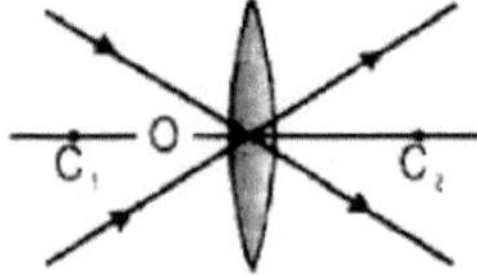

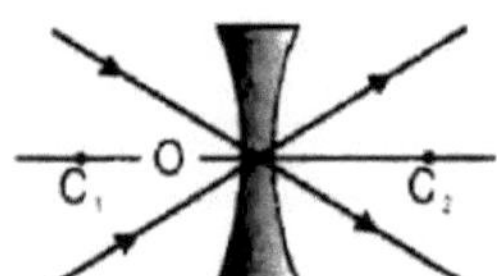

(c) **Principal Focus (f) :** It is defined as the point where the parallel beam of light converges or appear to diverge i.e. focus.

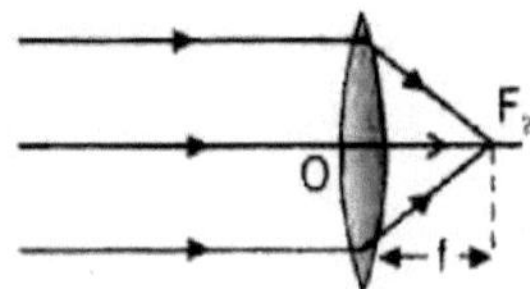

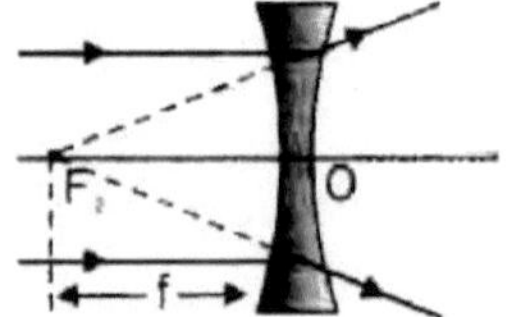

(d) **Aperture :** In reference to lens, aperture means to effective diameter of its light transmitting area so that brightness i.e. intensity of image formed by a lens which depends on the light passing through the lens will depend on the square of aperture i.e. $I \propto (\text{aperture})^2$.

Terms related to thin spherical Lenses

(i) **Principal axis** : Line passing through the optical centre and joining the centres of curvature of the two curved surface.

(ii) **Optical centre**: It is a point lying within a lens through which the ray of light pass undeviated.

(iii) **Principal focus** : It is a point on the principal axis of the lens where all the rays of light coming parallel to the principal axis either converge actually (convex lens) or appear to diverge (concave).

(iv) **Focal length (f)** : The distance between the optical centre and the principal focus. For a convex lens : f = +ve. For a concave lens : f = –ve

(v) **Focal plane** : A plane passing through the principal focus and perpendicular to the principal axis.

(vi) **Aperture** : The effective diameter of the light transmitting portion of the lens. Brightness of image is directly proportional to square of aperture of the lens.

4.12.4 Rules for image formation by a Lens

(i) A ray of light travelling parallel to the principal axis, after refraction passes through (convex lens) or appears to come from (concave lens) its principal focus.

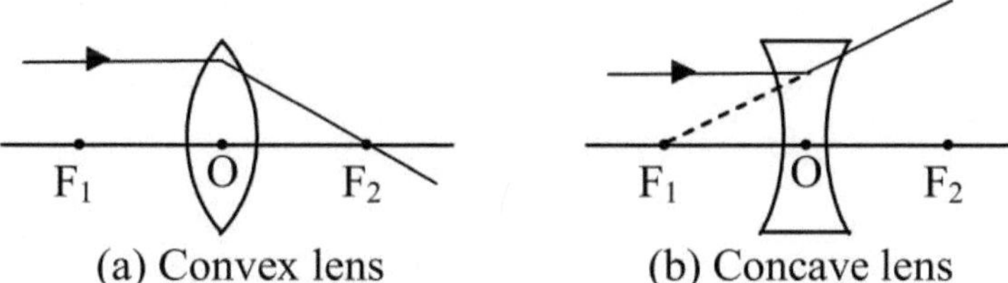

(a) Convex lens (b) Concave lens

(ii) A ray of light initially travelling through (convex lens) or along the direction of principal focus after refraction, travels parallel to the principal axis.

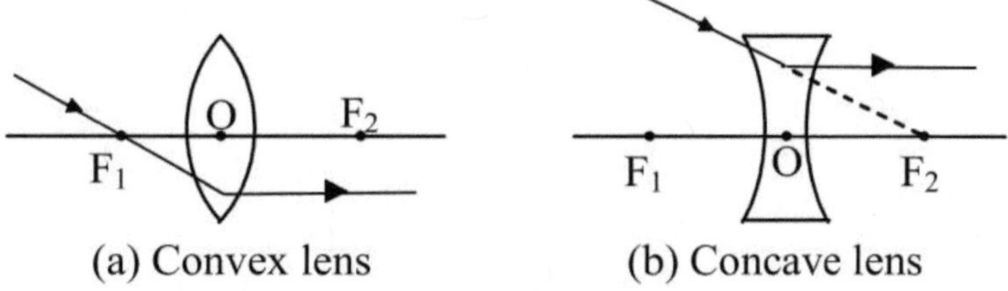

(a) Convex lens (b) Concave lens

(iii) A ray of light which passes through the optical centre, does not suffer any refraction.

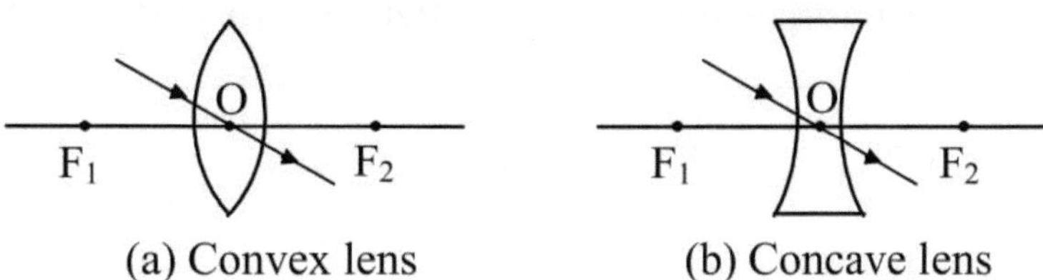

(a) Convex lens (b) Concave lens

4.12.5 Image formation in Lenses Using Ray Diagrams

(a) Image formation by a lens

Position of object	Details of Image	Figure
At infinity	Real, inverted, diminished (m << – 1), At F	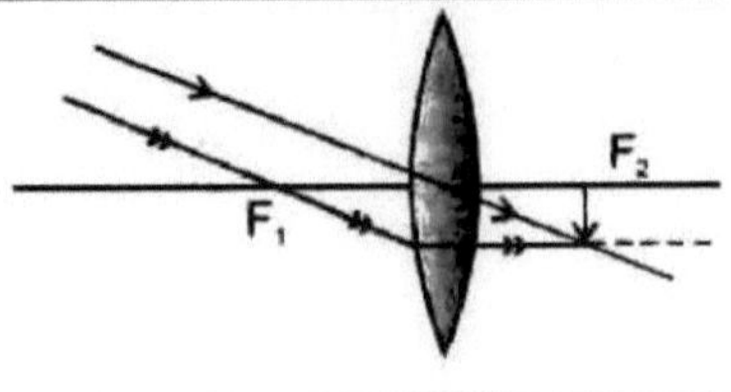 F_1, F_2
Between infinity and 2F	Real, inverted, diminished (m < – 1), between 2F and F	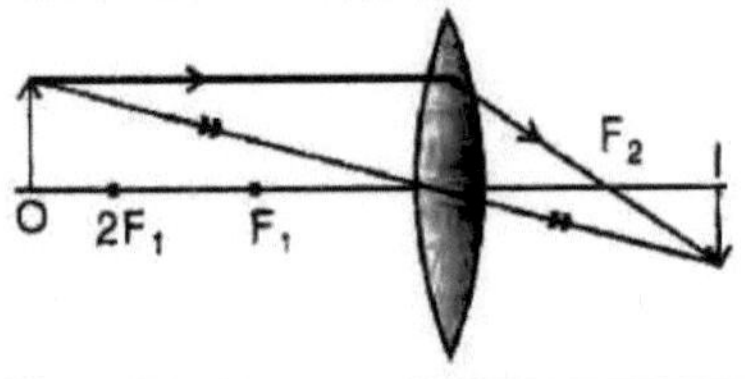 O, $2F_1$, F_1, F_2, I
At 2F	Real, inverted, equal in size (m = – 1), At 2F	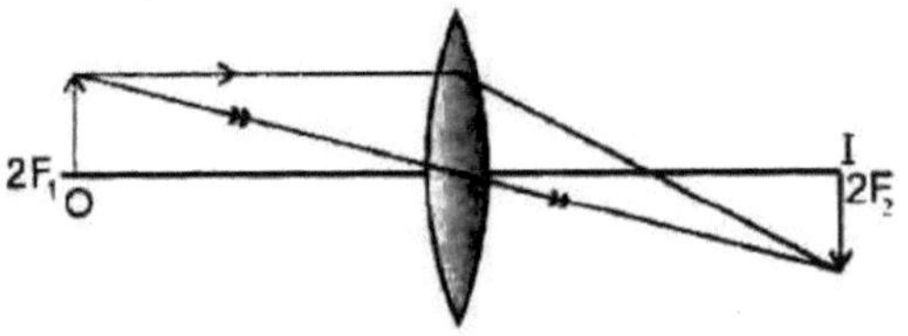 $2F_1$, O, I, $2F_2$
Between 2F and F	Real, inverted, enlarged (m > – 1), Between 2F and ∝	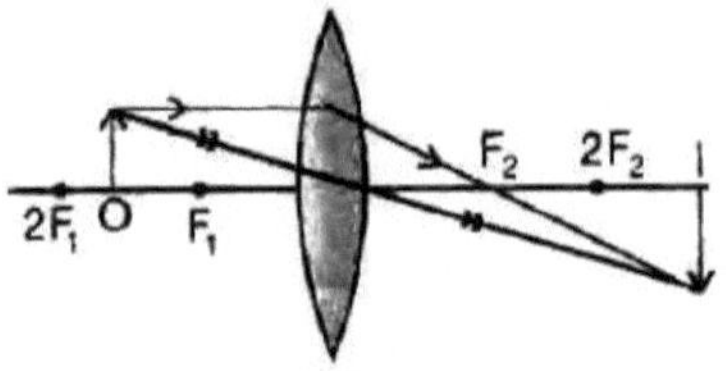 $2F_1$, O, F_1, F_2, $2F_2$, I
At F	Real, inverted, enlarged (m >> – 1), At infinity	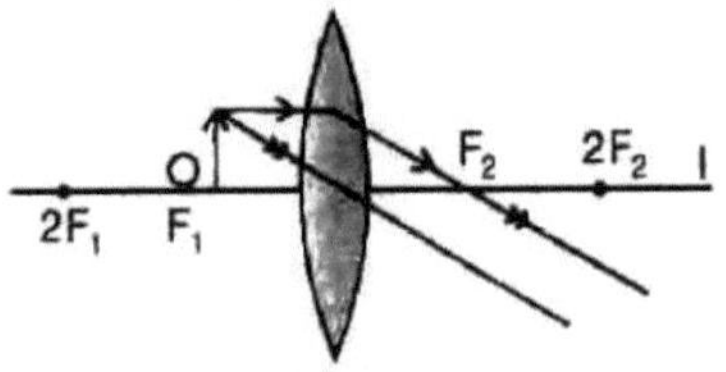 $2F_1$, F_1, O, F_2, $2F_2$, I
Between Focus and Pole	Virtual, erect, enlarged (m > +1), Between ∞ and Object, on same side of object	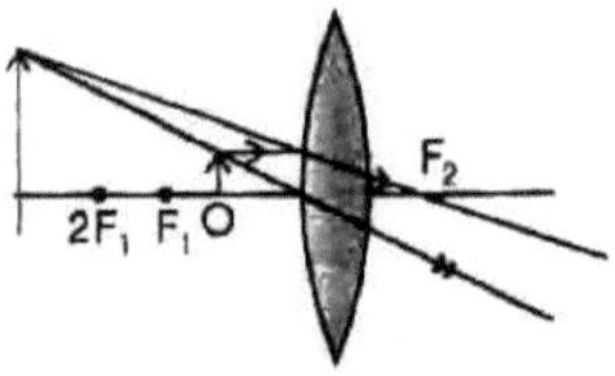 $2F_1$, F_1, O, F_2

(b) Image formed by a concave lens

Position of the object	Position of the image	Relative size of the image	Nature of the image
At infinity (figure a)	At the focus F_1	Highly diminished, point-sized	Virtual and erect
Between infinity and optical centre O of the lens (figure b)	Between focus F_1 and optical centre O	Diminished	Virtual and erect

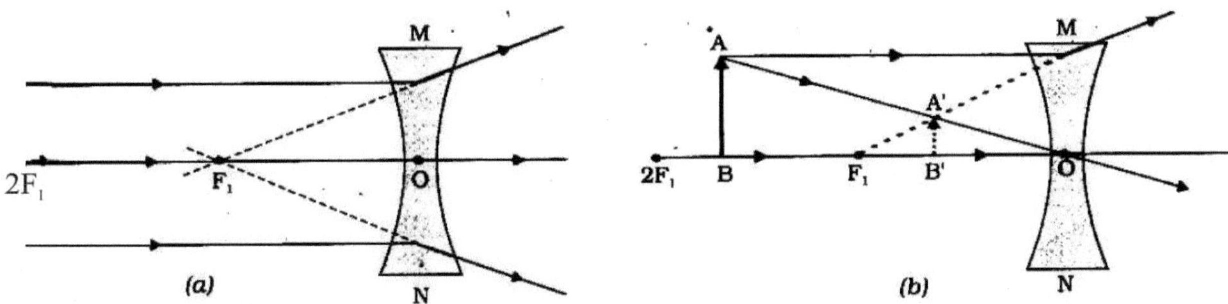

(fig. The position, size and the nature of the image formed by a concave lens for various positions of the object)

4.12.6 Sign Convention for spherical Lenses

(i) All the distances are measured from the optical centre of the lens.

(ii) The **distance measured** in the **same direction** as that of **incident light are taken as positive**.

(iii) The **distance measured against the direction of incident light** are taken as **negative**.

(iv) The **distances measured upward** and perpendicular to the principal axis are taken as **positive**.

(v) The **distances measured downward** and perpendicular to the principal axis are taken as **negative**.

Direction of incident ray
+ve
F_1
–ve
O
+ve
F_2
–ve

4.12.7 The Lens Formula $\frac{1}{v}-\frac{1}{u}=\frac{1}{f}$

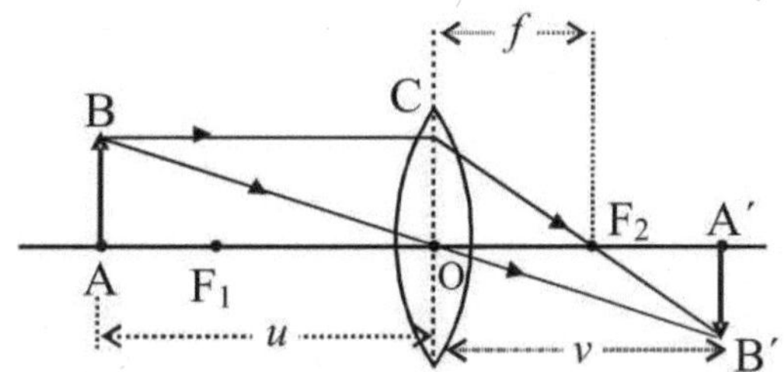

4.12.8 Magnification (m)

It is defined as the ratio of the height of the image and the height of the object

$$m=\frac{\text{Height of the image}}{\text{Height of the object}}=\frac{h_i}{h_o}$$

From equation (i)

$$\frac{A'B'}{AB}=\frac{OA'}{OA} \quad \text{or} \quad \frac{h_i}{h_o}=\frac{v}{u} \quad \text{or} \quad m=\frac{h_i}{h_o}=\frac{v}{u}$$

(i) If the image is real and inverted (i.e.. I is negative) m is – ve.

(ii) If the image is virtual and erect (i.e.. I is positive), m is +ve.

$$m=\frac{I}{O}=\frac{v}{u}=\frac{f-v}{f}=\frac{f}{f+u}$$

4.12.9 Power of Lens (P)

$$P = \frac{1}{f(\text{in meter})} = \frac{100}{f(\text{in cm})}$$

SI unit of power is diopter (D).

(i) Power of a convex lens is +ve. (ii) Power of a concave lens is -ve.

- Power of a lens is the measure of its degree of convergence or divergence of light rays falling on it.

Illustration 17

The image of a needle placed 45 cm from a lens is formed on a screen placed 90 cm on the other side of the lens. Find the displacement of the image, if the object is moved by 5 cm away from the lens. Also find the power of the lens.

Solution

Case I: u = –45 cm, v = 90 cm, f = ?

Using, $\frac{1}{f} = \frac{1}{v} - \frac{1}{u}$ or $\frac{1}{f} = \frac{1}{90} + \frac{1}{45} = \frac{3}{90} = \frac{1}{30}$ or $f = 30$ cm

Case II: u′ = –45 – 5 = –50 cm

$\frac{1}{v'} - \frac{1}{u'} = \frac{1}{f}$ or $\frac{1}{v'} = \frac{1}{f} + \frac{1}{u'} = \frac{1}{30} - \frac{1}{50}$ or $\frac{1}{v'} = \frac{2}{150}$

or $v' = \frac{150}{2} = 75$ cm

or Displacement of image = 90 – 75 = 15 cm

Power of lens, $P = \frac{1}{f} = \frac{100}{30} = +3.33$ D

Illustration 18

Two converging lenses with focal lengths 15 cm and 25 cm are placed 18 cm apart. An object is located 8.0 cm in the left of the 15 cm focal length lens. Where will be the final image formed.

Solution:

Find the image location for the first lens using the thin lens equation

$\frac{1}{v_1} = \frac{1}{f_1} + \frac{1}{u_1} = \frac{1}{15\text{cm}} + \frac{1}{-8.0\,\text{cm}}$ which gives $V_1 = -17.14$ cm

This image forms the object of the second lens located 17.14 cm + 18 cm = 35.14 cm away. The thin lens equation gives for the second lens

$\frac{1}{v_2} = \frac{1}{f_2} + \frac{1}{u_2} = \frac{1}{25\text{cm}} + \frac{1}{-35.14\,\text{cm}}$ which gives $v_2 = 86.64$ cm

The final image lies 86.64 cm to the right of the second lens (25 cm) lens

Illustration 19

A converging lens is used to read the small print in a contract. The lens is held 9.0 cm from the print and produces a magnification of + 2.5. What is the focal length of the lens?

Solution:

The fine print serves as the object for the lens u = 9.0 cm. The image distance is then

$$v = mu = -(2.5 \text{ cm})(9.0 \text{ cm}) = -22.5 \text{ cm}$$

The thin lens equation gives $\frac{1}{f} = \frac{1}{v} - \frac{1}{u} = \frac{1}{-22.5} - \frac{1}{-9} = \frac{1}{f}$

So, $f = +15$ cm

Try yourself

6. An object 10 cm high is placed at the principal focus of a concave lens of focal length 20 cm. Find the size, position and nature of the image. Also find the power of lens.

4.13 LENSES IN CONTACT

Consider two thin lens of focal lengths, f_1 and f_2 respectively placed in contact with each other.

Let O be the point object placed on the principal axis of the lenses. If second lens is not present, then the first lens forms an image I_1 of the object O at a distance v_1 from it.

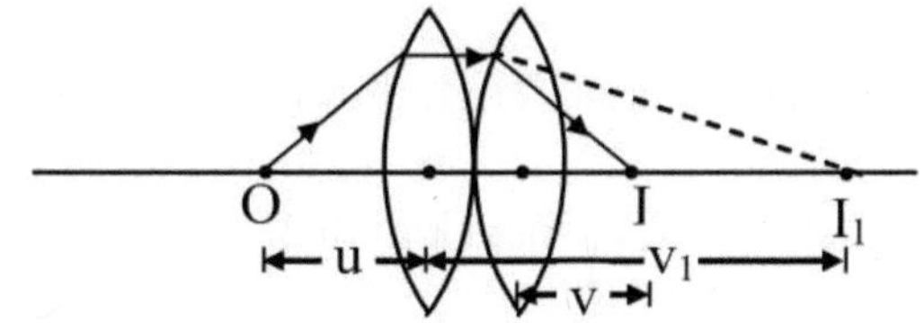

Using lens formula $\frac{1}{v_1} - \frac{1}{-u} = \frac{1}{f_1}$ or $\frac{1}{v_1} + \frac{1}{u} = \frac{1}{f_1}$ .....(i)

Since second lens is in contact with the first, So I_1 acts as an object for the second lens which forms the image I at a distance v from it.

or $-\frac{1}{v_1} + \frac{1}{v} = \frac{1}{f_2}$ .....(ii)

Adding equation (i) and (ii), we get

$\frac{1}{u} + \frac{1}{v} = \frac{1}{f_1} + \frac{1}{f_2}$ or $\frac{1}{u} + \frac{1}{v} = \frac{1}{F}$

where, $\frac{1}{F} = \frac{1}{f_1} + \frac{1}{f_2}$

F is equivalent focal length.

The power of the equivalent lens is given by $P = P_1 + P_2$

Magnification, $m = m_1 \times m_2$

(i) If two thin lens of equal focal length but of opposite nature (i.e. one convergent and other divergent) are put in contact, the resultant focal length of the combination will be

$$\frac{1}{f}=\frac{1}{+f}+\frac{1}{-f}=0$$

i.e., $F=\infty$ and $P=0$

i.e., the system will behave as a plane glass plate.

(ii) If two thin lens of the same nature are put in contact then as

$$\frac{1}{F}=\frac{1}{f_1}+\frac{1}{f_2}$$

$$\frac{1}{F}>\frac{1}{f_1} \text{ and } \frac{1}{F}>\frac{1}{f_2} \qquad \text{i.e., } F< f_1 \text{ and } F<f_2$$

i.e. The resultant focal length will be lesser than smallest individual.

(iii) If two thin lenses of same nature with different focal lengths are put in contact the resultant focal length will be of same nature as that of the lens of shorter focal length but its magnitude will be more than that of shorter focal length. If a lens of focal length f is divided into two equal parts (as shown in figure A)

Each part has focal length f' then as $\frac{1}{f}=\frac{1}{f'}+\frac{1}{f'} \Rightarrow f'=2f$

i.e. Each part have focal length 2f now if these parts are put in contact (as shown in figure B or C), the resultant focal length of the combination will be $\frac{1}{f}=\frac{1}{2f}+\frac{1}{2f}$

i.e., $F=f(=\text{initial value})$

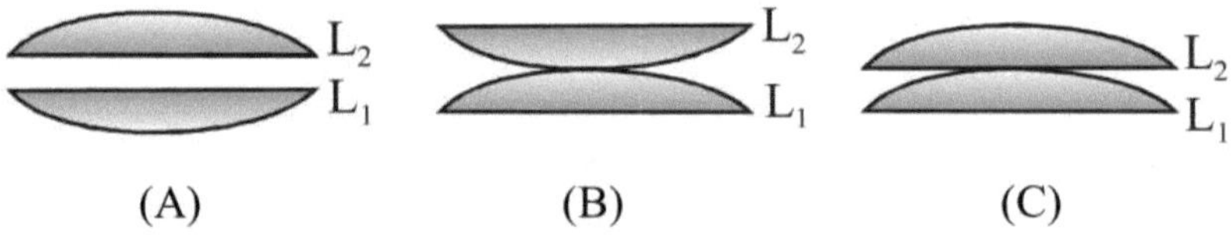

(A) (B) (C)

Note:

(1) when two lenses of focal lengths f_1 and f_2 are placed co-axially at a distance x from each other, then the equivalent focal length and power is given by

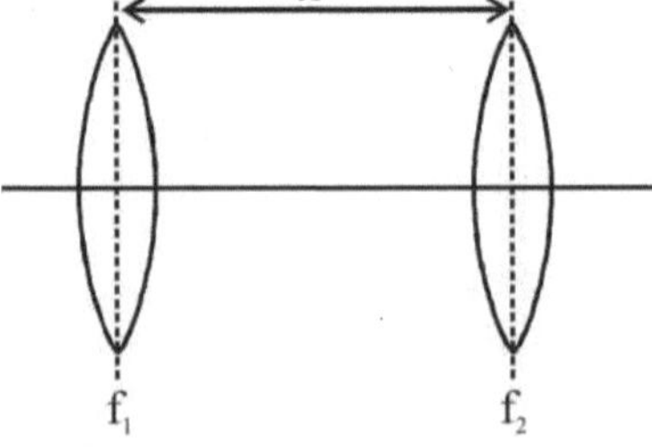

$$\frac{1}{F}=\frac{1}{f_1}+\frac{1}{f_2}-\frac{x}{f_1 f_2} \text{ and } P=P_1+P_2-xP_1P_2$$

4.13.1 Lens maker formula

This formula gives a relation among the focal length (f) the refractive index of a lens with respect to the medium in which it is placed $({}_m\mu_l - 1)$ and its radii of curvatures (R_1 and R_2). This formula is expressed as

$$\frac{1}{f} = ({}_m\mu_l - 1) \times \left(\frac{1}{R_1} - \frac{1}{R_2}\right) \quad \text{or} \quad \frac{1}{f} = \left(\frac{{}_a\mu_l}{{}_a\mu_m} - 1\right)\left(\frac{1}{R_1} - \frac{1}{R_2}\right)$$

where ${}_a\mu_\ell$ = refractive index of lens with respect to air

${}_a\mu_m$ = refractive index of medium with respect to air.

R_1 = radius of curvature of first surface of lens.

R_2 = radius of curvature of second surface of lens.

If lens is placed in air then

$${}_a\mu_m = 1 \text{ and } {}_a\mu_l = \mu \text{(say)} \quad \therefore \quad \frac{1}{f} = (\mu - 1)\left(\frac{1}{R_1} - \frac{1}{R_2}\right)$$

Knowledge Enhancer

Sign convention for R_1 and R_2 : Observe the sign convention for R_1 and R_2 in following figures.

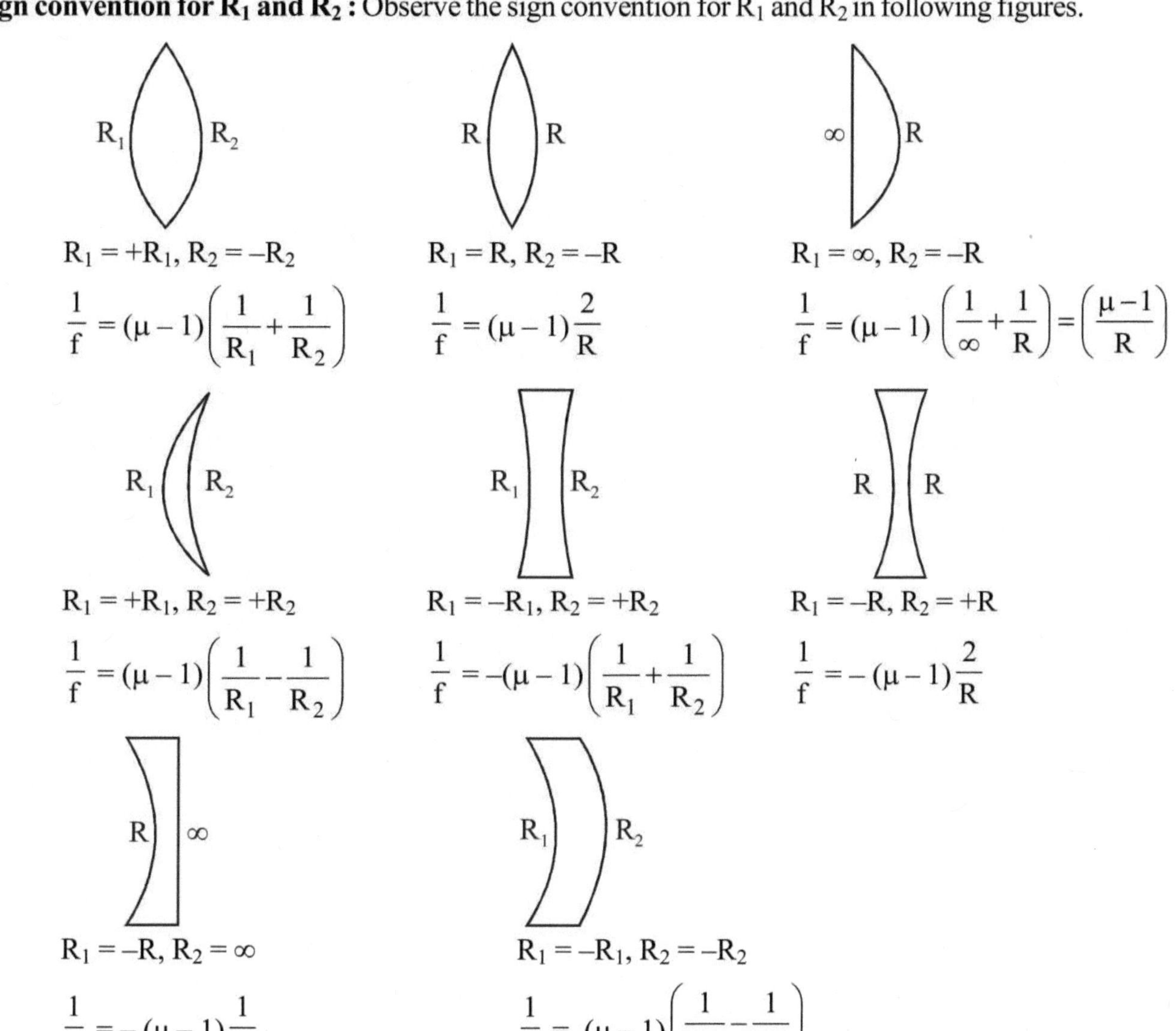

$R_1 = +R_1, R_2 = -R_2$

$\therefore \quad \frac{1}{f} = (\mu - 1)\left(\frac{1}{R_1} + \frac{1}{R_2}\right)$

$R_1 = R, R_2 = -R$

$\frac{1}{f} = (\mu - 1)\frac{2}{R}$

$R_1 = \infty, R_2 = -R$

$\frac{1}{f} = (\mu - 1)\left(\frac{1}{\infty} + \frac{1}{R}\right) = \left(\frac{\mu - 1}{R}\right)$

$R_1 = +R_1, R_2 = +R_2$

$\frac{1}{f} = (\mu - 1)\left(\frac{1}{R_1} - \frac{1}{R_2}\right)$

$R_1 = -R_1, R_2 = +R_2$

$\frac{1}{f} = -(\mu - 1)\left(\frac{1}{R_1} + \frac{1}{R_2}\right)$

$R_1 = -R, R_2 = +R$

$\frac{1}{f} = -(\mu - 1)\frac{2}{R}$

$R_1 = -R, R_2 = \infty$

$\frac{1}{f} = -(\mu - 1)\frac{1}{R}$

$R_1 = -R_1, R_2 = -R_2$

$\frac{1}{f} = (\mu - 1)\left(\frac{1}{R_2} - \frac{1}{R_1}\right)$

Illustration 20

A convex lens of focal length 10.0 cm is placed in contact with a convex lens of 15.0 cm focal length. What is the focal length of the combination.

Solution:

For combination of lenses

$$\frac{1}{f}=\frac{1}{f_1}+\frac{1}{f_2}=\frac{1}{10}+\frac{1}{15}=\frac{1}{6}$$

Therefore, $f = 6$ cm

Illustration 21

Ten identical converging thin lenses, each of focal length 10 cm, are in contact. What is the power of the combined lens.

Solution:

For thin lenses in contact

$$P = P_1 + P_2 + \ldots\ldots\ldots\ldots + P_{10}$$

$$= 10\ P_1 = \frac{10\times100}{10} = 100\ D$$

Knowledge Enhancer

A lens has two surface. If one of the surfaces are silvered, the lens behave as a mirror. The mechanism of the image formation can be understood in brief as given below.

Light from the object falls on the lens which produces a virtual image I_1. This image acts as object for the silvered surface (which acts as a mirror) and a second virtual image I_2 is formed. Finally, this image acts as object for the lens and final image I_3 is formed. Thus, refraction takes place two times at the lens and reflection takes one time at the mirror .

Thus on silvering, the lens behave as a mirror of focal length F given by.

$$\frac{1}{f}=\frac{2}{f_l}+\frac{1}{f_m} \qquad \ldots..(1)$$

Where f_l = focal length of lens from which refraction takes place two times.

f_m = focal length of mirror from which reflection takes place one time.

Case I : When a double convex lens is silvered.

Clearly, $f_m = \frac{R}{2}$

Also, by lens maker formula

$$\frac{1}{f_l} = (\mu - 1)\left(\frac{1}{R} + \frac{1}{R}\right) = (\mu - 1)\frac{2}{R} \qquad \therefore \quad f_l = \frac{R}{2(\mu - 1)}$$

Putting the values of f_m and f_ℓ in (1) we get

$$\frac{1}{f} = \frac{2 \times 2(\mu - 1)}{R} + \frac{2}{R} = \frac{2(2\mu - 1)}{R} \qquad \therefore \quad \boxed{f = \frac{R}{2(2\mu - 1)}}$$

Case II : When a plano convex lens is silvered

(i) If curved surface is silvered

In this case,

$$f_m = \frac{R}{2} \text{ and } f_l = \frac{R}{(\mu - 1)} \qquad \therefore \quad \boxed{f = \frac{R}{2\mu}}$$

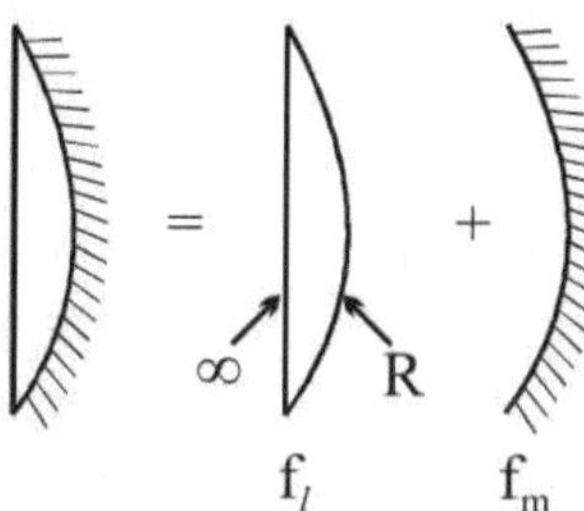

(ii) If plane surface is silvered

In this case, $f_m = \infty$ ($\because$ $R = \infty$)

and $f_l = \frac{R}{\mu - 1}$ $\qquad \therefore \quad \boxed{f = \frac{R}{2(\mu - 1)}}$

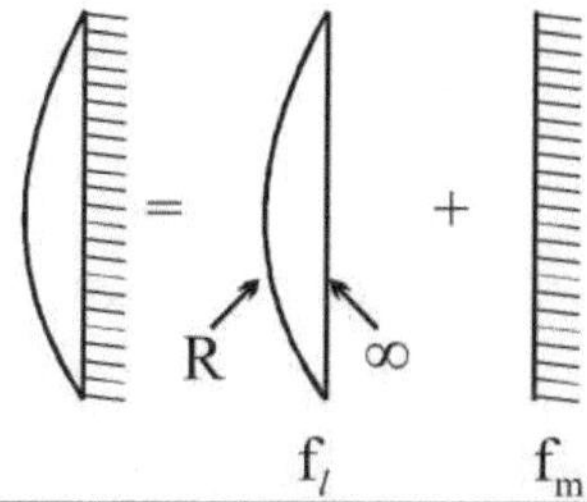

Illustration 22

The radius of curvature of a thin plano - convex lens is 10 cm (of curved surface) and the refraction index is 1.5. If the plane surface is silvered then it behaves like a concave mirror of focal length.

(a) 10 cm (b) 15 cm (c) 20 cm (d) 5 cm

Solution:

(a) The silvered plano convex lens behaves as a concave mirror, whose focal length is given by

$$\frac{1}{f} = \frac{2}{f_1} + \frac{1}{f_m}$$

If plane surface is silvered, $f_m = \frac{R_2}{2} = \frac{\infty}{2} = \infty$

$$\therefore \quad \frac{1}{f_1} = (\mu - 1)\left[\frac{1}{R_1} - \frac{1}{R_2}\right] = (\mu - 1)\left[\frac{1}{R} - \frac{1}{\infty}\right] = \frac{\mu - 1}{R}$$

$$\therefore \quad \frac{1}{f} = \frac{2(\mu - 1)}{R} + \frac{1}{\infty} = \frac{2(\mu - 1)}{R} \quad \Rightarrow \quad f = \frac{R}{2(\mu - 1)}$$

Here R = 10 cm, μ = 1.5

$$\therefore \quad f = \frac{10}{2(1.5 - 1)} = 10\text{cm}$$

SOME OTHER PROPERTIES OF LIGHT

As we know light shows dual nature - the nature of a particle in some cases and the nature of a wave in some other. When light behaves as a wave, it shows the following characteristics -

(A) Interference (B) Diffraction (C) Polarisation

When light behaves as a particle, it performs phenomenon like photoelectric effect.

(A) Interference of light

The colour in soap bubbles and oil slicks are due to this property of light. When two light waves of exactly same frequency travels in a medium, in the same direction simultaneously then due to their superposition, the intensity of light is maximum at some points while the intensity is minimum at other points. This phenomenon is called interference of light. It is of two types:

(i) Constructive interference and (ii) Destructive interference

When the waves meet the point with same phase, constructive interference is obtained at that point. Hence, at that point bright spot of light is seen.

But when the waves meet a point with opposite phase, destructive interference is obtained at that point. Hence, at that point dark spot of light is seen.

(A.1) Young's double slit experiment

Fringes are produced by interference which we discussed. Constructive and destructive interference is reviewed in figure. We see that the addition, or superposition of a pair of identical waves in phase with each other produces a wave of the same frequency but with twice the amplitude. If the waves are exactly one half wavelength out of phase, their superposition results in complete cancellation. If they are out of phase by order other amounts partial cancellation occurs

In 1801, the wave nature of light was convincingly demonstrated when the British physician Thomas Young performed his now famous interference experiment. Young found that light directed through two closely spaced pinholes recombined to produce fringes of brightness and darkness on a screen behind. The bright fringes of light resulted from light waves from the two holes arriving crest to crest, while the dark area resulted from light waves arriving through to crest. Figure shows Young's drawing of the pattern of superimposed waves from the two sources. His experiment is now done with two closely spaced slits instead of with pinhole, so the fringe patterns are straight lines (as shown in figure below).

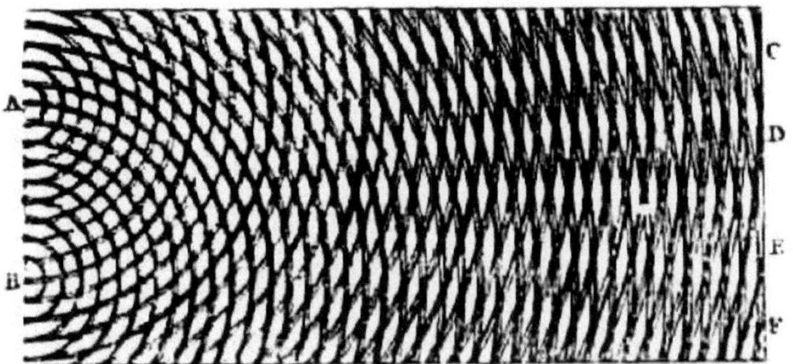

Thomas Young's original drawing of a two-source interference pattern. Letter C, D, E and F mark regions of destructive interference.

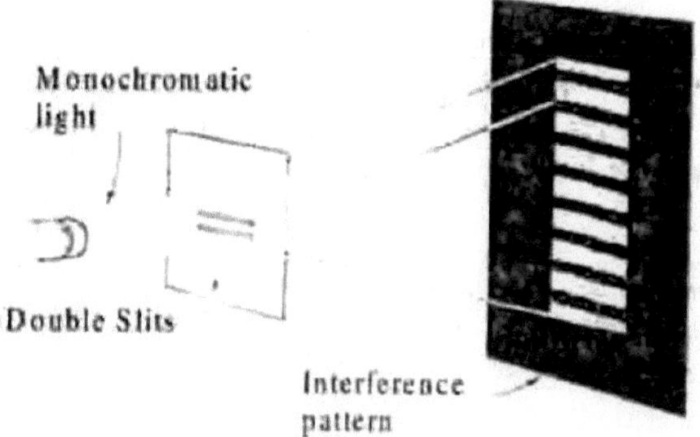

We see in figures and how the series of bright and dark lines results from the different path lengths from the slits to the screen. For the central bright fringe, the path from each slit are the same length, and the waves arrive in phase and reinforce each other. The dark fringes on either side of the central fringe result from one path being longer (or shorter) by one half of wavelength where the wave arrive half a wave length where the wave arrive half wavelength out of phase. The other sets of dark fringes occur where the paths differ by odd multiples of one - half wave length : 3/2, 5/2 so on.

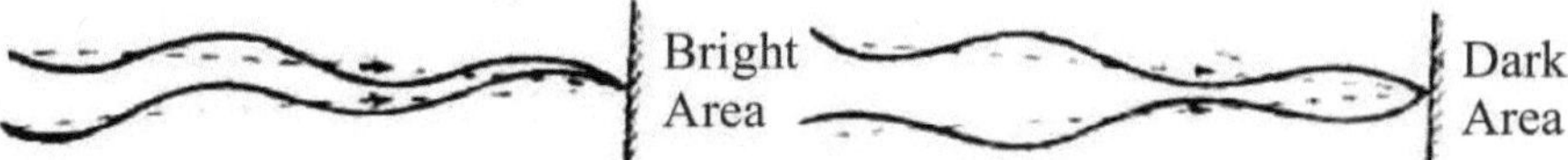

Bright fringes occur when waves from both slits arrive in phase dark areas result from the overlapping of waves that are out of phase.

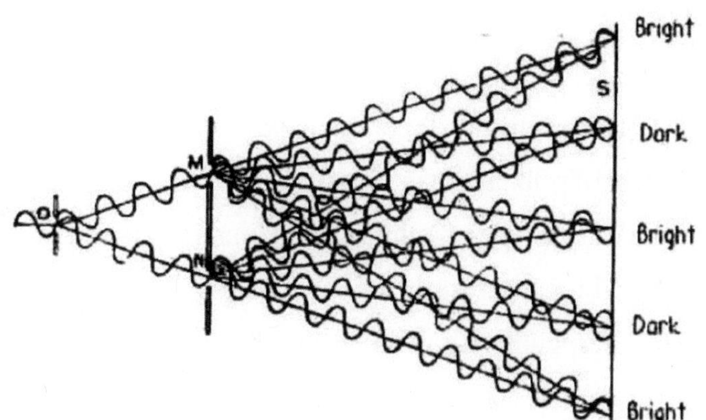

Light from O passes through slits M and N and produces an interference pattern on the screen S.

+ = Reinforcement + = Cancellation + = Partial cancellation

Wave interference

(B) DIFFRACTION OF LIGHT.

The wavelength of light is of the order of an angstroms. So, when light waves encounter obstacles of very small size, the light waves bend around the edges of the obstacle and travel. This is known as diffraction of light. It is due to the diffraction of light that a sharp shadow of an object cannot be obtained on any screen placed behind it. Due to diffraction, light bend and travels into the region of geometrical shadow of the object and thus complete darkness is not found in the shadow. The brightness of light gradually decreases towards complete darkness as we go gradually into the geometrical shadow of the obstacle.

(C) POLARISATION OF LIGHT

An ordinary source of light such as bulb consist of a large number of waves emitted by atoms or molecules in all directions symmetrically. Such light is called unpolarized light (as shown in figure a)

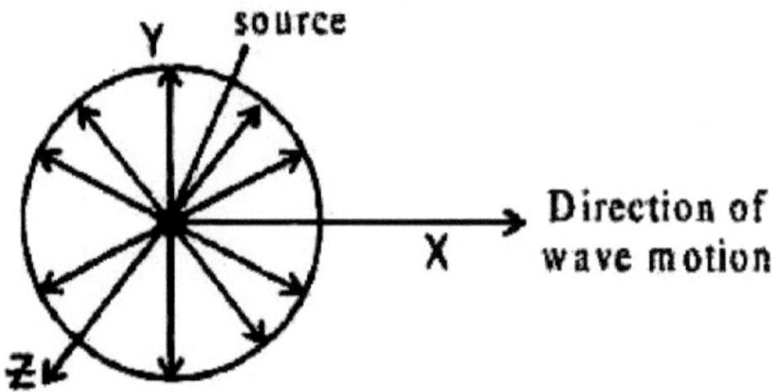

(a) Unpolarised light

If we confine the direction of wave vibration of electric vector in one direction (with the help of polkaroids or Nicol prism) perpendicular to the direction of wave propagation, then such type of light is called plane polarised or linearly polarised. The phenomenon by which, we restrict the vibrations of wave in a particular direction (as shown in figure b). Perpendicular to direction of wave propagation is called polarisation.

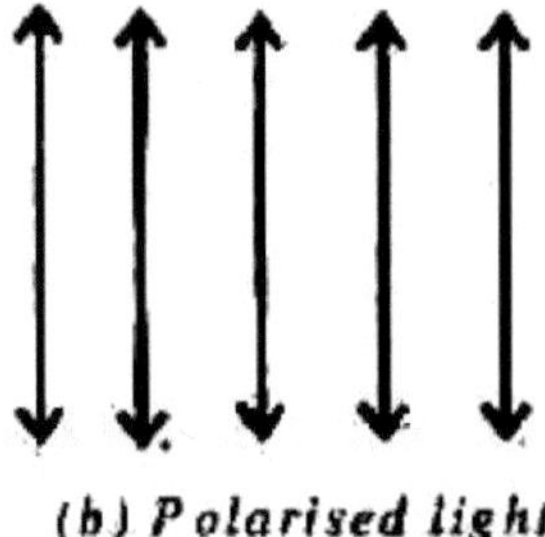

(b) Polarised light

4.14 APPLICATION OF LENSES

Lenses are used in cameras, telescopes, cinema projectors, search lights and microscopes.

(i) A convex lens is used from the image of an object on the film of a camera.

(ii) A convex lens is used in an astronomical telescope to see the heavenly objects like moon, stars, galaxies etc.

(iii) A convex lens of small focal length is used as a reading glass.

(iv) A convex lens of small focal length is used in microscopes to study biological specimens.

(v) A convex lens is used to correct hypermetropia or long - sightedness defect of human eye.

(vi) A concave lens is used to correct myopia or short - sightedness defect of human eye.

Illustration 23

Two thin lenses of focal lengths +10 cm and –5 cm are kept in contact. What is the

(a) focal length (b) power of the combination.

Solution

$$\frac{1}{f} = \frac{1}{f_1} + \frac{1}{f_2}$$

or $\frac{1}{f} = \frac{1}{10} - \frac{1}{5}$ or $\frac{1}{f} = -\frac{1}{10}$ or $f = -10$ cm

Power, $P = \frac{100}{f} = \frac{100}{-10} = -10D$

Try yourself

7. Find the focal length and power of combination of two lenses, one converging of power 8 diopter and the other diverging of power 4 diopter are combined together.

4.14.1 Defects of lenses

(i) **Chromatic aberration** : Due to dispersion the image has coloured edges.

(ii) **Spherical aberration** : Due to different focal length for marginal rays and paraxial rays.

(iii) **Coma** : Comet like tail added to all images.

(iv) **Astigmatism** : Defect in image shape when the rays from horizontal plane and rays from vertical plane focus at different points.

(v) **Distortion** : Due to different magnification of a lens for the upper or lower portion and central portion.

4.14.2 Uses of lenses

(i) Concave, convex and other types of lenses are used in spectacles for correcting the defects of vision.

(ii) Almost all the optical instruments such as projector, telescope, microscope, camera, periscope etc. make use of lenses.

(iii) Now-a-days powerful lenses of large aperture are used to focus solar energy.

4.14.3 Behaviour of lenses in different optical medium

Case I: $n_m < n_l$

where n_m = Absolute refractive index of medium.

n_l = Absolute refractive index of material of lens

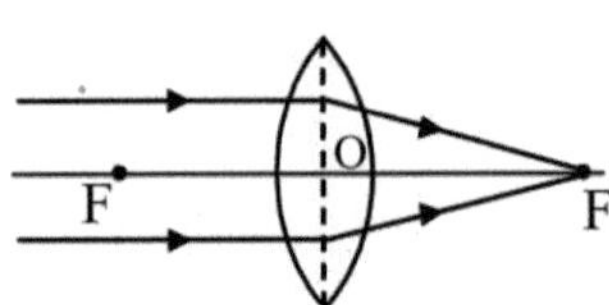

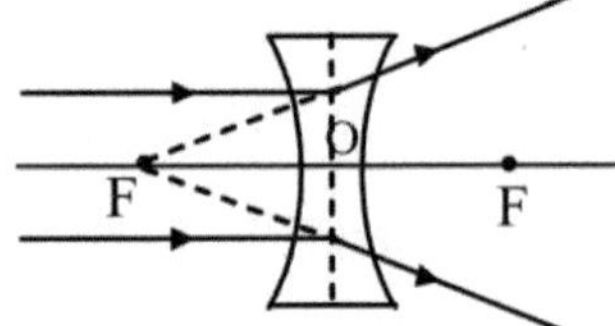

Case II: $n_m = n_l$

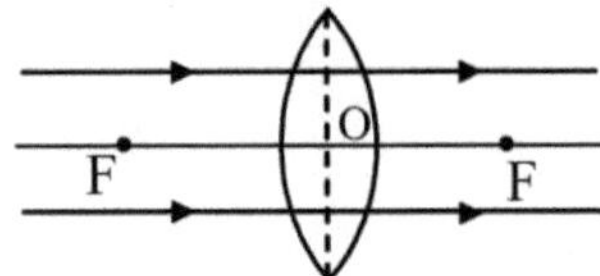

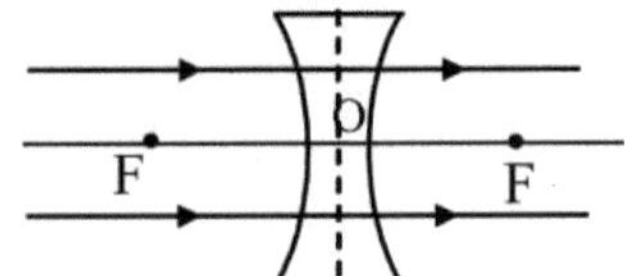

Case III: $n_m > n_l$

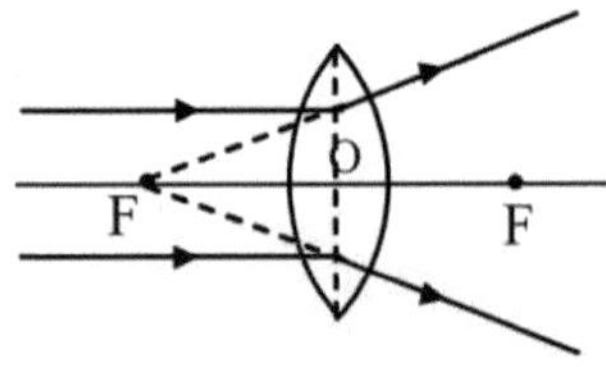

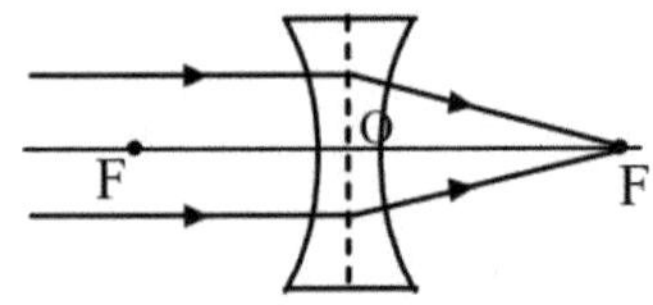

IMPORTANT NOTE

(1) Intensity or brightness of the image is proportional to the square of the aperture of the lens i.e. Intensity of image $\propto$ (Aperture)^2.

(2) If a lens is cut horizontally into two equal halves as shown in figure, then focal length remains unchanged.

(3) If a lens is cut vertically into two equal halves as shown in figure, then focal length becomes double.

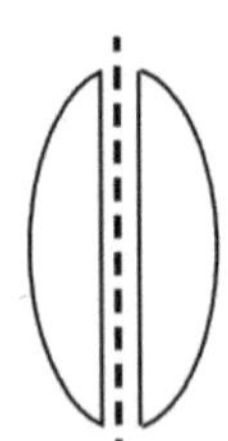

CONCEPT MAP

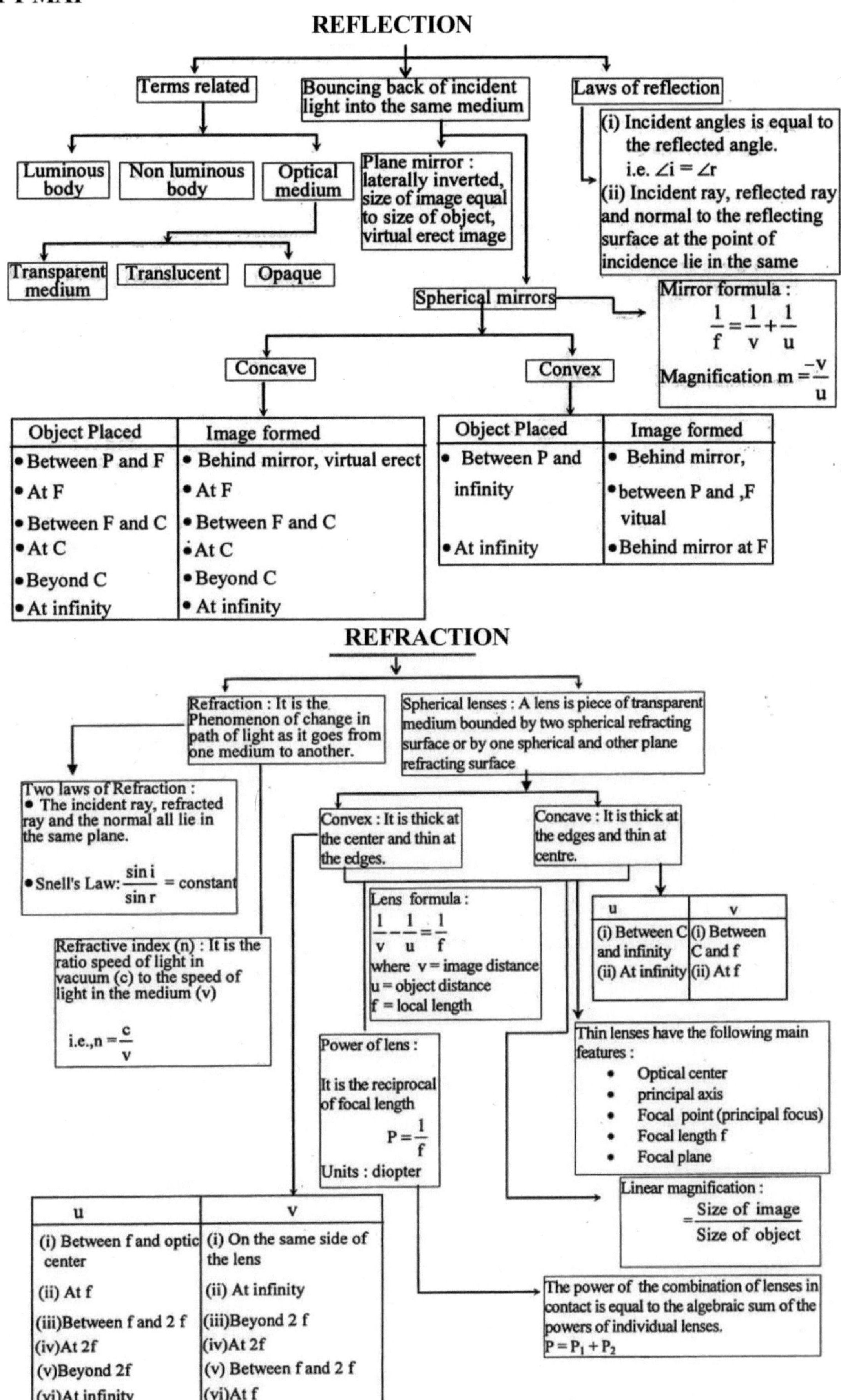
REFLECTION
Terms related
Bouncing back of incident light into the same medium
Laws of reflection
Luminous body
Non luminous body
Optical medium
Transparent medium
Translucent
Opaque
Plane mirror : laterally inverted, size of image equal to size of object, virtual erect image
(i) Incident angles is equal to the reflected angle. i.e. ∠i = ∠r
(ii) Incident ray, reflected ray and normal to the reflecting surface at the point of incidence lie in the same
Spherical mirrors
Mirror formula : 1/f = 1/v + 1/u
Magnification m = −v/u
Concave
Convex
Object Placed | Image formed
• Between P and F | • Behind mirror, virtual erect
• At F | • At F
• Between F and C | • Between F and C
• At C | • At C
• Beyond C | • Beyond C
• At infinity | • At infinity
Object Placed | Image formed
• Between P and infinity | • Behind mirror, • between P and ,F vitual
• At infinity | • Behind mirror at F
REFRACTION
Refraction : It is the Phenomenon of change in path of light as it goes from one medium to another.
Spherical lenses : A lens is piece of transparent medium bounded by two spherical refracting surface or by one spherical and other plane refracting surface
Two laws of Refraction :
• The incident ray, refracted ray and the normal all lie in the same plane.
• Snell's Law: sin i / sin r = constant
Convex : It is thick at the center and thin at the edges.
Concave : It is thick at the edges and thin at centre.
Lens formula : 1/v − 1/u = 1/f where v = image distance u = object distance f = local length
u | v
(i) Between C and infinity | (i) Between C and f
(ii) At infinity | (ii) At f
Refractive index (n) : It is the ratio speed of light in vacuum (c) to the speed of light in the medium (v) i.e., n = c/v
Power of lens : It is the reciprocal of focal length P = 1/f Units : diopter
Thin lenses have the following main features :
• Optical center
• principal axis
• Focal point (principal focus)
• Focal length f
• Focal plane
Linear magnification : = Size of image / Size of object
The power of the combination of lenses in contact is equal to the algebraic sum of the powers of individual lenses. P = P1 + P2
u | v
(i) Between f and optic center | (i) On the same side of the lens
(ii) At f | (ii) At infinity
(iii) Between f and 2 f | (iii) Beyond 2 f
(iv) At 2f | (iv) At 2f
(v) Beyond 2f | (v) Between f and 2 f
(vi) At infinity | (vi) At f

LET US RECAPITULATE

- **Light** is a form of energy which produces the sensation of sight.
- Speed of light in vacuum / air = 3×10^8 ms^{-1}
- **Ray of light :** A line drawn in the direction of propagation of light is called ray of light.
- **Beam of light :** A group of parallel rays light emitted by a source of light is called beam of light.
- **Reflection of light :** The phenomenon of returning of light in the same medium after striking a surface is called reflection of light.
- **Laws of reflection :** The reflection of light from a surface obeys certain laws called laws of reflection.
  - (i) incident angle is equal to reflected angle i.e. $\angle i = \angle r$.
  - (ii) Incident ray, reflected ray and normal to the reflecting surface at the point on incident lie in the same plane.
- **Concave mirror :** concave mirror is a part of a hollow sphere whose outer part is silvered and the inner part is reflecting surface.
- **Convex mirror :** convex mirror is a part of a hollow sphere whose outer part is reflecting surface and inner part is silvered.
- **Centre of curvature :** The centre of a hollow sphere of which the spherical mirror forms a part is called centre of curvature. It is denoted by C
- **Radius of curvature :** The radius of a hollow sphere of which the spherical mirror forms a part is called radius of curvature. It is denoted by R
- **Pole :** The mid point of a spherical mirror is called its pole. It is denoted by P
- **Aperture:** The part of spherical mirror exposed to the incident light is called the aperture of the mirror.
- **Principal Axis:** A line joining the centre of curvature (C) and pole (P) of a spherical mirror and extend on either side is called principal axis of the spherical mirror.
- **Principal Focus :** A point on the principal axis of a spherical mirror where the rays of light parallel to the principal axis meet or appears to meet after reflection from the spherical mirror is called principal focus. It is denoted by F.
- **Focal Plane :** A plane normal or perpendicular to the principal axis and passing through the principal focus (F) of the spherical mirror is called focal plane of the spherical mirror.
- **Focal length (f):** The distance between the pole (P) and the principal focus (F) of a spherical mirror is called the focal length of the spherical mirror.
- $f = \frac{R}{2}$, Where R is the radius of the curvature of the mirror.
- Focal length and radius of curvature of a concave mirror are **negative**.
- Focal length and radius of curvature of a convex mirror are **positive**.

- **Sign Conventions for reflection by spherical mirrors**
  (1) All distance are measured from the pole of a spherical mirror.
  (2) Distance measured in the direction of incident light are taken as positive. Distance measured in the direction opposite to that of the incident light are taken negative.
  (3) The upward distance perpendicular to the principal axis are taken as positive, while the downward distance perpendicular to the principal axis are taken as negative.
- Radius of curvature plane mirror = ∞ (infinite)
- Focal length of a plane mirror = ∞
- **Mirror Formula :** The relation between *u, v,* and focal length (*f*) of a spherical mirror is known as mirror formula.

  That is $\frac{1}{u}+\frac{1}{v}=\frac{1}{f}$
- **Linear magnification :** Linear magnification produced by a mirror is defined as the ratio of the size (or height) of the image to the size of the object . It is denoted by m.

  That is $m=\frac{h'}{h}=\frac{-v}{u}$
- Power of mirror (P) = $\frac{-1}{f(\text{in m})}=\frac{-100}{f(\text{in cm})}$
- Linear magnification produced by a plane mirror = + 1.
- **Refraction of light:** The bending of light rays when they pass obsessively from one medium to the other medium is called refraction of light .
- A transparent medium through which light travels fast is known as optically rarer medium.
- A transparent medium through which light travels slow is known as optically denser medium.
- **Laws of refraction**
  (i) The incident ray, the refracted ray and the normal to the surface separating two media all lie in the same plane.
  (ii) The ratio of the sine of the incident angle ($\angle i$) to the sine of the refracted angle ($\angle r$) is constant

  i.e. $\frac{\sin i}{\sin r}=\text{constant}$

  This constant is known as the refractive index of second medium w.r.t the first medium.
- Absolute refractive index of a medium is defined as the ratio of the speed of light in vacuum (c) to the speed of light in the medium (v)

  i.e. $n=\frac{c}{v}$
- Relative refractive index of medium. 2 w.r.t. the medium 1 is defined as the ratio of the speed of light in medium 1 (v_1) to the speed of light in medium 2 (v_2).

  i.e. $n_{21}=\frac{v_1}{v_2}$

- $n_{21} = \frac{n_2}{n_1}$
- $n_{21} = \frac{1}{n_{12}}$
- A medium whose refractive index is large is known as optically denser medium.
- A medium whose refractive index is small is known as optically rarer medium.
- Lateral shift (displacement) . The perpendicular distance between the original part of the incident ray and the emergent ray coming out of the glass slab is called lateral shift.
- Lens is a transparent medium bounded by two spherical refracting surfaces one spherical and other plane refracting surface .
- Lens are of two types :
  - (i) Convex lens or converging lens: it is thick in the middle and thin at the edge.
  - (ii) Concave lens or diverging lens: it is thin in the middle and thick at the edge.
- Convex lens converges the rays of light falling on it and acts as a magnifying glass.
- Concave lens diverges the rays of light falling on it.
- Principal axis of a lens is a line joining the centres of curvature of two spherical surfaces forming a lens
- Optical centre of a lens is a point inside or outside a lens through which rays of light passes without deviation.
- Principal focus of a lens is a point on the principal axis where all the rays of light parallel to the principal axis meet or appear to meet after refracting through the lens.
- Focal length of a lens is the distance between the optical centre and the principal focus of the lens.
- Focal length of a convex lens is positive.
- Focal length of a concave length is negative.
- Lens formula: $-\frac{1}{u}+\frac{1}{v}=\frac{1}{f}$
- Magnification produced by a lens: $m = \frac{\text{Size of image}}{\text{Size of object}} = \frac{h'}{h}$

  Also $m = \frac{v}{u}$
- Power of lens $P = \frac{1}{f(\text{in m})} = \frac{100}{f(\text{in cm})}$
- Unit of power is **diopter** (D).
- Power of a lens is 1 diopter if its focal length is 1 m or 100 cm.
- Power of a convex lens is **positive**.
- Power of concave lens is **negative**.

CONCEPT APPLICATION LEVEL - I [NCERT Questions]

TEACHER'S ADVICE

1. ***Always take value of u (object distance) –ve, in any of the problem either it is of Lens or Mirror directly.***
2. ***Take focal length of convex (either mirror or either lens) +ve, each problem directly.***
3. ***Take focal length of the concave (either mirror or lens) – ve, each problem directly.***

Q.1 Which one of the following materials cannot be used to make a lens?
(A) Water (B) Glass (C) Plastic (D) Clay

Ans. (D). This is because clay is opaque (i.e. light cannot pass through it).

Q.2 The image formed by a concave mirror is observed to be virtual, erect and larger than the object. Where should be the position of the object?
(A) Between the principal focus and the centre of curvature.
(B) At the centre of curvature.
(C) Beyond the centre of curvature.
(D) Between the pole of the mirror and its principal focus.

Ans. (D) Between the pole of the mirror and its principal focus.

Q.3 Where should an object be placed in front of a convex lens to get a real image of the size of the object?
(A) At the principal focus of the lens.
(B) At twice the focal length.
(C) At infinity.
(D) Between the optical centre of the lens and its principal focus.

Ans. (B) At twice the focal length.

Q.4 A spherical mirror and a thin spherical lens have each a focal length of –15 cm. The mirror and the lens are likely to be
(A) Both are concave.
(B) Both are convex.
(C) The mirror is concave and the lens is convex.
(D) The mirror is convex but the lens is concave.

Ans. (A) Both are concave

Q.5 No matter how far you stand from a mirror, your image appears erect. The mirror is likely to be
(A) Plane only. (B) Concave only.
(C) Convex only. (D) Either plane or convex.

Ans. (D) Either plane or convex

Q.6 Which of the following lenses would you prefer to use while reading small letters found in a dictionary?

(A) A convex lens of focal length 50 cm. **(B) A concave lens of focal length 50 cm.**

(C) A convex lens of focal length 5 cm. **(D) A concave lens of focal length 5 cm.**

Ans. (D) A concave lens of focal length 5 cm

Q.7 We wish to obtain an erect image of an object, using a concave mirror of focal length 15 cm. What should be the range of distance of the object from the mirror? What is the nature of the image? Is the image larger or smaller than the object? Draw a ray diagram to show the image formation in this case.

Ans. A concave mirror produces an erect image if the object is placed between the pole and the focus of the concave mirror. Thus, object may be placed at any position whose distance is less than 15 cm from the concave mirror. The image is virtual and erect. The image is larger than the object.

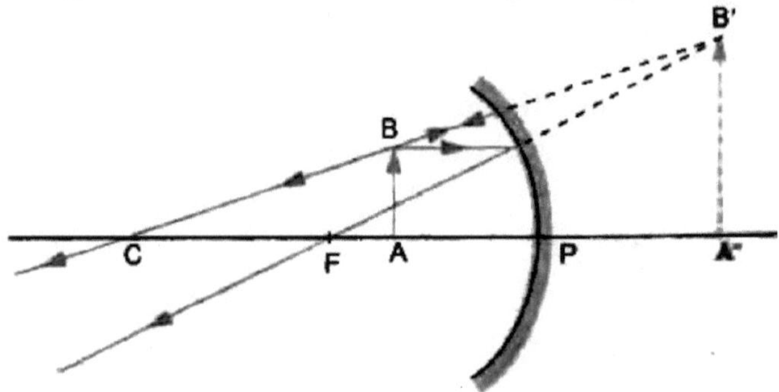

Q.8 Name the type of mirror used in the following situation

(a) Head lights of a car **(b) Side rear view mirror of a vehicle** **(c) Solar furnace**

Support your answer with reason.

Ans. (a) **Concave mirror :** When a bulb is placed at the focus of a concave mirror, then the beam of light from the bulb after reflection from the concave mirror goes as a parallel beam which lights up the front road.

(b) **Convex mirror :** Image formed by a convex mirror is erect and small in size. The field of view behind the vehicle is large.

(c) **Concave mirror :** Concave mirror focuses rays of light coming from the sun at its focus. So, the temperature at the focus is raised.

Q.9 One-half of a convex lens is covered with a black paper. Will this lens produce a complete image of the object?

Ans. A complete image of the object is formed as shown in figure (but with less intensity).

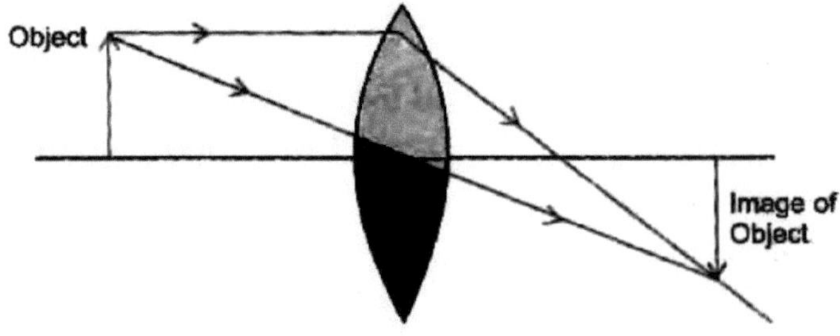

Q.10 An object 5 cm in length is held 25 cm away from a converging lens of focal length 10 cm. Draw the ray diagram and find the position, size and the nature of the image formed.

Ans.

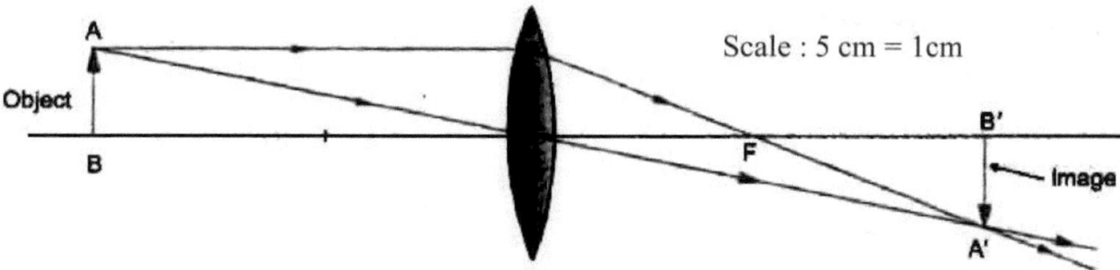

Here, u = –25, f = 10 cm

Using $-\frac{1}{u}+\frac{1}{v}=\frac{1}{f}$, we get

$$\Rightarrow \quad \frac{1}{v}=\frac{1}{f}+\frac{1}{u} = \frac{1}{10}-\frac{1}{25} = \frac{5-2}{50} = \frac{3}{50}$$

$$\therefore \quad v=\frac{50}{3} = 16.67 \text{ cm (position of image)}$$

Size of Image :

$$m=\frac{h'}{h}=\frac{v}{u}=+\frac{50}{3\times -25}=-\frac{2}{3}$$

or $$h' = -\frac{2}{3}\times h = -\frac{2}{3}\times 5 = -\frac{10}{3} = -3.33 \text{ cm}$$

Image is real and inverted.

Q.11 A concave lens of focal length 15 cm forms an image 10 cm from the lens. How far is the object placed from the lens? Draw the ray diagram.

Ans. Here, f = –15 cm, v = –10 cm, u = ?

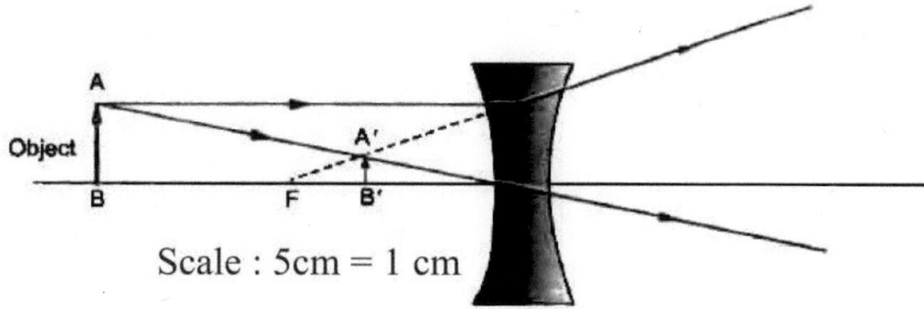

Using, $-\frac{1}{u}+\frac{1}{v}=\frac{1}{f}$,

we get $-\frac{1}{u}=-\frac{1}{v}+\frac{1}{f}$

$$\Rightarrow \frac{-1}{u}=\frac{1}{10}-\frac{1}{15}=\frac{1}{30}$$

$\therefore$ u = – 30 cm.

Q.12 An object is placed at a distance of 10 cm from a convex mirror of focal length 15 cm. Find the position and nature of the image.

Ans. Here, $u = -10$ cm, $f = +15$ cm, $v = ?$

Using, $\frac{1}{u} + \frac{1}{v} = \frac{1}{f}$

we get, $\frac{1}{v} = \frac{1}{f} - \frac{1}{u} = \frac{1}{15} + \frac{1}{10} = \frac{1}{6}$ $\therefore$ $v = 6$ cm.

Now, $m = \frac{-v}{u} = \frac{6}{10} = 0.6$. Since, m is positive, so the orientation of both object and image is same.

Thus, image is erect and virtual.

Q.13 The magnification produced by a plane mirror is +1. What does this means?

Ans. $m = \frac{h'}{h} = 1$ or $h' = h$

It means, size of the image formed by plane mirror is equal to the size of the object. Positive sign with m tells that both object and image are erect.

Q.14 An object 5.0 cm in length is placed at a distance of 20 cm in front of a convex mirror of radius of curvature 30 cm. Find the position of the image, its nature and size.

Ans. $h = 5$ cm, $u = -20$ cm, $R = 30$ cm,

$\therefore$ $f = \frac{R}{2} = 15$ cm

(i) Using, $\frac{1}{u} + \frac{1}{v} = \frac{1}{f}$, we get $\frac{1}{v} = \frac{1}{f} - \frac{1}{u} = \frac{1}{15} + \frac{1}{20} = \frac{7}{60}$

$\therefore$ $v = \frac{60}{7} = 8.57$ cm (Position of image)

(ii) $\frac{h'}{h} = -\frac{v}{u} = \frac{60}{7 \times 20} = \frac{3}{7}$

or $h' = \frac{3}{7} \times 5 = \frac{15}{7} = 2.14$ cm

Since h' is positive, so image is erect and virtual.

Q.15 An object of size 7.0 cm is placed at 27 cm in front of a concave mirror of focal length 18 cm. At what distance from the mirror should a screen be placed, so that a sharp focussed image can be obtained? Find the size and the nature of the image.

Ans. $h = +7.0$ cm, $u = -27$ cm, $f = -18$ cm

(i) Using, $\frac{1}{u} + \frac{1}{v} = \frac{1}{f}$,

we get $\frac{1}{v}=\frac{1}{f}-\frac{1}{u} = -\frac{1}{18}+\frac{1}{27} = -\frac{1}{54}$

$\therefore$ v = – 54 cm

So the screen must be placed at distance of 54 cm in front of the concave mirror.

(ii) $\frac{h'}{h} = -\frac{v}{u}$ or $h' = -\frac{v}{u}\times h = \frac{54}{-27}\times 7 = -14$ cm

Since h' is negative, so image is inverted & real.

Q.16 Find the focal length of a lens of power –2.0 D. What type of lens is this?

Ans. $P = \frac{1}{f(\text{in m})}$ $\therefore$ $f=\frac{1}{P}=\frac{1}{-2} = -0.5$ m = –50 cm

The lens is concave.

Q.17 A doctor has prescribed a corrective lens of power + 1.5 D. Find the focal length of the lens. Is the prescribed lens diverging of converging?

Ans. $f=\frac{1}{P}=\frac{1}{1.5} = +0.67$ m = +67 cm

Since focal length is positive, so the lens is converging.

Q.18 Define the principal focus of a concave mirror.

Ans. A point on the principal axis where the parallel rays of light after reflecting from a concave mirror meet.

Q.19 The radius of curvature of a spherical mirror is 20 cm. What is focal length?

Ans. Radius of curvature, R = 20 cm

$\therefore$ Focal length, $f=\frac{R}{2}=\frac{\pm 20}{2} = \pm 10$ cm

Note : '+' for covex mirror, '–' for concave mirror.

Q.20 Name a mirror that can give an erect and magnified image of an object.

Ans. A concave mirror

Q.21 Why do we prefer a convex mirror as a rear-view mirror in vehicles?

Ans. This because a convex mirror forms an erect and diminished (small in size) images of the objects behind the vehicle and hence the field of view behind the vehicle is also increased.

Q.22 Find the focal length of a convex mirror whose radius of curvature is 32 cm.

Ans. R = + 32 cm. Therefore, f = R/2 = +32/2 = +16 cm

Thus, focal length of the convex mirror is 16 cm.

Q.23 A concave mirror produces three times magnified (enlarged) real image of an object placed at 10 cm in front of it. Where is the image located?

Ans. m = –3,

But m = –v/u, so, v = 3u

u = –10 cm, v = 3 (–10 cm) = –30 cm

Thus, the image is located at a distance of 30 cm to the left side of the concave mirror.

Q.24 A ray of light travelling in air enters obliquely into water. Does the light ray bend towards the normal or away from the normal? Why?

Ans. The ray of light bends towards the normal because the speed of light decreases when it goes from air (rarer medium) into water (denser medium).

Q.25 Light enters from air to glass having refractive index 1.50. What is the speed of light in the glass? The speed of light in vacuum in 3×10^8 ms^{-1}.

Ans. $n = \frac{c}{v}$ $\quad \therefore \quad$ $v = \frac{3\times10^8 \text{ms}^{-1}}{1.50} = 2 \times 10^8 \text{ ms}^{-1}$

Thus, speed of light in glass is 2×10^8 ms^{-1}.

Q.26 You are given kerosene, turpentine and water. In which of these does the light travel faster?

Ans. We know, $v = \frac{c}{n}$ Refractive index (n) of water is 1.333, whereas refractive index of kerosene is 1.44 and that of turpentine is 1.47. As refractive index of water is least, so speed of light in water is more than in kerosene and turpentine. Hence, light travels faster in water.

Q.27 The refractive index of diamond is 2.72. What is the meaning of this statement?

Ans. We know, $n = \frac{c}{v}$ $\quad$ or $\quad$ $v = \frac{c}{n} = \frac{1}{2.42} \times c$

Then, speed of light in diamond is $\frac{1}{2.42}$ times the speed a light in vacuum.

Q.28 Define 1 dioptre of power of a lens.

Ans. Power = 1/f (in m)

Power of a lens in 1 dioptre if focal length of the lens is 1 metre or 100 cm.

Q.29 A convex lens forms a real and inverted image of a needle at a distance of 50 cm. from it. Where is the needle placed in front of the convex lens if the image is equal to the size of the object? Also find the power of the lens.

Ans. (i) $v = 50$ cm

$m = \frac{h'}{h} = -1$ $\quad$ ($\because$ Image is real and inverted & of same size as that of object)

Also, $m = \frac{v}{u}$ $\quad$ or $\quad$ $u = -v = -50$ cm

Thus, needle is to be placed at 50 cm in front of the lens.

(ii) Using, $-\frac{1}{u} + \frac{1}{v} = \frac{1}{f}$, we get $\frac{1}{f} = \frac{1}{50} + \frac{1}{50} = \frac{2}{50} = \frac{1}{25}$ $\quad$ or $\quad$ $f = 25$ cm

$\therefore \quad P = \frac{100}{f(\text{in cm})} = \frac{100}{25} = +4.0$ D

Q.30 Find the power of a concave lens of focal length 2 m.

Ans. Here $f = -2$ m

$\therefore \quad P = \frac{1}{f} = -\frac{1}{2} = -0.5$ D

CONCEPT APPLICATION LEVEL - II

SECTION - A

VERY SHORT ANSWER QUESTIONS

Q.1 What type of waves are light waves?

Ans. Light waves are electromagnetic waves.

Q.2 What is the radius of a plane mirror?

Ans. The radius of a plane mirror is infinity.

Q.3 What is the angle of reflection if a ray falls normally on a plane mirror?

Ans. The angle of reflection is 0°.

Q.4 Relate the focal length f and radius of curvature R.

Ans. Focal length = $\frac{\text{Radius of curvature}}{2}$ or f = R/2

Q.5 What is a real image?

Ans. If the rays of light after reflection or refraction actually meet at a point, the image is known as real image.

Q.6 What is a virtual image?

Ans. If the rays do not actually meet but appear to meet when produced backwards, then the image is known as virtual image.

Q.7 What type of image is formed:

(i) In a plane mirror (ii) On a cinema screen?

Ans. (i) Virtual image (ii) Real image

Q.8 Write the mirror formula.

Ans. $\frac{1}{v}+\frac{1}{u}=\frac{1}{f}$ (u = object distance, v = image distance and f = focal length)

Q.9 Name the type of mirror which always forms a virtual and diminished image.

Ans. Convex mirror

Q.10 Which mirror convex or concave has more field of view?

Ans. Convex mirror

Q.11 For what position of an object, a concave mirror forms a real image equal in size to the object?

Ans. At C, centre of curvature.

Q.12 What should be the position of the object when a concave mirror is to be used?

(i) As a shaving mirror and (ii) As a doctor's mirror?

Ans. (i) Between pole P and focus F.
(ii) Between pole P and focus F.

Q.13 Differentiate between virtual image of a concave mirror and of a convex mirror.

Ans. The virtual image of a concave mirror is always magnified whereas the virtual image of a convex mirror is diminished.

Q.14 The angle between an incident ray and the mirror is θ. The total angle turned by the ray of light is 80°. What is the value of θ?

Ans. Since angle of incidence is equal to angle of reflection, $\theta = 90° - 40° = 50°$.

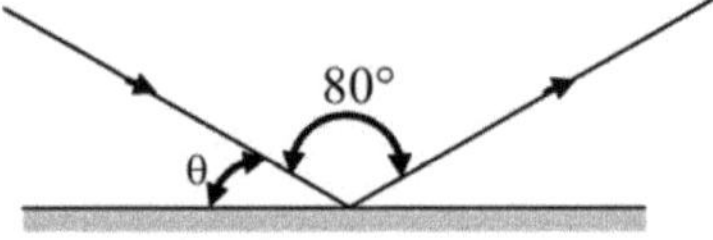

Q.15 What is the value of θ in the following ray diagram?

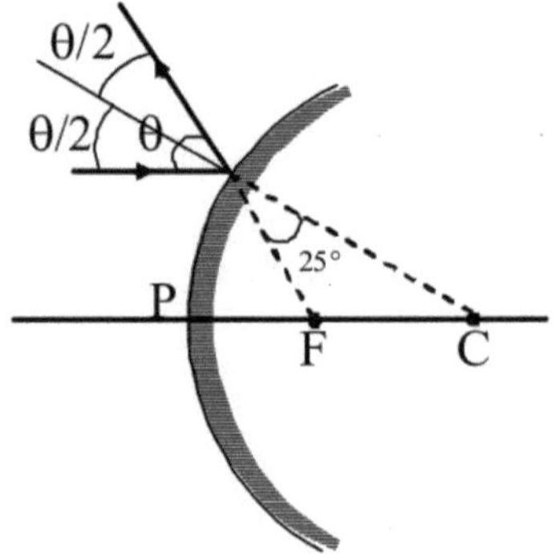

Ans. 50°

Q.16 What is a rarer medium?

Ans. A medium, in which the speed of light is more, is known as optically rarer medium.

Q.17 What is the unit of refractive index?

Ans. Refractive index has no units as it is a ratio of two similar quantities.

Q.18 Name a point inside a lens through which the light passes undeviated.

Ans. Optical centre.

Q.19 Define the power of a lens. Give its SI unit. State whether the power of a converging lens is positive or negative.

Ans. Power of a lens is defined as the reciprocal of its focal length f (in metres)

$$P = \frac{1}{f(\text{in m})}$$

The SI unit of a lens is dioptre. The power of a converging lens is positive.

Q.20 A spherical mirror and a lens both have focal length of –20 cm. What type of mirror and lens are these?

Ans. A concave mirror and concave lens have negative focal length.

Q.21 What is dioptre?

Ans. One dioptre is the power of a lens whose focal length is 1 metre.

Q.22 What is the nature of light?

Ans. Light is an electromagnetic wave which does not require a material medium for propagation.

Q.23 What is a ray?

Ans. The path of light is called a ray.

Q.24 If the angle of incidence (i) for a light ray in air be 45° and the angle of refraction (r) in glass be 30°. Find the refractive index

Ans. Refractive index of glass, $n = \frac{\sin 45°}{\sin 30°} = \frac{1/\sqrt{2}}{1/2} = \sqrt{2}$

Q.25 A point object is 24 cm above the surface of water ($\mu = 4/3$) in a lake. A fish inside the water will observe the image to be at distance.

(A) 32 cm above the water surface **(B) 18 cm above the water surface**

(C) 6 cm above the water surface **(D) 6 cm below the water surface**

Ans. Apparent depth= $n_{dr} \times$ Real depth $= \frac{4}{3} \times 24 = 32$ cm

SECTION - B

CONCEPTUAL QUESTIONS

Q.1 State two effects caused by the refraction of light

Ans. Two effects caused by the refraction of light

(i) A stick partly immersed in water appears to be bent at the water surface.

(ii) A pool of water appears less deeper than it's actual position.

Q.2 Distinguish between real and virtual image.

Ans.

	Real Image		Virtual Image
(i)	It is formed by the actual meeting of reflected (or refracted) rays.	(i)	It is formed when reflected (or refracted) rays appear to meet when produced backwards.
(ii)	It can be obtained on the screen.	(ii)	It cannot be obtained on the screen.
(iii)	It is always inverted.	(iii)	It is always erect.
(iv)	It is always formed by concave mirror and convex lens.	(iv)	It is formed by concave, convex and plane mirrors, concave and convex lens.

Q.3 If you are driving a car, what type of mirror would you prefer to use for observing traffic at your back and why?

Ans. Convex mirror, because it formes virtual, erect and diminished image of an object. Thus have larger field of view.

Q.4 Define Snell's law of Refraction.

Ans. The second law of refraction is called Snell's law of refraction. According to Snell's law "The ratio of sine of the angle of incidence to the sine of the angle of refraction is a constant for a pair of medium"

$$\frac{\sin i}{\sin r} = \text{constant}$$

This constant is called refractive index.

Q.5 A convex lens of focal length 40 cm is in contact with a concave lens of focal length 25 cm. Find the power of the combination.

Ans. $\frac{1}{f} = \frac{1}{f_1} + \frac{1}{f_2} = \frac{1}{0.4} + \frac{1}{-0.25} = \frac{1}{0.4} - \frac{1}{0.25} = \frac{0.25 - 0.4}{0.4 \times 0.25} = \frac{-0.15}{0.4 \times 0.25}$

or $\frac{1}{f} = \frac{-0.15}{0.4 \times 0.25} = -1.5 \text{ cm}$ or $P = \frac{1}{f} = -1.5$ Dioptre

Q.6 The speed of light in water 2.25 × 10⁸ m/s. If the speed of light in vacuum be 3 × 10⁸ m/s, calculate the refractive index of water.

Ans. Refractive index of water $= \frac{\text{Speed of light in vacuum}}{\text{Speed of light in water}} = \frac{3 \times 10^8}{2.25 \times 10^8} = \frac{3 \times 100}{225} = 1.33$

Q.7 A person having a myopic eye uses a concave lens of focal length 50 cm. What is the power of the lens?

Ans. Focal length, f = –50 cm (concave lens)

Now, power, $P = \frac{1}{f\,(in\ metre)} = \frac{1}{-50/100\ m} = -\frac{100}{50} = -2D$

Thus, the power of this concave lens is –2 dioptres.

Q.8 A glass slab placed over a page on which VIBGYOR is printed with each letter in its corresponding color.

(i) Will the image of all the letters be at same place

(ii) If not, give reason for your answer

Ans. (i) No, the image of letters of different. color will be raised by slightly different heights from each other.

(ii) Violet raised to maximum height because of refractive index of violet is maixmum. Its apparent depth will be minimum, hence maximum height.

SECTION C

NUMERICAL PROBLEMS

Q.1 An object is situated at a distance of f/2 from a convex lens of focal length f. Find the distance of the image.

Ans. For a spherical lens $\frac{1}{v}-\frac{1}{u}=\frac{1}{f}$

For convex lens u = – f/2 and f is +ve

$$\frac{1}{v}=\frac{1}{f}+\frac{1}{u}=+\frac{1}{f}-\frac{2}{f}=-\frac{1}{f} \qquad \therefore v=-f$$

Therefore distance of image v = – f.

Q.2 An object of length 1 cm is placed at a distance of 15 cm from a concave mirror of focal length 10 cm. Find the nature and size of the image.

Ans. Given, u = – 15 cm f = –10 cm, O = 1 cm

By using mirror formula

$$\frac{1}{v}+\frac{1}{u}=\frac{1}{f}, \qquad \frac{1}{v}=\frac{1}{f}-\frac{1}{u}=\frac{1}{-10}-\frac{1}{-15}$$

$\therefore$ V = –30 cm

By magnification formula

$$\frac{I}{O}=\frac{-v}{u}=-\frac{-30}{-15}=-2$$

I = –2 × 1 = –2 cm

Image is real and inverted and placed on the same side of size 2 cm of mirror.

Q.3 A biconvex lens whose both the surfaces have same radii of curvature has a power of 5D. The refractive index of material of lens is 1.5. Find the radius of curvature of each surface.

Ans. $P=\frac{1}{f}$, $\therefore$ $f=\frac{1}{p}=\frac{1}{5}m=20\text{ cm}$

For an equiconvex lens

$$\frac{1}{f}=\frac{2(\mu-1)}{R} \qquad \therefore R=2(\mu-1)\,f=2\times 0.5\times 20=20\text{ cm}$$

Q.4 A lens placed at a distance of 20 cm from an object produces a virtual image 2/3 the size of the object. Find the position of the image, kind of lens and its focal lens

Ans. Virtual image means I is positive and it is given that I = (2/3)O. Thus m = + 2/3

Further because u = –20 cm (given), using

$$m = \frac{f}{f+u}$$

we get $\frac{2}{3} = \frac{f}{f+(-20)}$ or f = –40 cm

Thus f is negative, thus the lens is a concave lens. Again using m = v/u

we get $\frac{2}{3} = \frac{v}{-20}$ or $v = -\frac{40}{3} = -13.33$ cm

Thus virtual and erect image is formed on the same side of the object.

Q.5 The focal length of a concave mirror is 30 cm. Find the position of the object in front of the mirror, so that the image is three times the size of the object.

Ans. Here image can be real or virtual. If the image is real.

f = –30 cm, u = ?, m = –3

$$m = \frac{f}{f-u} \Rightarrow -3 = \frac{-30}{-30-u} \Rightarrow u = -40 \text{ cm}$$

If the image is virtual

$$m = \frac{f}{f-u} \Rightarrow 3 = \frac{-30}{-30-u} \Rightarrow u = -20 \text{ cm}$$

Q.6 A square ABCD of side 1 mm is kept at distance 15 cm infront of the concave mirror as shown in the figure. The focal length of the mirror is 10 cm. Find the length of the perimeter of its image.

Ans. Given that u = –15 cm, f = – 10 cm

By using mirror formula, $\frac{1}{f} = \frac{1}{v} + \frac{1}{u}$

$\therefore \quad \frac{1}{v} = \frac{-3+2}{30}$

$\therefore \quad v = -30, m = -\frac{v}{u} = -2$

$\therefore \quad A'B' = C'D' = 2 \times 1 = 2$ mm

Now, $\frac{B'C'}{BC} = \frac{A'D'}{AD} = \frac{v^2}{u^2} = 4$ mm

$\Rightarrow \quad B'C' = A'D' = 4$ mm

$\therefore \quad$ Length = 2 + 2 + 4 + 4 = 12 mm

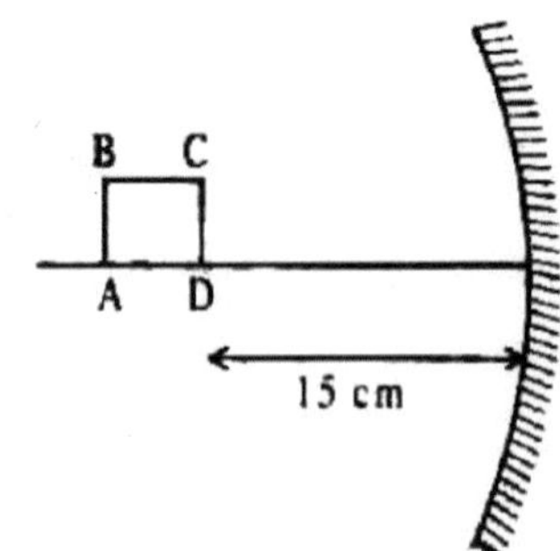

Q.7 A convex mirror has its radius of curvature 20 cm. Find the position of the image of object placed at a distance of 12 cm from the mirror.

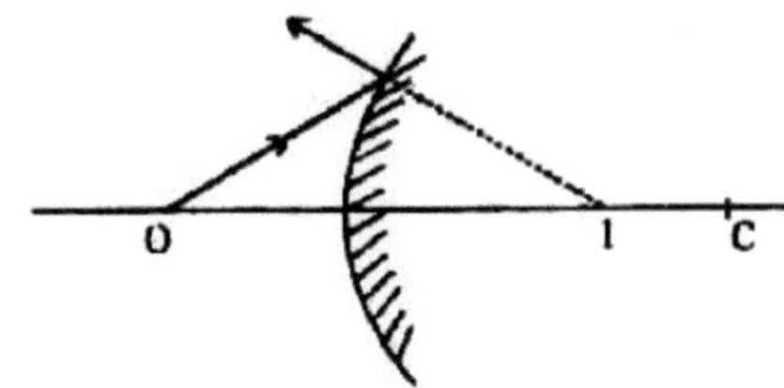

Ans. The situation is shown in figure above.

Here, u = – 12 cm and R = + 20 cm. We have

$$\frac{1}{u}+\frac{1}{v}=\frac{2}{R} \text{ or } \frac{1}{v}=\frac{2}{R}-\frac{1}{u}$$

$$\Rightarrow \quad \frac{1}{v}=\frac{2}{20}-\frac{1}{-12}=\frac{11}{60}\text{ cm}$$

$$\Rightarrow \quad v=\frac{60}{11}\text{ cm}$$

Hence, distance of images 5.45 cm

Q.8 An object of length 2.5 cm is placed at a distance of 1.5 f from a concave mirror where f is the magnitude of the focal length of the mirror. The length of the object is perpendicular to the principal axis. Find the length of the image. Is the image erect or inverted?

Ans. The given situation is shown in the figure

The focal length f= – f and u =–1.5 f, h_i = 2.5 cm

We know

$$\frac{1}{u}+\frac{1}{v}=\frac{1}{f} \quad \text{or} \quad \frac{-1}{1.5f}+\frac{1}{v}=-\frac{1}{f}$$

$$\text{or} \quad \frac{1}{v}=\frac{1}{1.5f}-\frac{1}{f}=\frac{-1}{3f} \quad \text{or} \quad v=-3f$$

$$\text{Now} \quad m=-\frac{v}{u}=\frac{3f}{1.5f}=-2.$$

$$\text{or} \quad \frac{h_2}{h_1}=-2.$$

or $h_2 = -2h_1 = -5.0$ cm

The image is 5.0 cm long. The minus sign shows that it is inverted.

Q.9 Sunlight is incident on a concave mirror, parallel to its principal axis. The image is formed at a distance of 12 cm from the pole. Find the radius of curvature of the mirror.

Ans. As the rays from the sun are parallel to the principal axis, they form the image at the focus. Thus, the focal length of the mirror is 12 cm. The radius of curvature will be twice the focal length, i.e. 24 cm

Q.10 An object is placed at a distance of 20 cm from a convex mirror of focal length 25 cm. Calculate the position of the image. Discuss its nature.

Ans. Here, u = 20 cm and f = 25 cm

We have $\frac{1}{v}+\frac{1}{u}=\frac{1}{f}$

$$\frac{1}{v}=\frac{1}{f}-\frac{1}{u}=\frac{1}{25\,\text{cm}}-\frac{1}{-20\,\text{cm}}=\frac{9}{100\,\text{cm}}$$

$$v=\frac{100}{9}\,\text{cm}=11.11\text{ cm}$$

The positive sign of v shows that the image is formed on the right i.e. behind the mirror. The image is virtual. Also,

$$m=-\frac{v}{u}=-\frac{11.11}{-20}=+0.55$$

Since the magnification, and hence, the height of the image is positive, the image is erect.

Q.11 A 2.0 cm high object is placed at a distance of 20 cm from a concave mirror. A real image is formed at 40 cm from the mirror. Calculate the focal length of the mirror and the size of the image.

Ans. As the image is real, it is formed on the same side as the reflected rays.
Here, u = – 20 cm and v = –40 cm

Thus, $\frac{1}{f}=\frac{1}{u}+\frac{1}{v}=\frac{1}{-20\,\text{cm}}+\frac{1}{-40\,\text{cm}}$ or f = – 13.3 cm

The magnification is, $m=-\frac{v}{u}=-\frac{-40\text{ cm}}{-20\,\text{cm}}=-2.0\text{ cm}$

The height of the image is 4.0 cm, and the negative sign of $h_e=-2h_o=-2\times 2.0\text{ cm}=-4.0\text{ cm}$
The height of the image is 4.0 cm, and the negative sign of h_e shows that the image is inverted.

Q.12 Find the position, size and the nature of the image formed by a spherical mirror from the following data
u = – 20 cm, f = –15 cm, h_o = 1.0 cm

Ans. We have $\frac{1}{v}+\frac{1}{u}=\frac{1}{f}$

or $\frac{1}{v}=\frac{1}{f}-\frac{1}{u}=\frac{1}{-15}-\frac{1}{-20\,\text{cm}}=\frac{-1}{60\text{cm}}$

or v = –60 cm

The image is formed at 60 cm from the mirror. Since the sign of u and v are the same, the image is on the same side as the object (to the left of the mirror) and hence, is real. The magnification is

$$m=\frac{h_i}{h_o}=-\frac{v}{u}=-\frac{-60\,\text{cm}}{-20\,\text{cm}}=-3$$

So $h_i=-3h_0=-3\times 1.0\text{ cm}=-3.0\text{ cm}$
The minus sign shows that the image is inverted. Its size is 3.0 cm.

Q.13 A 2 cm high object is placed at a distance of 32 cm from a concave mirror. The image is real, inverted and 3 cm in size. Find the focal length of the mirror and the position of the image.

Ans. We have $m = -\frac{v}{u} = \frac{h_i}{h_o}$

From the question h_e = –3 cm and h_o = 2 cm

$$\therefore \quad m = \frac{h_i}{h_o} = \frac{-3\,cm}{2\,cm} = -1.5 \quad \text{or} \quad -\frac{v}{u} = -1.5$$

$$\text{or} \quad \frac{v}{-32\,cm} = 1.5 \quad \text{or} \quad v = -48\ cm$$

$$\text{We have } \frac{1}{f} = \frac{1}{u} + \frac{1}{v} = \frac{1}{-32\,cm} + \frac{1}{-48\,cm} = \frac{-5}{96\,cm}$$

$$\text{or} \quad f = \frac{-96\,cm}{5} = -19.2\ cm$$

So the focal length of the concave mirror is 19.2 cm, and the image is formed 48 cm in front of it .

Q.14 A concave mirror forms an inverted image of an object placed at a distance of 12 cm from it. If the image is twice as large as the object, where is it formed.

Ans. From the question

$$\frac{h_i}{h_o} = -2 \text{ (inverted image)}$$

$$\text{But} \quad \frac{h_i}{h_o} = -\frac{v}{u}$$

$$\frac{v}{u} = 2$$

or $v = 2u = 2(-12\ cm) = -24\ cm$

The image is formed 24 cm in front of the mirror.

Q.15 A concave mirror forms an erect image of an object placed at a distance of 10 cm from it. The size of the image is double that of the object. Where is the image formed ?

Ans. From the question,

$$\frac{h_i}{h_o} = +2 \text{ (erect image)}$$

$$\text{or} \quad -\frac{v}{u} = 2 \quad \text{or} \quad v = -2u = -2(-10\ cm) = +20\ cm$$

Thus the image is formed 20 cm behind the mirror (from the positive sign of v)

Q.16 A concave lens of glass, refractive index 1.5 has both surfaces of same radius of curvature R. On immersion in a medium of refractive index 1.75, it will behave as a

(A) convergent lens of focal length 3.5 R (B) convergent lens of focal length 3.0 R

(C) divergent lens of focal length 3.5 R (D) divergent lens of focal length 3.0 R

Ans. According to lens maker's formula

$$\frac{1}{f} = (n_{gm} - 1)\left(\frac{1}{R_1} - \frac{1}{R_2}\right) \qquad \text{Now, } n_{gm} = \frac{n_g}{n_m} = \frac{1.5}{1.75}$$

For concave lens as shown in figure in this case $R_1 = -R$ and $R_2 = R$

n_m n_g n_m R_1 R_2

$$\therefore \frac{1}{f} = \left(\frac{1.5}{1.75} - 1\right)\left(-\frac{1}{R} - \frac{1}{R}\right) = +\frac{0.25 \times 2}{1.75R}$$

or $f = +3.5$ R

The positive sign shows that the lens behaves as convergent lens.

Q.17 A ray of light travelling in air falls on the surface of a rectangular slab of a plastic material whose refractive index is 1.6. If the incident ray makes an angle of 53° with the normal, find the angle made by the refractive ray with the normal (sin 53° = 4/5).

Ans. The angle of incidence is 53° and the refractive index is n = 1.6.

We have, $\frac{\sin i}{\sin r} = n$ or $\sin r = \frac{\sin i}{n}$

or $\frac{\sin 53^\circ}{1.6} = \frac{4}{5 \times 1.6} \Rightarrow \sin r = \frac{1}{2}$ or $r = 30^\circ$

Q.18 Find the refractive index of glass with respect of water. The refractive indices of these with respect to air are 3/2 and 4/3 respectively.

Ans. We have $n_{21} = \frac{n_2}{n_1}$. Here, glass is the second medium

Here $n_2 = \frac{3}{2}$, $n_1 = \frac{4}{3}$, So, $n_{21} = \frac{9}{8}$

Q.19 A point object is placed at a distance of 12 cm from a convex lens on its principal axis. Its image is formed on the other side of the lens at a distance of 18 cm from the lens. Find the focal length of the lens.

Ans. According to convention, let the object be on the left of the lens. Therefore u is negative, i.e.u = –12 cm. Since the image is on the other side, it is formed on the right of the lens. Thus v is positive, i.e. v = +18 cm. (you can also say that since u is measured opposite to the direction of the incident ray, it is negative. And since v is measured along the direction of the incident rays, it is positive)

We have, $\frac{1}{f} = \frac{1}{v} - \frac{1}{u}$

or $\frac{1}{f} = \frac{1}{18\,\text{cm}} - \frac{1}{-12\,\text{cm}} = \frac{5}{36\,\text{cm}}$ or $f = \frac{36}{5}$ cm = 7.2 cm

Q.20 The image of an object formed by a convex lens is of the same size as the object. If the image is formed at a distance of 40 cm, find the focal length of the lens. Also find the power of the lens. At what distance from the lens is the object placed?

Ans. A same sized image is formed when an object is placed at a distance of 2f from the convex lens. The image is formed at a distance of 2f from the lens. Here this distance is given as 40 cm. So

$2f = 40 \text{ cm}$ or $f = 20 \text{ cm}$

Power $p = \frac{1}{f} = \frac{1}{0.2\,m} = 5\text{ D}$

The object is placed at a distance of 2f = 40 cm from the lens .

Q.21 An object is placed on the principal axis of a concave lens at a distance of 20 cm from it. If the focal length of the lens is also 20 cm, find the location of the image.

Ans. Given u = –20 cm, f = –20 cm

We have $\frac{1}{v} - \frac{1}{u} = \frac{1}{f}$

or $\frac{1}{v} - \frac{1}{-20\,cm} = \frac{1}{-20\,cm}$

or $\frac{1}{v} = \frac{1}{-20\,cm} + \frac{1}{-20\,cm} = \frac{-1}{10}$ or $v = -10$ cm.

Thus, the image is formed at a distance of 10 cm from the lens. As v has turned out to be negative, the image just be on the left of the lens.

Q.22 A beam of light travelling parallel to the principal axis of a concave lens appears to diverge from a point 20 cm behind the lens after passing through the lens. Find the power of the lens.

Ans. By definition, the point from where the beam appears to diverge is the focus of the lens. Thus the focal length is 20 cm. As it is a concave lens, f is negative

$f = -20 \text{ cm} = -0.2 \text{ m}$

The power is $P = \frac{1}{f} = \frac{1}{-0.2\,m} = -5\text{ D}$

Q.23 A convex lens of power 4 D is placed at a distance of 40 cm from a wall. At what distance from the lens should a candle be placed so that its image is formed on the wall ?

Ans. Here, $f = \frac{1}{P} = \frac{1}{4\,D} = \frac{1}{4}\,m = 25\,cm$, and v = +40 cm

We have $\frac{1}{v} - \frac{1}{u} = \frac{1}{f}$ or $\frac{1}{u} = \frac{1}{v} - \frac{1}{f} = \frac{1}{40} - \frac{1}{25} = -\frac{3}{200\,cm}$

So the candle should be placed $\frac{-200}{3}$ cm from the lens

Q.24 A pin which is 2 cm long is placed at a distance of 16 cm from a convex lens. Assuming it to be perpendicular to the principal axis, find the position, size and the nature of the image if the focal length of the lens is 12 cm.

Ans. Here u = –16 cm and f = + 12 cm

We have $\frac{1}{v} - \frac{1}{u} = \frac{1}{f}$ or $\frac{1}{v} = \frac{1}{u} + \frac{1}{f} = \frac{1}{-16\,cm} + \frac{1}{12\,cm} = \frac{1}{48}$

or $v = +48$ cm

The image is formed 48 cm from the lens on the side of the transmitted rays. The image is therefore real.

The magnification is

$$m = \frac{v}{u} = = \frac{48\,cm}{-16\,cm} = -3 \quad \text{or} \quad \frac{h_i}{h_o} = -3$$

or $h_i = -3h_o = -3 \times 2$ cm $= -6$ cm

The image is inverted and is 6 cm in size. So an inverted and real image of size 6 cm is formed 48 cm from the lens.

Q.25 A 4.0 cm high object is place at a distance of 60 cm from a concave lens of focal length 20 cm. Find the size of the image.

Ans. We have f = – 20 cm and u = –60 cm

For a lens $\frac{1}{v} - \frac{1}{u} = \frac{1}{f}$

or $\frac{1}{v} = \frac{1}{u} + \frac{1}{f} = \frac{1}{-60\,cm} + \frac{1}{-20\,cm} = -\frac{1}{15\,cm}$

or $v = -15$ cm

The magnification is

$$m = \frac{h_i}{h_o} = \frac{v}{u} = \frac{-15\,cm}{-60\,cm} = \frac{1}{4} \quad \text{or} \quad h_i = \frac{h_o}{4} \Rightarrow \frac{4.0\,cm}{4} = 1.0\text{ cm}$$

So the image is 1.0 cm high. The positive sign shows that it is erect.

Q.26 A convex lens of focal length 20 cm is placed in contact with a concave lens of focal length 12.5 cm in such a way that they have the same principal axis. Find the power of combination.

Ans. $P = P_1 + P_2$

Here $P_1 = +\frac{1}{20\,cm} = +\frac{1}{0.20\,m} = 5D$

and $P_2 = \frac{1}{125\,cm} = -\frac{1}{0.125\,m} = -8D$

So the power of the combination is $P_1 + P_2 = -3$ D.

Q.27 A plane mirror is approaching you at 10 cm/sec. You can see your image in it. At what speed will your image approach you.

Ans. Relative speed of image with respect to person/observer = 2 × Speed of object with respect to mirror

$= 2 \times 10$ cm/sec $= 20$ cm/sec.

Q.28 Two mirrors are kept at 72° to each other and a body is placed at middle. Find the total number of images formed?

Ans. Here, $\frac{360}{\theta} = \frac{360}{72} = 5$

$\because \frac{360}{\theta}$ is odd integer and placement is symmetrical.

So, number of images $= \frac{360}{\theta} - 1 = 5 - 1 = 4.$

Q.29 An object is placed in front of a concave mirror of radius of curvature 40 cm at a distance of 10 cm. Find the position, nature and magnification of the image.

Ans. Here, R = –40 cm, u = –10 cm

Focal length of concave mirror,

$$f = \frac{R}{2} = -\frac{40}{2} = -20 \text{ cm}$$

Using $\frac{1}{u} + \frac{1}{v} = \frac{1}{f}$, we get

$$\frac{1}{v} = \frac{1}{f} - \frac{1}{u} = -\frac{1}{20} - \frac{1}{(-10)} = -\frac{1}{20} + \frac{1}{10} = \frac{-1+2}{20} = \frac{1}{20}$$

$\therefore$ v = +20 cm

Thus position of the image is at 20 cm to the right side of the pole of the mirror.

Since v is positive, so virtual image is formed.

$$m = -\frac{v}{u} = \frac{-20}{(-10)} = 2 \quad \text{Since, } m = \frac{I}{O} = 2$$

$\therefore$ I = 2 × O

Therefore, size of image is double than the size of the object, Moreover image is erect.

Q.30 An object is situated at a distance of 15 cm from a convex lens of focal length 30 cm. Find the position of the image formed by it.

Ans. u = –15 cm, f = 30 cm, v = ?

$$\because \frac{1}{v} = \frac{1}{f} + \frac{1}{u} = \frac{1}{30} - \frac{1}{15} = \frac{1-2}{30}$$

or $\frac{1}{v} = -\frac{1}{30}$ or v = –30 cm

Q.31 Find the time taken by light in travelling a water column of length 1000 m if the refractive index of water is 4/3.

Ans. $n_{aw} = \frac{v_a}{v_w}$

$\therefore \quad v_w = \frac{v_a}{n_{aw}} = \frac{3\times10^8}{4/3}$ or $v_w = 2.25 \times 10^8$ m/s

or $t = \frac{d}{v_w} = \frac{1000}{2.25\times10^8}$ or $t = 4.4 \times 10^{-6}$ sec.

Q.32 A rectangular glass slab of thickness 8 cm is placed on a figure. Eye is kept exactly above this slab. If the refractive index of glass is 1.6, then the figure will appear to raised by

(A) 8 cm (B) 2.4 cm (C) 4.2 cm (D) 3 cm

Ans. Let the figure get raised by d cm on placing the slab, then its apparent depth will be (8–d) cm

$$n_{ag} = \frac{real\, depth}{apparent\ depth}$$

$$1.6 = \frac{8}{8-d}$$

or $1.6(8-d) = 8$ or $12.8 - 1.6\,d = 8$

or $d = \frac{4.8}{1.6} = 3$ cm

Q.33 The focal length of a convex lens is 10 cm and its refractive index is 1.5. If the radius of curvature of one surface is 7.5 cm. Find the radius of curvature of the second surface.

Ans. We know,

$$\frac{1}{f} = (n-1)\left(\frac{1}{R_1} - \frac{1}{R_2}\right)$$

$f = 10$ cm, $R_1 = 7.5$ cm, $n = 1.5$

or $\frac{1}{10} = (1.5-1)\left(\frac{1}{7.5} - \frac{1}{R_2}\right)$

or $R_2 = -15$ cm

Q.34 Find the size, nature and position of image formed when an object of size 1 cm is placed at a distance of 15 cm from a concave mirror of focal length 10 cm.

Ans. Given that :
Object size = 1 cm
Object distance u = –15 cm
Focal length f = –10 cm

By using mirror formula, $\frac{1}{v} + \frac{1}{u} = \frac{1}{f} \Rightarrow \frac{-1}{10} + \frac{1}{15} = \frac{-3+2}{30} = \frac{-1}{30}$

$\therefore$ v = –30 cm

Magnificatiion $m = \frac{-v}{u} = \frac{h_i}{n_0}$

$\Rightarrow \frac{-(-30)}{-15} = \frac{h_i}{h_0} \Rightarrow h_i = \frac{-30}{15} \times 1 = -2$ cm

Image distance is at 30 cm in same side of mirror which is real and inverted. Image size is larger than object.

Q.35 A concave mirror of focal length 10 cm is placed at a distance of 25 cm from a wall. How far from the wall an object be placed so that its image formed by the mirror falls on the wall?

Ans. Given that focal length (f) = –10 cm
image distance (v) = –25 cm
object distance (u) = ?
by using mirror formula

$$\frac{1}{v} + \frac{1}{u} = \frac{1}{f} \Rightarrow \frac{1}{u} = \frac{1}{f} - \frac{1}{v}$$

$$\Rightarrow \frac{1}{u} = -\frac{1}{10} - \left(-\frac{1}{25}\right) = \frac{1}{10} + \frac{1}{25} = \frac{-5+2}{50}$$

$\therefore$ $u = \frac{-50}{3}$ cm = – 16.66 cm

Object distance is 16.66 cm from the mirror.

Q.36 An object is placed at a distance of 15 cm from a convex mirror of focal length 30 cm. Find the position and the nature of the image.

Ans. Given that object distance u = – 15 cm
focal length f = +30 cm
By mirror formula,

$$\frac{1}{v} + \frac{1}{u} = \frac{1}{f} \Rightarrow \frac{1}{v} - \frac{1}{15} = \frac{1}{30}$$

$$\Rightarrow \frac{1}{v} = \frac{1}{30} + \frac{1}{15} = \frac{1+2}{30} = \frac{3}{30}$$

$\therefore$ v = + 10 cm

Therefore image distance is 10 cm behind the mirror.

Q.37 A convex mirror used for rear-view on an automobile has a radius of curvature of 3 m. If a bus is located at 5 m from this mirror, find the position, nature and size of the image.

Ans. Given that radius of curvature (R) = 3 m

$\therefore$ Focal length $= \frac{R}{2} = \frac{3}{2} = 1.5$ m

object distance = – 5 cm

Position of image (v) = ?

By using mirror formula,

$$\frac{1}{v} + \frac{1}{u} = \frac{1}{f}$$

$$\Rightarrow \frac{1}{v} = \frac{1}{f} - \frac{1}{u} = \frac{2}{3} - \left(\frac{-1}{5}\right) = \frac{2}{3} + \frac{1}{5} = \frac{10+3}{15} = \frac{13}{15}$$

$$\therefore \quad v = \frac{15}{13} = 1.15 \text{ cm}$$

Thus, Image is placed at a distance of 1.15 cm behind the mirror which is virtual & erect

New magnification $m = -\frac{v}{u} = \frac{-1.15}{-5} = 0.23$

Then image size is a factor of 0.23 by the object size.

Q.38 An object 4 cm in size is placed at 25 cm in front of a concave mirror of focal length 15 cm. At what distance from the mirror should a screen by placed in order to obtain a sharp image? Find the nature and the size of this image.

Ans. Given that size of object $h_0 = 4$cm

object distance = –25 cm = u

focal length f = – 15 cm

By using mirror formula,

$$\frac{1}{v} + \frac{1}{u} = \frac{1}{f} \quad \Rightarrow \quad \frac{1}{v} = \frac{1}{f} - \frac{1}{u}$$

$$\Rightarrow \quad \frac{-1}{15} - \left(\frac{-1}{25}\right) = \frac{-1}{15} + \frac{1}{25} = \frac{-5+3}{75} = \frac{-2}{75}$$

$$\therefore \quad v = \frac{-75}{2} = -37.5 \text{ cm}$$

This image is formed at a distance of 37.5 cm from the mirror which is same side of object. It is real and inverted.

By using magnification

$$m = \frac{-v}{u} = \frac{h_i \text{ (height of image)}}{h_0 \text{(height of object)}} \quad \Rightarrow \quad \frac{h_i}{h_0} = \frac{-v}{u}$$

$$h_i = \frac{-v}{u} \times h_0 = \frac{-(-37.5)}{-25} \times 4 = 6 \text{ cm}$$

Image size is larger than the object size.

Q.39 Light of wavelength 6000 Å in air enters a medium of refractive index 1.5. What will be the frequency in the medium?

Ans. Given that wavelength $\lambda = 6000Å$
refractive index $\mu = 1.5$
frequency = ?
By using formula,

$\because \quad C = f.\lambda$ where c is speed of light.

$$\therefore \quad f = \frac{c}{\lambda} = \frac{3\times10^8}{6\times10^{-7}} = 0.5 \times 10^{15}$$

Frequency (f) = 5×10^{14} Hz

Q.40 If the refractive index of water for light going from air to water be 1.33, what will be the refractive index for light going from water to air?

Ans. Refractive index of water with repect to air

$$\mu_w{}^a = 1.33 = \frac{4}{3}$$

$$\therefore \quad \mu_a{}^w = \frac{1}{\mu_w^a} = \frac{1}{\frac{4}{3}} = \frac{3}{4} = 0.75$$

Q.41 Refractive index of water is 4/3 and glass is 3/2 with regard to air. What is the refractive index of glass with respect to water?

Ans. Refractive Index of water $= \frac{4}{3} = \mu_g$

Refractive index of glass $= \frac{3}{2} = \mu_w$

$\therefore$ R.I of glass with respect to water $= \frac{\mu_w}{\mu_g} = \frac{3}{2}\Big/\frac{4}{3} = \frac{9}{8}$

Q.42 Light of wavelength of 500 nm in air, enters a glass plate of refractive index 1.5. Find (i) speed (ii) frequency and (iii) wavelength of light in glass. Assume that the frequency of light remains the same in both media.

Ans. Given that wavelength $(\lambda) = 500 \times 10^{-9}$ m
Refractive index of glass plate $(\mu) = 1.5$
To find speed, frequency & wavelength.

(i) $\quad \mu = \frac{c}{v} \frac{\text{(speed of light in air / vaccum)}}{\text{(speed of light in medium)}}$

$$1.5 = \frac{3\times10^8}{v} \quad \Rightarrow \quad v = \frac{3\times10^8}{1.5} = 2\times 10^8 \text{ m/s.}$$

(ii) Since, velocity = frequency × wavelength

$$\Rightarrow \quad f = \frac{v}{\lambda} = \frac{2\times10^{8}}{500\times10^{-9}} = 0.4\times10^{15}\ \text{Hz}$$

(iii) Refractive index $(\mu) = \dfrac{f(\lambda_a)}{f(\lambda_g)}$

$$1.5 = \frac{500\times10^{-9}}{\lambda_g}$$

$$\Rightarrow \quad \lambda_g = \frac{500\times10^{-9}}{1.5} = 333.33\ \text{nm}$$

Q.43 A needle placed 45 cm from the lens forms an image on a screen placed 98 cm on the other side of the lens. Identify the type of the lens and determine its focal length.

Ans. Given that object (needle) distance (u) = – 45 cm
Screen placed or image formed at a
distance (v) = 98 cm
focal length (f) = ?
By using lens formula,

$$\frac{1}{v} - \frac{1}{u} = \frac{1}{f}$$

$$\frac{1}{f} = \frac{1}{98} + \frac{1}{45} = \frac{45+98}{98\times45}$$

∴ f = +30.8 cm
Focal length positive then lens is convex in nature.

Q.44 A concave lens has a focal length of 10 cm. An object 2.5 cm high is placed at 30 cm from the lens. Determine the position and size of the image.

Ans. Given that focal length (f) = – 10 cm
object height (h_0) = 2.5 cm
object distance u = –30 cm
by using lens formula

$$\Rightarrow \quad \frac{1}{v} - \frac{1}{u} = \frac{1}{f}$$

$$\Rightarrow \quad \frac{1}{v} = \frac{1}{f} + \frac{1}{u} = \frac{-1}{10} - \frac{1}{30} = \frac{-4}{30}$$

$$\therefore \quad v = \frac{-30}{4} = -7.5\ \text{cm}$$

$$\text{magnification (m)} = \frac{v}{u} = \frac{h_i\,\text{(image size)}}{h_0\,\text{(ojbect size)}}$$

$$\Rightarrow \quad \frac{-7.5}{-30} = \frac{h_i}{2.5} \qquad \Rightarrow \quad h_i = \frac{5}{8}\ \text{cm}$$

Q.45 A real image 4/5 size of the object is formed 18 cm from a lens. Calculate the focal length of the lens.

Ans. Given that image size $= \frac{4}{5}$ times of object size.

$\Rightarrow \quad h_i = \frac{4}{5} h_0 \qquad \Rightarrow \quad \frac{h_i}{h_0} = \frac{4}{5}$

$\because$ magnification $(m) = \frac{v}{u} = \frac{h_i}{h_0}$

$\Rightarrow \quad \frac{4}{5} = \frac{18}{-u} \qquad \Rightarrow \quad u = \frac{-18 \times 5}{4} = -22.5$ cm

u is object disatnce

Now by using lens formula

$\frac{1}{v} - \frac{1}{u} = \frac{1}{f} \qquad \Rightarrow \quad \frac{1}{18} - \left(\frac{-1}{22.5}\right) = \frac{1}{f} \qquad (\because$ Image distance v = 18 cm)

$\Rightarrow \quad \frac{1}{f} = \frac{1}{18} + \frac{1}{22.5} = \frac{1}{10}$

$\therefore$ focal length = 10 cm

Q.46 A 5 cm tall object is placed on the principal axis of a convex lens of focal length 50 cm at a distance of 40 cm from it. Find the nature, position and size of the image.

Ans. Given that: Object height h_0 = 5cm

Focal length f = 50 cm

Object distance v = –40 cm

By using lens formula, Image height = h_i = ?

Image distance = v ?

$$\frac{1}{v} - \frac{1}{u} = \frac{1}{f}$$

$$\Rightarrow \quad \frac{1}{v} = \frac{1}{f} + \frac{1}{u}$$

$$\Rightarrow \quad \frac{1}{50} + \left(\frac{-1}{40}\right) = \frac{1}{50} - \frac{1}{40} = \frac{4-5}{200} = \frac{-1}{200}$$

$\therefore$ v = –200 cm

Therefore image formed at a distance of 200 cm from the lens.

by magnification $m = \frac{v}{u} = \frac{h_i}{h_O}$

$\Rightarrow \quad \frac{v}{u} = \frac{h_i}{h_O} = \frac{h_i}{5} \qquad \Rightarrow \quad h_i = 5 \times 5 = +25$ cm

Image is 25 cm tall which is virtual & erect.

Q.47 A 5 cm tall object is placed perpendicular to the principal axis of a convex lens of focal length 20 cm. The distance of the object from the lens is 30. Find the (i) position and (ii) nature of the image formed.

Ans. Given that Object height $h_0 = 5cm$

Focal length $f = 20$ cm

Object distance $u = -30$ cm

To find (i) Position of image $v = ?$

(ii) Nasture of image = ?

(i) By using lens formula,

$$\Rightarrow \frac{1}{v} - \frac{1}{u} = \frac{1}{f}$$

$$\Rightarrow \frac{1}{v} = \frac{1}{f} + \frac{1}{u} = \frac{1}{20} + \left(\frac{-1}{30}\right) = \frac{3-2}{60} = \frac{1}{60}$$

$$\frac{1}{v} = \frac{1}{60}$$

The image is situated 60 cm on the other side of the lens.

(ii) Image formed real and Inverted.

Q.48 A 2 cm tall object is placed perpendicular to the principal axis of a convex lens of focal length 10 cm. The distance of the object from the lens is 15 cm. Find the nature, position and size of the image. Also find its magnification.

Ans. Given that : Object height $h_0 = 2$ cm

(f) focal length $= +\ 10cm$

(u) object distance $= -15$ cm

By using lens formula,

$$\frac{1}{v} - \frac{1}{u} = \frac{1}{f}$$

$$\Rightarrow \frac{1}{v} = \frac{1}{f} + \frac{1}{u} = \frac{1}{10} - \frac{1}{15} = \frac{3-2}{30}$$

$$\Rightarrow \frac{1}{v} = \frac{1}{30} \qquad \therefore v = 30 \text{ cm}$$

Image is formed at a distance of 30 cm behind the lens.

Now, magnification $= \frac{v}{u} = \frac{h_i}{h_0}$

$$\Rightarrow \frac{30}{-15} = \frac{h_i}{2} \qquad \Rightarrow \qquad h_i = -4 \text{ cm}$$

The image size is 4 cm which is real and inverted.

Magnification $m = \frac{v}{u}$

$$\Rightarrow \quad m = -2$$

Q.49 A convex lens has focal length of 20 cm. Calculate at what distance from the lens should the object be placed so that the image is formed at 40 cm on the other side of the lens? Also state the nature of the image formed.

Ans. Here, f = 20 cm, v = 40 cm, u = ?

Step 1: Using $-\frac{1}{u}+\frac{1}{v}=\frac{1}{f}$,

we have $-\frac{1}{u}=\frac{1}{f}-\frac{1}{v}=\frac{1}{20}-\frac{1}{40}$ or $-\frac{1}{u}=\frac{1}{40}$ or $u=-40$ cm

Thus, the object should be placed at a distance of 40 cm in front of the convex lens.

Step 2: $m=\frac{v}{u}=\frac{40}{-40}=-1$

Negative sign shows that the image is real and inverted (Nature of image).

Q.50 An object 4 cm high is placed at a distance of 27 cm in front of a convex lens of focal length 18 cm. Find the position, nature and size of the image formed.

Ans. Here, u = –27 cm (sign convention), f = 18 cm, h = 4 cm

Step 1: Determination of 'v'

Using $-\frac{1}{u}+\frac{1}{v}=\frac{1}{f}$,

we get $\frac{1}{(-27)}+\frac{1}{v}=\frac{1}{18}$ or $\frac{1}{v}=\frac{1}{18}-\frac{1}{27}=\frac{1}{54}$

∴ v = 54 cm (Position of image)

Step 2 : Determination of h'

Using, $\frac{h'}{h}=\frac{v}{u}$

we get, $h'=\frac{v}{u}\times h=\frac{54}{-27}\times 4=-8.0$ cm

Thus, size of image is 8 cm. Negative sign shows that the image is **inverted**.

Q.51 A 4.0 cm tall object is placed perpendicular to the principal axis of a convex lens of focal length 20 cm. If the distance of the object is 30 cm from the lens, find the position, nature and size of the image. Also find its magnification.

Ans. Here, h = 4.0 cm, f = 20 cm; u = –30 cm, h' = ?, v = ?, m = ?

Step 1: Determination of v

Using lens formula $-\frac{1}{u}+\frac{1}{v}=\frac{1}{f}$

we have $-\frac{1}{(-30)}+\frac{1}{v}=\frac{1}{20}$

or $\frac{1}{v}=\frac{1}{20}-\frac{1}{30}$ or $\frac{1}{v}=\frac{1}{60}$ or $v=+60$ cm

Thus, the image is formed at 60 cm on other side (i.e. right side) of the lens.

Step 2: Determination of h'

Using, $\frac{h'}{h} = \frac{v}{u}$

We have $h' = \frac{v}{u}h = \frac{60}{-30} \times 4 = -8.0$ cm

Thus, size of the image is 8.0 cm. Negative sign shows that the image is inverted. So, a real and inverted image of large size is formed.

Step 3: Determination of Magnification

Using, $m = \frac{h'}{h}$

we get, $m = \frac{-8.0\text{ cm}}{4.0\text{ cm}} = -2$

Q.52 A concave lens of focal length 20 cm forms an image at a distance of 10 cm from the lens. What is the distance of the object from the lens? Also draw ray diagram.

Ans. Here, f = –20 cm (Sign convention), v = –10 cm (∵ image formed by concave lens is virtual)

Step 1: Using lens formula $-\frac{1}{u} + \frac{1}{v} = \frac{1}{f}$

We have, $-\frac{1}{u} - \frac{1}{10} = -\frac{1}{20}$

$\Rightarrow -\frac{1}{u} = \frac{-1}{20} + \frac{1}{10}$

or $u = -20$ cm

Thus, the object is placed at 20 cm from the concave lens.

Step 2:

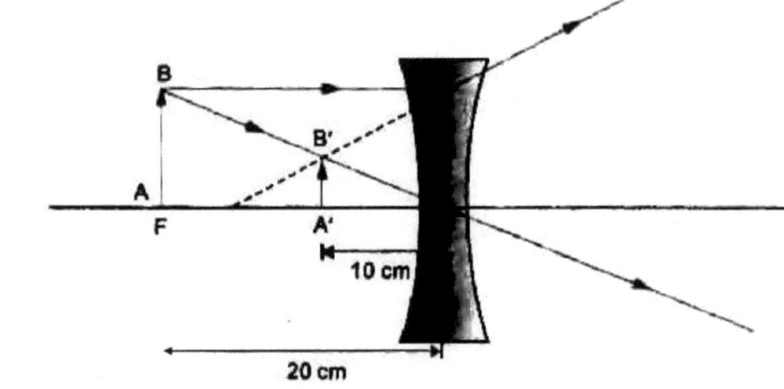

Q.53 What will be the focal length of a lens whose power is given as + 2.0 D?

Ans. Here, P = 2.0 D

Using $P = \frac{1}{f(\text{in m})}$ we get, $f = \frac{1}{P} = \frac{1}{2} = 0.5\text{ m} = 50$ cm

Q.54 What is the power of a convex lens of focal length 40 cm?

Ans. Here, $f = 40$ cm

Using $P = \frac{100}{f(\text{in cm})}$ we get, $f = \frac{100}{40} = +2.5$ D

Q.55 (a) Two lenses have power of (i) + 2D, (ii) –4D. What is the nature and focal length of each lens?

(b) An object is kept at a distance of 100 cm from each of above lenses. Calculate (i) image distance, (ii) magnification in each of the two cases.

Ans. (a) (i) $P = +2D$. Since power is positive, so the lens is convex lens.

Focal length, $f = \frac{1}{P} = \frac{1}{2} = 0.5 \text{ m} = 50 \text{ cm}$

(ii) $P = -4D$. Since power is negative. So the lens is concave lens.

Focal length, $f = \frac{1}{P} = \frac{1}{-4} = -0.25 \text{ m} = -25 \text{ cm}$

(b) (i) Here, $u = -100$ cm (sign convention)

1st case : $f = 50$ cm

Using $-\frac{1}{u} + \frac{1}{v} = \frac{1}{f}$

We get, $\frac{1}{v} = \frac{1}{f} + \frac{1}{u} = \frac{1}{50} - \frac{1}{100} = \frac{1}{100}$

or $v = 100$ cm

2nd case : $f = -25$ cm

Using $-\frac{1}{u} + \frac{1}{v} = \frac{1}{f}$

We get, $\frac{1}{v} = \frac{1}{f} + \frac{1}{u} = -\frac{1}{25} - \frac{1}{100} = \frac{-5}{100} = \frac{-1}{20}$

or $v = -20$ cm

(ii) $m = \frac{v}{u}$

1st case : $u = -100$ cm, $v = 100$ cm

$\therefore$ $m = \frac{100 \text{ cm}}{-100 \text{ cm}} = -1$

2nd case : $u = -100$ cm, $v = -20$ cm

$\therefore$ $m = \frac{-20 \text{ cm}}{-100 \text{ cm}} = \frac{1}{5} = 0.2$

Q.56 An object of size 5 cm is kept at a distance 25 cm from the optical centre of a converging lens of focal length 10 cm. Calculate the distance of the image from the lens and size of the image.

Ans. Here, size of object, h = 5 cm, u = –25 cm (sign convention), f = 10 cm (sign convention)

Step 1: Using $-\frac{1}{u}+\frac{1}{v}=\frac{1}{f}$

We get, $\frac{1}{v}=\frac{1}{f}+\frac{1}{u}=\frac{1}{10}-\frac{1}{25}=\frac{3}{50}$

$\therefore \quad v=\frac{50}{3}=16.67$ cm

Thus, image distance = 16.67 cm

Step 2: $m=\frac{h'}{h}=\frac{v}{u}$

$h'=\frac{v}{u}\times h=\frac{50}{3\times(-25)}\times 5=-\frac{10}{3}=-3.33$ cm

Thus, size of image = 3.33 cm. Negative sign show that image is inverted.

Q.57 A concave lens has focal length of 20 cm. At what distance from the lens, a 5 cm tall object be placed so that it formed an image at 15 cm from the lens? Also calculate the size of the image formed.

Ans. Here, f = –20 cm (sign convention), h = 5 cm, v = – 15 cm (sign convention), u = ?, h' = ?

Step 1: Using $-\frac{1}{u}+\frac{1}{v}=\frac{1}{f}$

We get, $-\frac{1}{u}-\frac{1}{15}=-\frac{1}{20}=\frac{1}{u}=\frac{1}{20}-\frac{1}{15}=\frac{3-4}{60}$

or $\frac{1}{u}=-\frac{1}{60} \quad \therefore \quad -u=60$ cm

Thus, object should be placed at a distance of 60 cm from the lens to the left side.

Step 2: Using $m=\frac{h'}{h}=\frac{v}{u}$

$h'=\frac{v}{u}\times h=\frac{-15}{-60}\times 5\text{ cm}=1.25$ cm

$\therefore$ Size of image = 1.25 cm

Q.58 An object 50 cm tall is placed on the principal axis of a convex lens. A 20 cm tall image is formed on the screen placed at a distance of 10 cm from the lens. Calculate the focal length of the lens.

Ans. Here, h = 50 cm, h' = –20 cm (sign convention), v = 10 cm, f = ?

Step 1: Using $\frac{h'}{h} = \frac{v}{u}$

we get $\frac{-20}{50} \times \frac{10}{u}$ or $u = -\frac{10 \times 50}{20} = -25$ cm

Step 2: Using $-\frac{1}{u} + \frac{1}{v} = \frac{1}{f}$

we get, $\frac{1}{25} + \frac{1}{10} = \frac{1}{f}$

or $\frac{1}{f} = \frac{2+5}{50} = \frac{7}{50}$ or $f = \frac{50}{7} = 7.14$ cm

Thus, focal length of the convex lens = 7.14 cm

SECTION D

PREVIOUS YEAR VERY SHORT ANSWER QUESTION (1 Mark)

Q.1 To find the focal length of a concave mirror, Sita should choose which one of the following set-ups? **[CBSE - 2011]**

(A) A mirror holder and a screen holder.
(B) A screen holder and a scale.
(C) A mirror holder, a screen holder and a scale.
(D) A screen, a mirror, holders for them and a scale.

Q.2 By using a convex lens, a student obtained a sharp image of his class-room window grill on a screen. In which direction should he move the lens to focus a distant tree instead of the grill? **[CBSE - 2007,11]**

(A) Towards the screen (B) Away from the screen
(C) Very for away from the screen (D) Behind the screen

Q.3 To determine the focal length of a convex lens by obtaining a sharp image of a distant object, the following steps were suggested which are given in proper sequence: **[CBSE - 2007, 11]**

(I) Hold the lens between the object and the screen.
(II) Adjust the position of the lens to form a sharp image.
(III) Select a suitable distant object.
(IV) Measure the distance between the lens and the screen.

The correct sequence of steps to determine the focal length of the lens is

(A) III, I, II, IV (B) III, I, IV, II (C) III, IV, II, I (D) I, II, III, IV

Q.4 In these diagrams, the angle of refraction r has been correctly marked? **[CBSE - 2007, 11]**

(I) 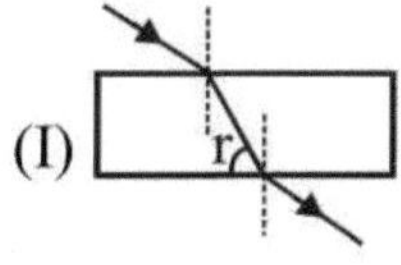

(II) 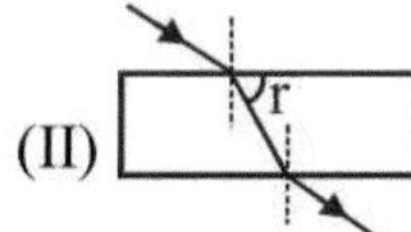

(III) 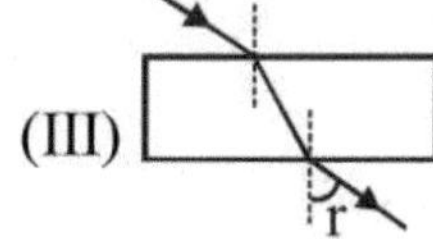

(IV) 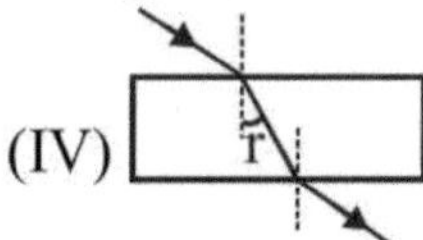

(A) I (B) II (C) III (D) IV

Q.5 For a ray of light passing through a glass slab **[CBSE - 2011]**

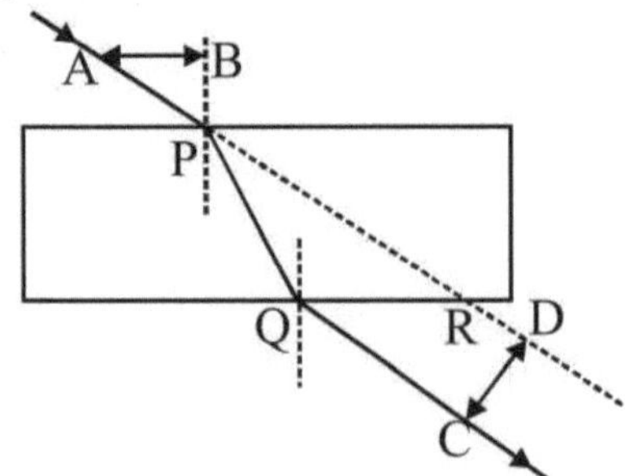

the lateral displacement was correctly measured as

(A) AB (B) PQ (C) CD (D) PR

Q.6 The steps involved in observing a slide under a microscope are given below. They are not in proper sequence. **[CBSE - 2011]**

(I) Focus the object under high power of the microscope.
(II) Place the slide on the stage of the microscope.
(III) Arrange the mirror to reflect maximum light to the slide.
(IV) Focus the object under low power of the microscope.
The proper sequence of steps is

(A) II, III, IV, I (B) I, II, III, IV (C) IV, III, II, I (D) III, I, II, IV

Q.7 A student has to determine the focal length of a concave mirror by obtaining the image of a distant object on screen. For getting best result he should focus **[CBSE - 2012]**

(A) A distant tree or an electric pole
(B) A well-illuminated distant building
(C) Well-lit grills of the nearest window
(D) A burning candle placed at the distant edge of the laboratory table

Q.8 If you have to determine the focal length of a convex lens, you should have **[CBSE - 2012]**

(A) A convex lens and a screen
(B) A convex lens and a lens holder
(C) A lens holder, a screen holder and a scale
(D) A convex lens, a screen, holders for them and a scale

Q.9 While performing the experiment on tracing the path of a ray of light through a rectangular glass slab, in which of the following experimental set-ups is a student likely to get best results? P_1 and P_2 are the positions of pins fixed by him. **[CBSE - 2007,11,13,14]**

(I) 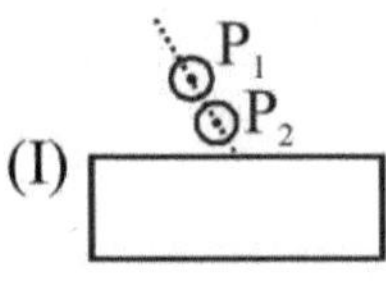

(II) 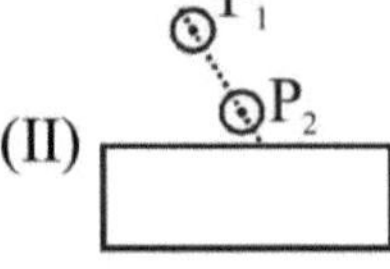

(III) 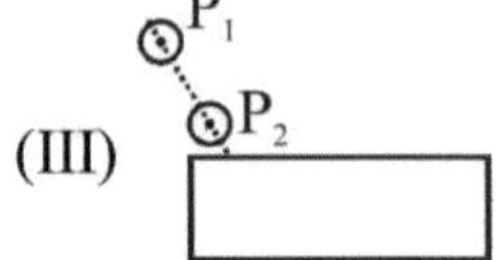

(IV) 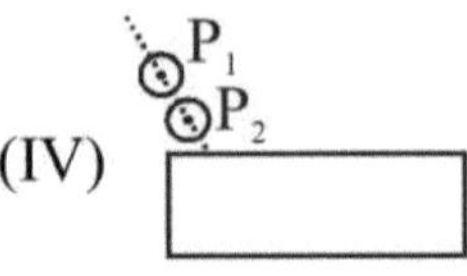

(A) I (B) II (C) III (D) IV

Q.10 Four students showed the following traces of the path of a ray of light passing through a rectangular glass slab. **[CBSE - 2007,11,12]**

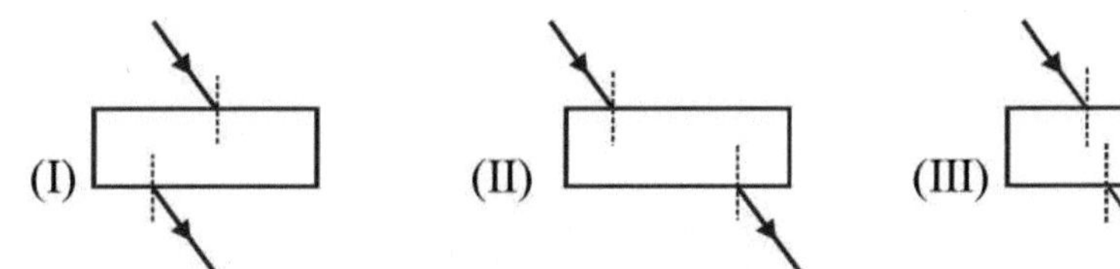

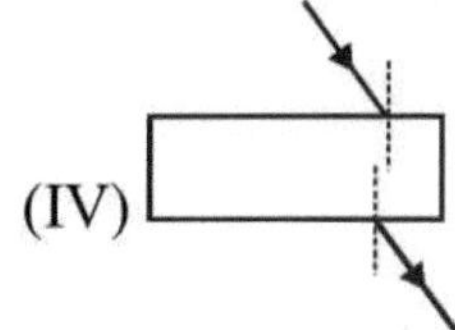

The trace most likely to be correct is that of student.

(A) I (B) II (C) III (D) IV

Q.11 Why does a ray of light bend when it travels from one medium to another medium? **[CBSE 2009]**

Sol. When a ray of light travels from one medium into another medium, its speed (wavelength) changes so it bends.

Q.12 Draw the given diagram in your answer book and complete it for the path of ray of light beyond the lens. **[CBSE- 2009]**

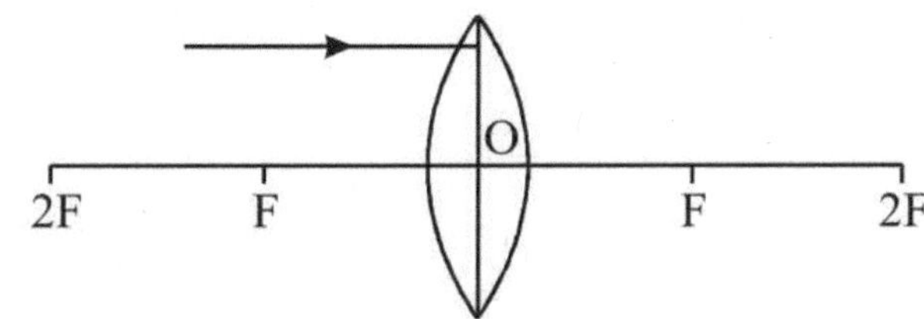

Sol.

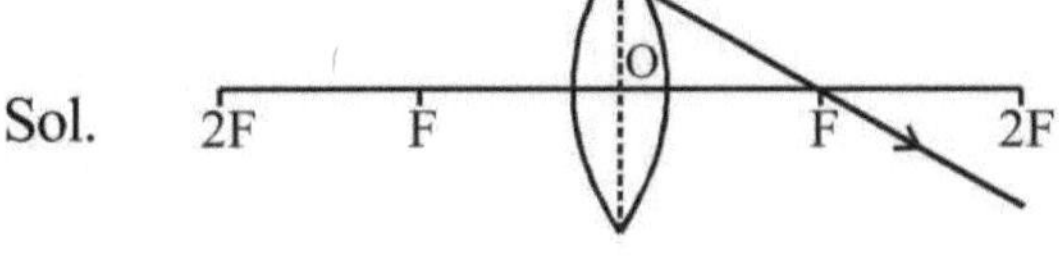

Q.13 Explain why a ray of light passing through the centre of curvature of a concave mirror gets reflected along the same path. **[CBSE - 2010]**

Sol. The normal of concave mirror at any point passes through centre, so incident angle ($\angle i$) is equal to zero.

Q.14 What is the nature of the image formed by a concave mirror if the magnification produced by the mirror is +3? **[CBSE- 2010]**

Sol. Magnification = + 3

so that nature of image virtual, erect and magnified.

Q.15 State one function of iris in human eye. **[CBSE - 2012]**

Sol. Functions of iris :

To control the amount of light entering the eye.

SECTION - E

PREVIOUS YEAR SHORT ANSWER QUESTIONS (2 & 3 Marks)

Q.1 What is the minimum number of rays required for location of the image formed by a concave mirror of an object. Draw a ray diagram to show the formation of a virtual image by a concave mirror.

[CBSE - 2009]

Ans. Two (minimum)

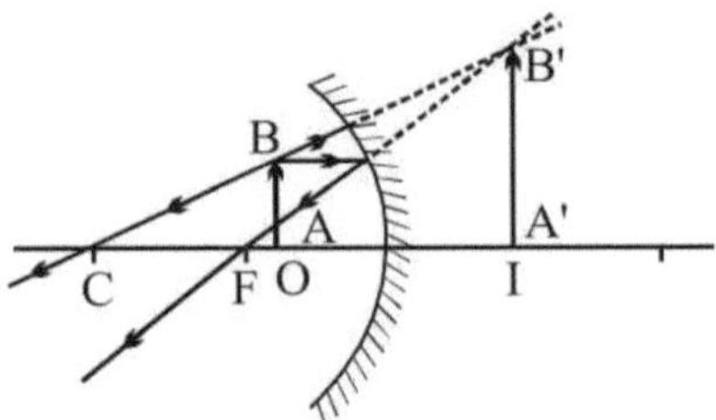

Q.2 At what distance should an object be placed from a convex lens of focal length 18 cm to obtain an image at 24 cm from it on the other side. What will be the magnification produced in this case?

[CBSE - 2010]

Ans. Given: f = 18 cm; v = 24 cm; u = ?; m = ?

By using len's formula,

$$\frac{1}{v} - \frac{1}{u} = \frac{1}{f}$$

$$\Rightarrow \quad \frac{1}{24} - \frac{1}{u} = \frac{1}{18} \qquad \Rightarrow \quad \frac{1}{u} = \frac{1}{24} - \frac{1}{18}$$

$$\Rightarrow \quad \frac{1}{u} = \frac{3-4}{72} \qquad \Rightarrow \quad \frac{1}{u} = -\frac{1}{72}$$

$$\Rightarrow \quad \square u = -72 \text{ cm}$$

Object distance is 72 cm infront of mirror.

Magnification :

$$m = \frac{v}{u} = \frac{24}{-72} = -\frac{1}{3}$$

Hence, final image is 3 times smaller than the object.

Negative sign shows image is real & inverted.

Q.3 State any four characteristics of the image of an object formed by a plane mirror. **[CBSE - 2010]**

Sol. (i) Distance of object from mirror is equal to distance of image from mirror.

(ii) The image is laterally inverted.

(iii) The line joining the object point with its image is normal to the reflecting surface.

(iv) The size of the image is same as that of the object.

Q.4 An object is placed between infinity and the pole of a convex mirror. Draw a ray diagram and also state the position, the relative size and the nature of the image formed. **[CBSE - 2010]**

Sol.

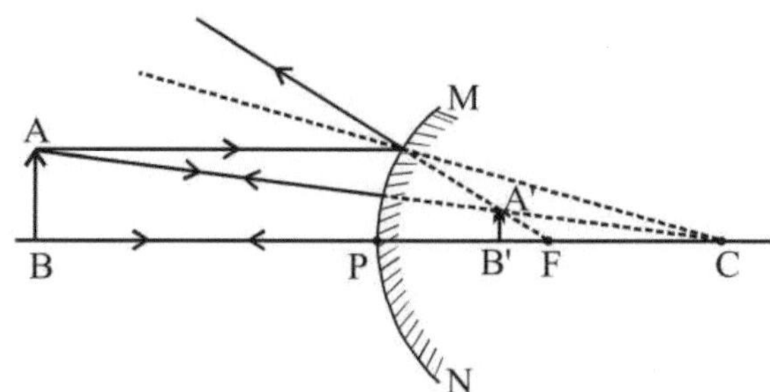

Position of the image – Between P and F, behind the mirror.
Size of the image – Diminished.
Nature of the image - Virtual and erect.

Q.5 What is the principal of reversibility of light? Show that the incident ray of light is parallel to the emergent ray of light when light falls obliquely on a side of a rectangular glass slab. **[CBSE - 2010]**

OR

"A ray of light incident on a rectangular glass slab immersed in any medium emerges parallel to itself." Draw labelled ray diagram to justify the statement. **[CBSE - 2010]**

Sol. Path of ray of light is reversible.

or

Light traces back it's path while travelling in reverse direction.

$$\frac{\sin i}{\sin r} = \frac{n_2}{n_1} \quad .... (1)$$

$$\frac{\sin r}{\sin e} = \frac{n_1}{n_2} \quad .... (2)$$

on multiplying eq. (1) and (2)

$$\frac{\sin i}{\sin r} \times \frac{\sin r}{\sin e} = \frac{n_2}{n_1} \times \frac{n_1}{n_2}$$

$$\Rightarrow \frac{\sin i}{\sin e} = 1 \Rightarrow \angle i = \angle e$$

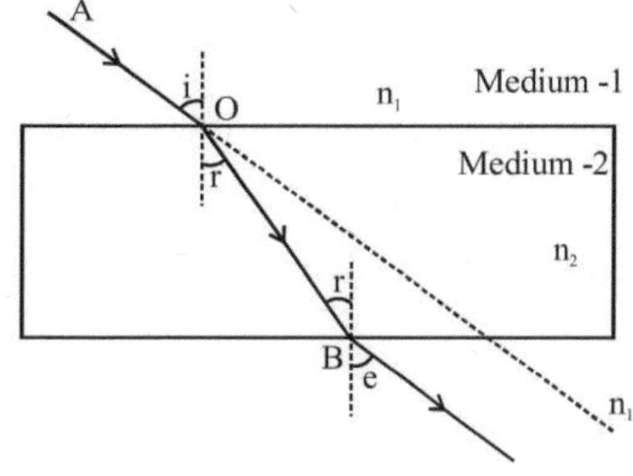

Q.6 To construct ray diagram we use two light rays which are so chosen that it is easy to know their directions after refractions from the lens. List these two rays and state the path of these rays after refraction. Use these rays to locate the image of an object placed between centre of curvature and focus of a convex lens. **[CBSE - 2010]**

Sol. (i) Any ray parallel to the principal axis after reflection will pass through the focus.
(ii) Any ray passing through the focus after refraction will go parallel to the principle axis.

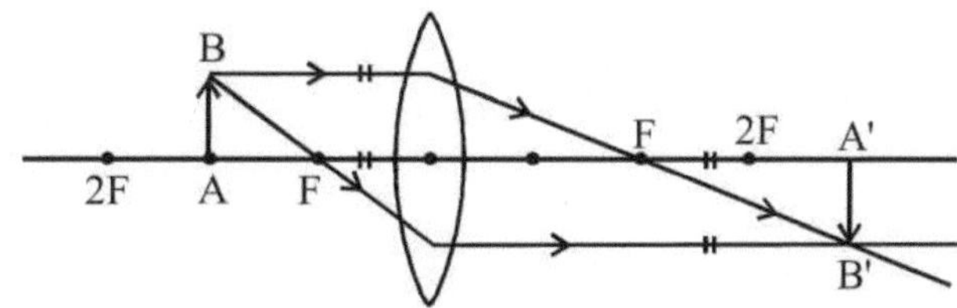

Q.7 A 4 cm tall object is placed perpendicular to the principal axis of a convex lens of focal length 24 cm. The distance of the object from the lens is 16 cm. Find the position, size & nature of the image formed by using lens formula. **[CBSE - 2012]**

Sol. A 4 cm tall object is given
So object height $h_0 = 4$ cm
focal length $f = +24$ cm
object distance $u = -16$ cm
To find : image height $h_i = ?$
image distance $v = ?$

using lens formula, $\frac{1}{f} = \frac{1}{v} - \frac{1}{u}$

$$\Rightarrow \quad \frac{1}{f} + \frac{1}{u} = \frac{1}{v} \quad \text{... (1)}$$

put the value of u and f in equation (1)

$$\frac{1}{v} = \frac{1}{24} - \frac{1}{16} = \frac{2-3}{48} = -\frac{1}{48}$$

$\therefore \quad v = -48$ cm

(–ve) sign shows that the image formed is same side of the object.
Now, magnification

$$m = \frac{h_i}{h_0} = \frac{v}{u}$$

$$\frac{h_i}{4} = \frac{-48}{-16} \Rightarrow h_i = 3 \times 4 = 12 \text{ cm}$$

Hence, image is formed at a distance of 48 cm infront of lens which is virtual and erect. Height of image is 12 cm.

Q.8 Draw a diagram and only these conventions for calculating the focal length and nature of a spherical mirror which forms a $\frac{1}{3}$ times magnified virtual image of an object placed 18 cm in front of it.
[CBSE - 2012]

Sol. Given that $u = -18$ cm
If object size is h_0 and image size is h_i,

then $h_i = \frac{1}{3} h_0 \quad \Rightarrow \quad \frac{h_i}{h_0} = \frac{1}{3}$

magnification $m = \frac{h_i}{h_0} = \frac{1}{3}$

$$\therefore \quad \frac{h_i}{h_0} = \frac{1}{3} \quad \Rightarrow \quad -\frac{v}{u} = \frac{1}{3}$$

$$\Rightarrow \quad v = \frac{-u}{3} = -\left(\frac{-18}{3}\right) = \frac{+18}{3} = +6\text{cm}$$

By using mirror formula

$$\frac{1}{v}+\frac{1}{u}=\frac{1}{f}$$

$$\Rightarrow \quad \frac{1}{6}-\frac{1}{18}=\frac{1}{f} \qquad \Rightarrow \quad \frac{1}{f}=\frac{3-1}{18}=\frac{2}{18}$$

$$\Rightarrow \quad \frac{1}{f}=\frac{1}{9} \qquad \Rightarrow \quad f=9\text{ cm}$$

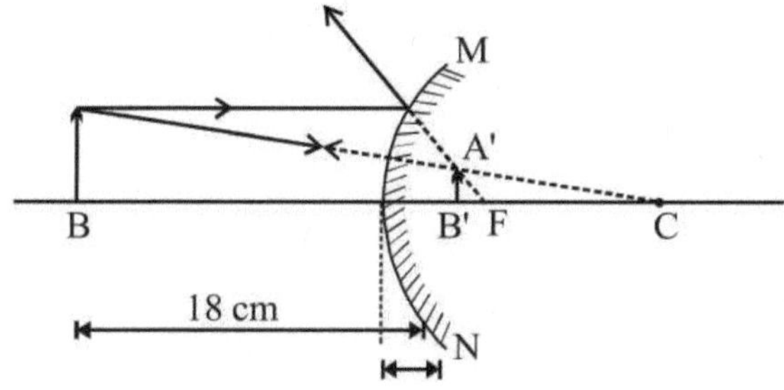

Hence, focal length is 9 cm behind the mirror and mirror is convex in nature. Image is virtual & erect and size of image is smaller than object.

Q.9 An object of height 6 cm is placed perpendicular to the principal axis of a concave lens of focal length 5 cm. Use lens formula to determine the position, size of nature of the image if the distance of the object from the lens is 10 cm. **[CBSE - 2013]**

Sol. Given that $h_0 = 6$ cm
$f = -5$ cm
$u = -10$ cm

by using lens formula,

$$\frac{1}{v}-\frac{1}{u}=\frac{1}{f}$$

$$\Rightarrow \quad \frac{1}{v}=\frac{1}{f}+\frac{1}{u}=\frac{1}{-5}+\frac{1}{-10}=\frac{-2-1}{10}=\frac{-3}{10}$$

$$v=\frac{-10}{3}\text{ cm}=-3.33\text{ cm}$$

Distance of image from the lens is 3.33 cm.

Now magnification $m=\frac{h_i}{h_0}=\frac{v}{u}$

$$\Rightarrow \quad \frac{h_i}{h_0}=\frac{v}{u} \Rightarrow \frac{h_i}{6}=\frac{-10/3}{-10}=\frac{1}{3}$$

$h_i = 2$ cm

Hence, image formed at a distnace of 3.33 cm infront of lens which is virtual & erect size of image is larger than the object i.e. image size is 3 times less than object size.

Q.10 If the image formed by the mirror for all positions of the object placed infront of it is always erect and diminished, what type of mirror it is? Draw a ray diagram to justify your answer. Where and why do we generally use this type of mirror. **[CBSE - 2015]**

Ans. A convex mirror always produces an erect and diminished image of the object placed in front of it irrespective of the position of the object.

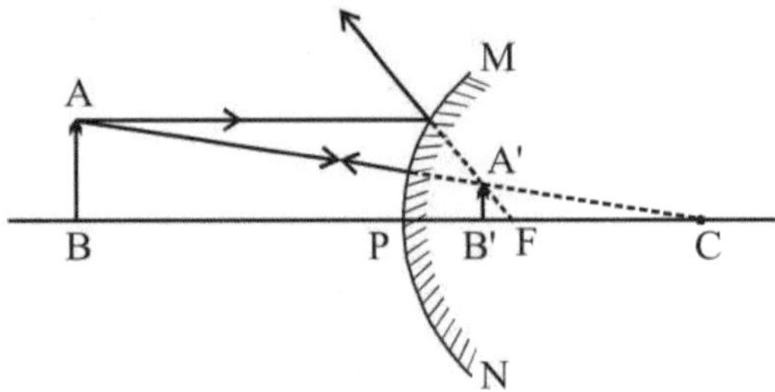

A virtual, erect and diminished image is formed behind the mirror between the pole and focus as shown in figure.As a convex mirror gives a wide field of view, it is used as a rear view mirror in vehicles. It enables the driver to view a much larger area of the traffic behind, it is also used as shop security cameras.

Q.11 An object of height 5 cm is placed perpendicular to the principle axis of a concave lens of focal length 10 cm. If the distance of the object from the optical centre of the lens is 20 cm, determine the position, nature & size of the image formed using the lens formula. **[CBSE - 2015]**

Sol. Given:

Height of object = 5cm

Focal length of concave lens = – 10 cm

Object distance u = – 20 cm

Using lens formula,

$$\frac{1}{f} = \frac{1}{v} - \frac{1}{u}$$

$$\frac{1}{v} = \frac{1}{f} + \frac{1}{u} = \frac{1}{-10} - \frac{1}{20} = \frac{-2-1}{20} = \frac{-3}{20}$$

$\therefore$ v = – 6.67 cm

Hence image is formed 6.67 infront of the lens on the same side as the object because v is negative, we can say that the image is virtual.

Now, magnification $m = \frac{h_i}{h_o} = \frac{v}{u}$

$$h_i = \frac{v}{u} \times h_o = -\frac{6.67 \times 5}{-20} = 1.67 \text{ cm}$$

Hence, the size of the image is $h_i = 1.67$ cm

Because the height of the image is positive and smaller than the height of the object, the image is erect and diminised.So, we can conclude that image is virtual, erect and diminished.

Q.12 The image of a candle flame placed at a distance of 45 cm from a spherical lens is formed on a screen placed at a distance of 90 cm from the lens. Identify the type of lens and calculate its focal length. If the height of the flame is 2 cm, find the height of its image. **[CBSE - 2016]**

Ans. Given that object distance $u = -45$ cm

Image distance $v = 90$ cm

The image of a candle flame is formed on the screen, so a convex lens is used.

$$\frac{1}{f} = \frac{1}{v} - \frac{1}{u}$$

$$\Rightarrow \quad \frac{1}{f} = \frac{1}{90} - \left(\frac{1}{-45}\right) = \frac{1}{90} + \frac{1}{45} = \frac{1+2}{90} = \frac{3}{90} = \frac{1}{30}$$

$\Rightarrow \quad f = +30$ cm

Hence, it is convex lens of focal length 30 cm

Now, height of image $h_i = ?$

$$\text{Magnification} \quad m = \frac{h_i}{h_o} = \frac{v}{u}$$

$$\Rightarrow \quad h_i = \frac{v \times h_o}{u}$$

$$\therefore \quad h_i = \frac{2 \times 90}{-45} = -4 \text{ cm}$$

Height of image $h_i = -4$ cm

Thus, height is 4 cm which is image minus (–1) sign indicates that the image is formed below the principal axis. So image is real & inverted.

Q.13 The image formed by a spherical mirror is real, inverted and is of magnification-2. If the image is at a distance of 30cm from the mirror, where the object placed? Find the focal length of the mirror. List two characteristic of the image formed if the object is moved 10 cm towards the mirror. **[CBSE - 2016]**

Sol. Given that $m = -2$

Distance of the image, $v = -30$ cm

$$\text{magnification } m = -\frac{v}{u}$$

$$u = \frac{-v}{m} = -\frac{(-30)}{(-2)} = -15\text{cm}$$

Now using mirror formula

$$\frac{1}{f} = \frac{1}{v} + \frac{1}{u}$$

$$= \frac{1}{(-30)} + \frac{1}{(-15)} = \frac{-1}{30} - \frac{1}{15} = \frac{-1-2}{30} = \frac{-3}{30}$$

$f = -10$ cm

When object is moved 10 cm towards the mirror the new position of the object is

$$u' = -(15 - 10) = -5 \text{ cm}$$

Again, using $\frac{1}{f}=\frac{1}{v'}+\frac{1}{u'}$

$$\frac{1}{v'}=\frac{1}{f}-\frac{1}{u'}=\frac{1}{-10}-\left(\frac{1}{-5}\right)=\frac{-1}{10}+\frac{1}{5}$$

$$\frac{1}{v'}=\frac{1}{10} \quad \Rightarrow \quad v'=10\text{cm}$$

Thus, the image formed 10 cm behind the mirror.

magnification $m'=\frac{v'}{u'}=-\frac{10}{(-5)}=2$

Since, magnification is positive the image is erect and virtual.
Thus, the image is erect, virtual and magnified in nature.

Q.14 Define the radius of curvature of spherical mirror. Find the nature and focal length of a spherical mirror whose radius of curvature is + 24 cm. **[CBSE - 2017]**

Ans. Radius of curvature : Radius of sphere from which a mirror is cut. It is denoted by R.

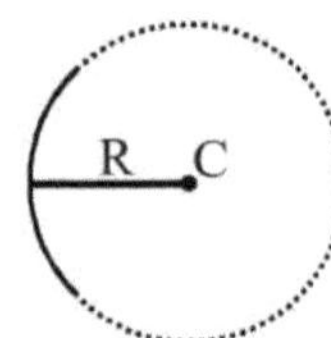

The radius of curvature of a spherical mirror is the radius of the sphere of which the reflecting surface of the spherical mirror is a part and it represented by 'R'.

Given that R = 24 cm

∴ focal length $f=\frac{R}{2}=12\text{cm}$

SECTION - F

PREVIOUS YEAR LONG ANSWER QUESTIONS (5 Marks)

Q.1 (a) What is meant by 'Power of a lens'? **[CBSE - 2010]**

(b) State and define the S.I. unit of power of a lens.

(c) A convex lens of focal length 25 cm and a concave lens of focal length 10cm are placed in close contact with each other. Calculate the lens power of this combination.

Sol. (a) It is the ability of lens to converge or diverge the incident light rays.
Power of a lens is the reciprocal of the focal length of a lens.

$$P=\frac{1}{f(\text{in m})}=\frac{100}{f(\text{in cm})}$$

(b) S.I. unit of power of a lens is dioptre (D)
Power of a lens in 1 dioptre if focal length of the lens is 1 metre or 100 cm.

(c) Given $f_1=25$ cm; $f_2=-10$ cm; $p_1=\frac{100}{25}=4D$; $p_2=\frac{100}{-10}=-10D$

$p=p_1+p_2=(4-10)\,D=-6\,D$

Q.2 (a) Draw a ray diagram to show the formation of image of object placed between infinity and the optical centre of a concave lens.

(b) A concave lens of focal length 15 cm forms an image 10 cm from the lens. Calculate :

(i) The distance of the object from the lens.

(ii) The magnification for the image formed.

(iii) The nature of the image formed. **[CBSE - 2010]**

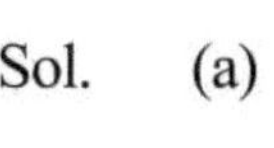

Sol. (a)

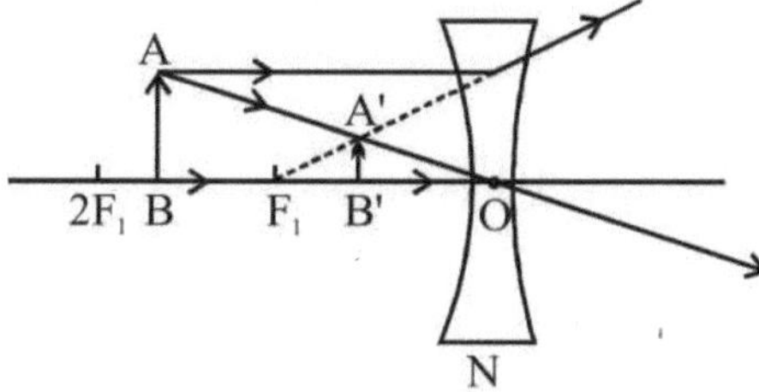

(b) f = – 15 cm

v = – 10 cm

(i) $\frac{1}{v} - \frac{1}{u} = \frac{1}{f}$ $\Rightarrow$ $\frac{1}{-10} - \frac{1}{u} = \frac{1}{-15}$

$\frac{1}{u} = \frac{1}{-10} + \frac{1}{15}$ $\Rightarrow$ u = – 30 cm

Object distance is 30 cm from lens.

(ii) $m = \frac{v}{u} = \frac{-10}{-30} = \frac{1}{3}$

Hence magnification is 1/3

(iii) Nature of image – virtual and erect.

Q.3 With the help of ray diagram, state what is meant by refraction of light. State snell's law of refraction of light and also express it mathematically. The refractive index of air with respect to glass is 2/3 and the refractive index of water with respect to air is 4/3. If the speed of light in glass is 2×10^8 m/s. Find the speed of light in (a) air (b) water. **[CBSE - 2012]**

Sol. Refraction of light :

The bending of light rays when they pass obliquely from one medium to another medium is called refraction of light.

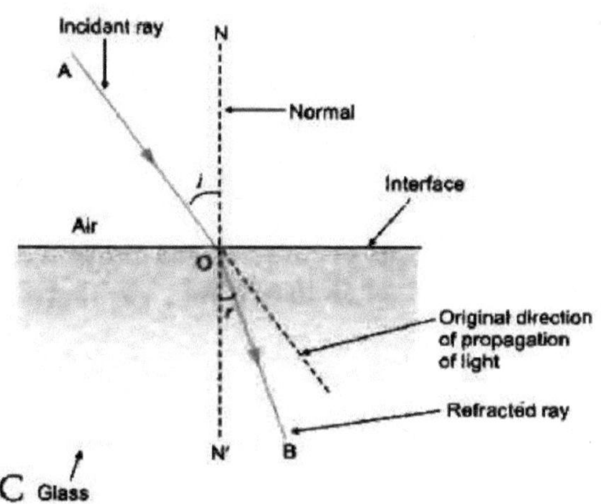

Snell's law :

The ratio of the sine of the incident angle ($\angle i$) to the sine of the refracted angle ($\angle r$) is constant for a pair of two media

i.e. $\frac{\sin i}{\sin r} = \text{constant}$

This constant is known as the refractive index of the medium in which refracted ray travels with respect to the medium in which incident ray travels.

Given that ${}^{a}\mu_{g} = \frac{2}{3} \Rightarrow {}^{g}\mu_{a} = \frac{3}{2}$ and ${}^{w}\mu_{a} = \frac{4}{3}$

Let velocity of light in glassis v_g & water is v_w then $v_g = 2 \times 10^8$ m/s

To find : $v_a = ?\ v_w = ?$

$$\text{Refractive index} = (\mu) = \frac{\text{speed of light in air}}{\text{speed of light in medium}}$$

(a) $${}^{g}\mu_{a} = \frac{\text{speed of light in glass}}{\text{speed of light in air}}$$

$$\Rightarrow \quad \frac{2}{3} = \frac{2\times10^8}{V_a} \quad \Rightarrow \quad V_a = 3 \times 10^8 \text{ m/s}$$

Hence, speed of light in air is 3×10^8 m/s.

(b) $${}^{a}\mu_{w} = \frac{\text{speed of light is air}}{\text{speed of light in water}}$$

$$\frac{4}{3} = \frac{3\times10^8}{V_W} \quad (\because \text{Speed of light is air} = 3 \times 10^8 \text{ m/s})$$

$$\Rightarrow \quad V_W = \frac{4}{9}\times10^8 = 2.25 \times 10^8 \text{ m/s}$$

Q.4 A convex lens of focal length 25 cm and a concave lens of focal length 10 cm are placed in close contact with each other. Calculate the lens power of this combination. **[CBSE - 2012]**

Sol. Focal length of convex lens $f_1 = 25$ cm

Focal length of concave lens $f_2 = -10$ cm

$$\because \quad \frac{1}{f} = \frac{1}{f_1} + \frac{1}{f_2} = \frac{1}{25} - \frac{1}{10} = \frac{2-5}{50} = \frac{-3}{50}$$

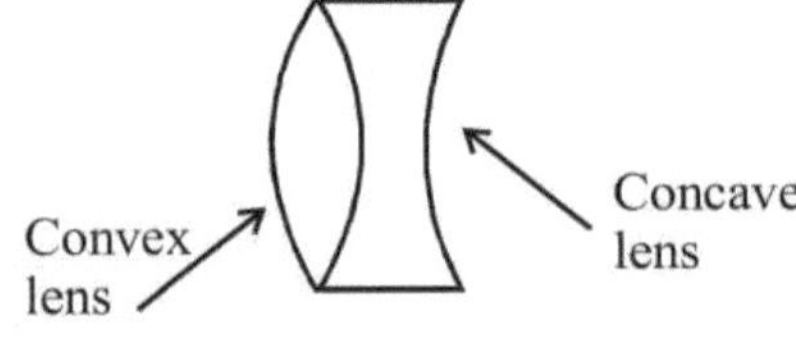

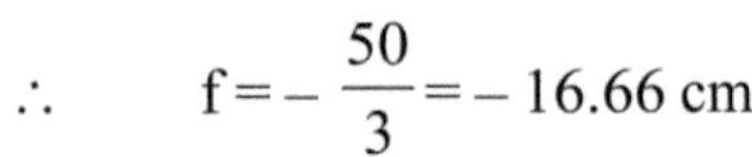

$$\therefore \quad f = -\frac{50}{3} = -16.66 \text{ cm}$$

Focal length of combination of lens is $\frac{-50}{3}$ cm

$$\therefore \quad \text{Power} = \frac{100}{f}, \text{ where f is in cm}$$

$$= \frac{-100\times3}{50} = -6\,D$$

Q.5 A concave lens of focal length 15 cm forms an image 10 cm from the lens. Calculate
(i) The distance of the object from the lens.
(ii) The magnification for the image formed.
(iii) The nature of the image formed. **[CBSE - 2012]**

Sol. Given that $f = -15\text{cm}, v = -10$ cm,
To find, $u = ?,\ m = ?$

(i) By using lens formula $\frac{1}{v} - \frac{1}{u} = \frac{1}{f}$

$$-\frac{1}{u} = \frac{1}{f} - \frac{1}{v} = -\frac{1}{15} + \frac{1}{10} = \frac{-2+3}{30} = \frac{1}{30} \quad \Rightarrow \quad u = -30 \text{ cm}$$

(ii) Magnification, $m = \frac{v}{u} = \frac{-10}{-30} = \frac{1}{3}$

(iii) $m = \frac{1}{3}$, and $m = \frac{h_i}{h_0} = \frac{\text{image size}}{\text{object size}}$

$$\therefore \quad \frac{h_i}{h_0} = \frac{1}{3}$$

$$h_i = \frac{1}{3} h_0$$

Hence image size is $\frac{1}{3}$ times of the object size. Image formed at the same side of object which is virtual and erect.

Q.6 (a) An object of size 7.6 cm is placed at 24 cm infront of a concave mirror of focal length 16 cm. At what distance from the mirror should a screen be placed, so that a sharp focused image can be obtained? Find the size and nature of the image.
(b) The diagram given below shows an object O. Copy the diagram and draw a suitable ray to locate the image. Name the type of lens used in this case. **[CBSE - 2013]**

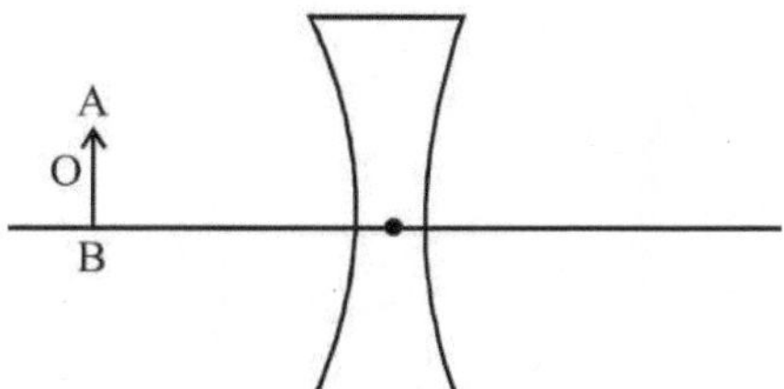

Sol. (a) Given that object height $h_0 = 7.6$ cm $= -24$ cm; $f = -16$ cm; $v = ?$

By using mirror formula, $\frac{1}{v} + \frac{1}{u} = \frac{1}{f}$

$$\frac{1}{v} = \frac{1}{f} - \frac{1}{u} = -\frac{1}{16} - \left(-\frac{1}{24}\right)$$

$$\frac{-1}{16} + \frac{1}{24} = \frac{-3+2}{48} = \frac{-1}{48}$$

$v = 48$ cm

Image distance with (-ve) sign shows that image formed at the same side of the object and screen also placed at that point.

Now, $m = \frac{h_i}{h_0} = \frac{-v}{u} \Rightarrow \frac{h_i}{h_0} = \frac{-v}{u}$

$\Rightarrow \frac{h_i}{7.6} = \frac{-(-48)}{-24} = 2$

$h_i = 2 \times 7.6 = 15.2$ cm

Image size is 15.2 cm which is lager than the oject. Image I real and inverted.

(b)

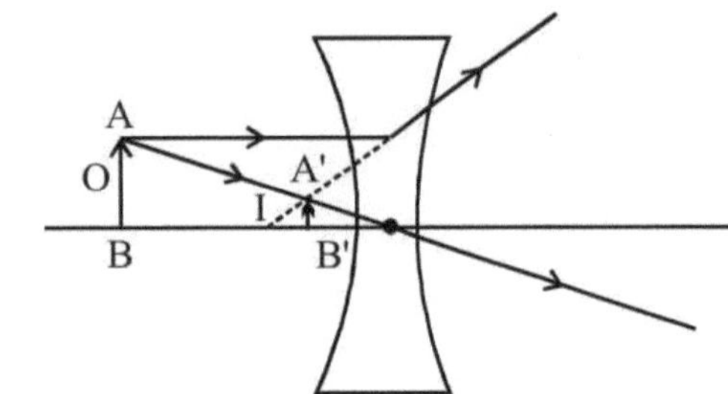

AB = object

A'B' = Image

Lens used here is concave.

Q.7 (a) Name the lens which can be used as a magnifying glass. For which position of the object a convex lens forms:

(i) A real & inverted image of the same size as that of the object.

(ii) A virtual & erect image.

Draw the ray diagram to justify your answer in each case.

(b) One half of a convex lens is covered with a black paper. Will this lens produce a complete image of the object?

Draw ray diagrm to justify your answer. **[CBSE - 2016]**

Ans. (a) Convex lens is used as a magnifying glass.

(i)

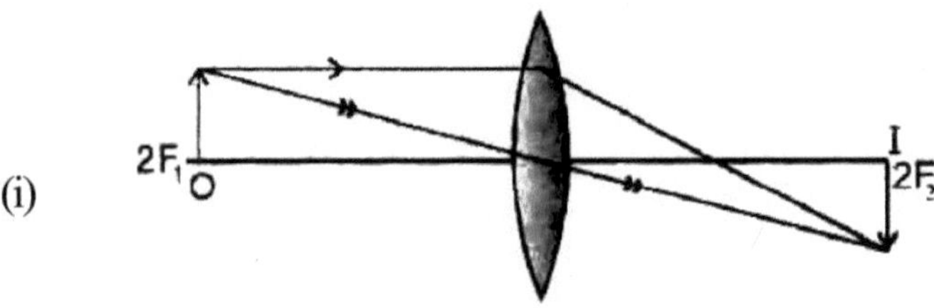

(ii)

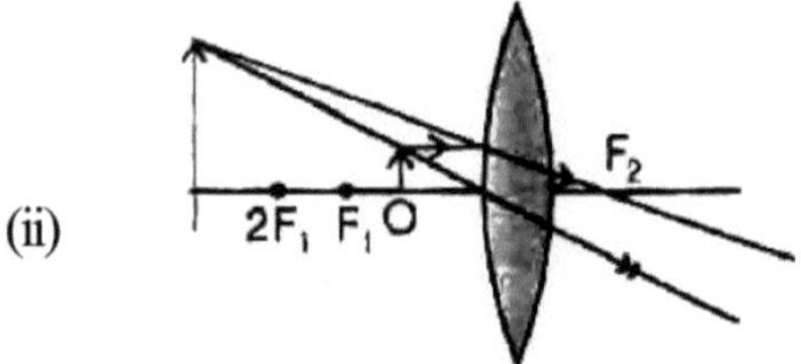

(b) The convex lens will form a complete image of an object, even if its one-half is covered with black paper. It can be understood by the following two cases :

Case I - When upper half of lens is covered

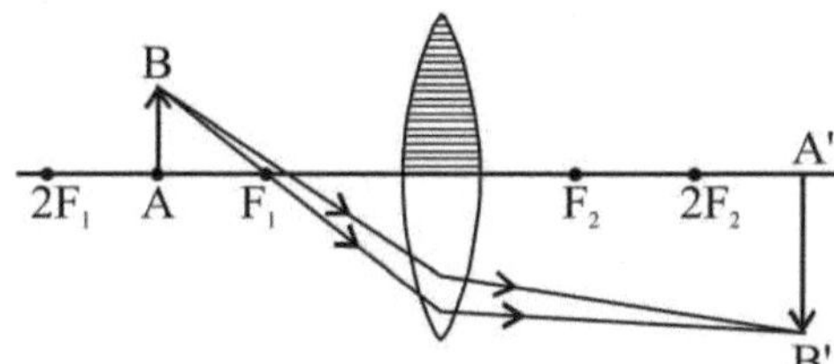

In this case, the ray of light coming from the object will be refracted by lower half of the lens. These rays meet at the other side of the lens to form the image of the given object.

Case-II - When the lower half of the lens is covered.

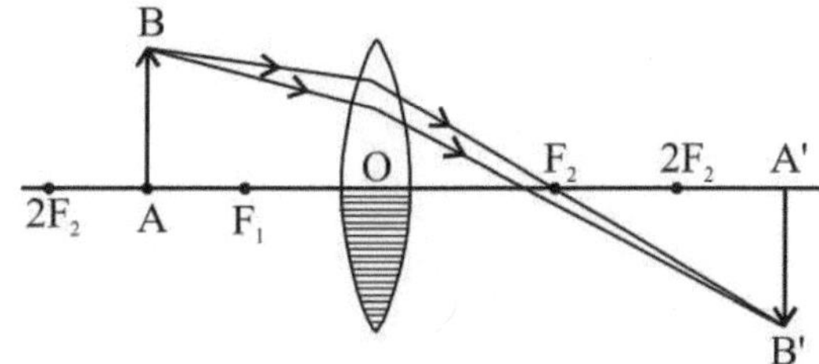

In this case, a ray of light coming from the object is refracted by the upper half of the lens. These rays meet at the other side of the lens to form the image of the given object, as shown in figure given above.

Note : The only difference between these two images will be that they will have less intensity.

Q.8 An object 4 cm in length is placed at a distance of 20 cm infront of a convex mirror of radius of curvature 20 cm. The mirror formula to find the position, nature and size of image. Also draw a ray diagram for the above situation and mark the position of pole, focus and centre of curvature on it.

[CBSE - 2016]

Sol. Given that :

Object distance $u = -20$ cm

Object height $h_0 = 4$ cm

Radius of curvature $R = 20$ cm

$$\therefore \quad f = \frac{R}{2}$$

$$\therefore \quad \text{Focal length } f = \frac{20}{2} = 10 \text{ cm}$$

According to mirror formula,

$$\frac{1}{v} + \frac{1}{u} = \frac{1}{f}$$

$$\frac{1}{v} = \frac{1}{f} - \frac{1}{u}$$

$$\frac{1}{v} = \frac{1}{10} - \left(\frac{1}{-20}\right) = \frac{1}{10} + \frac{1}{20} = \frac{2+1}{20} = \frac{3}{20}$$

$$\therefore \quad v = \frac{20}{3} = 6.67 \text{ cm}$$

The positive value of v indicates that the image is formed behind the mirror. So,it is virtual in nature

magnification $m = -\frac{v}{u}$

$$m = -\frac{v}{u} = -\frac{6.67}{-20} = 0.33$$

and $m = \frac{h_i}{h_0} \Rightarrow h_i = m \times h_0$

$$= 0.33 \times 4 = 1.32 \text{ cm}$$

The positive value of the image height indicates that the image formed is erect.

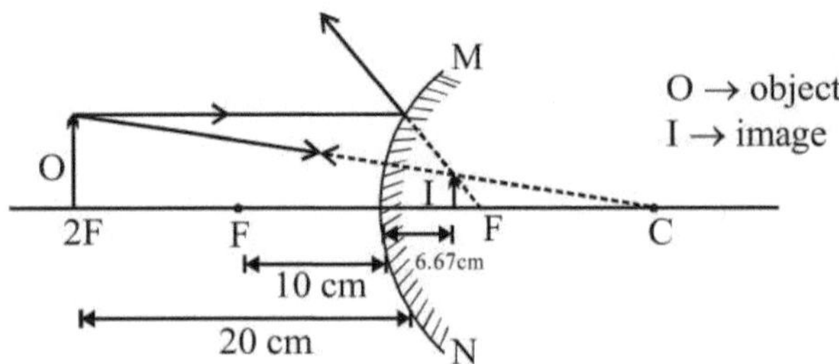

SECTION - G
PRACTICAL BASED QUESTIONS

Q.1 A student focused the image of a distant object using a device 'X' on a white screen 'S' as shown in the figure. If the distance of the screen from the device is 40 cm, select the correct statement about the device.

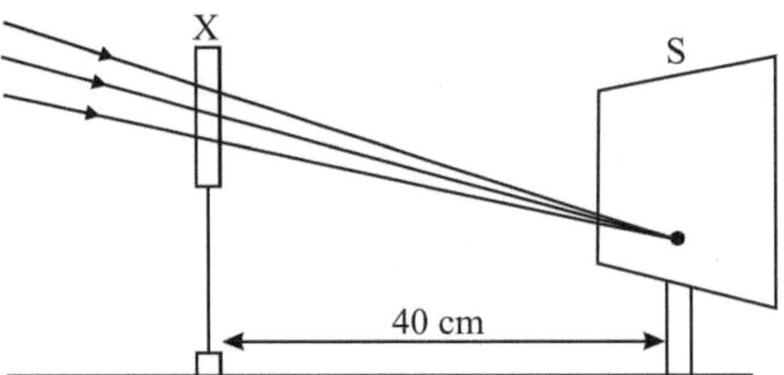

(A) The device X is a convex lens of focal length 20 cm.
(B) The device X is a concave mirror of focal length 40 cm.
(C) The device X is concave mirror of radius of curvature 40 cm.
(D) The device X is a convex lens of focal length 40 cm.

Q.2 A student obtained a sharp image of a burning candle, placed at the farther end of a laboratory table, on a screen using a concave mirror. For getting better value of focal length of the mirror, the subject teacher suggested him for focussing a well illuminated distant object. What should the student do?
(A) He should move the mirror away from the screen.
(B) He should move the mirror slightly towards the screen.
(C) He should move the mirror as well as the screen towards the newly selected object.
(D) He should move only the screen towards the newly selected object.

Q.3 After tracing the path of rays of light through a glass slab for three different angles of incidence, a student measured the corresponding values angle of refraction (r) and angle of emergence (e) and recorded them in the table given below:

S.No.	$\angle i$	$\angle r$	$\angle e$
I	30°	20°	31°
II	40°	25°	40°
III	50°	31°	49°

correct observations are :

(A) only I (B) only II (C) I and III (D) I, II and III

Q.4 Study the following ray diagrams:

(I) 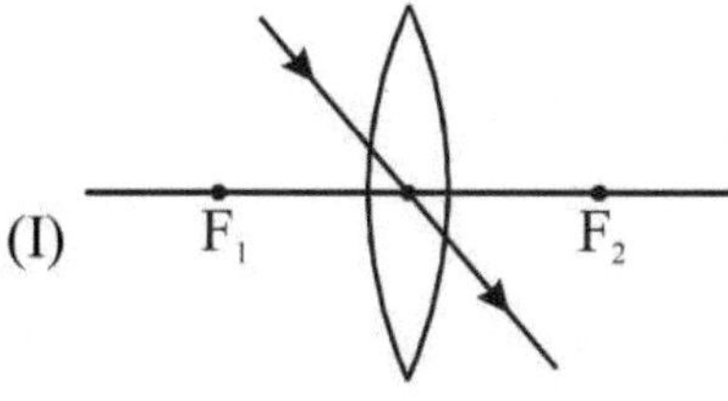

(II) 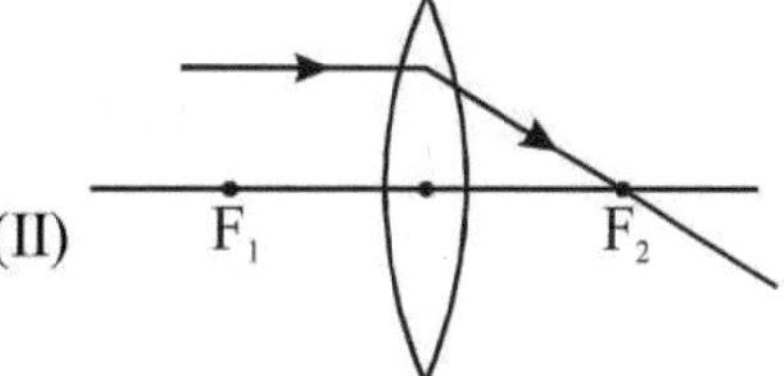

(III) 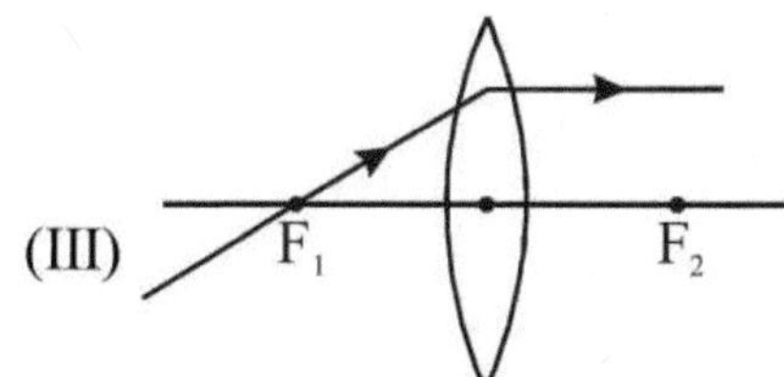

(IV) 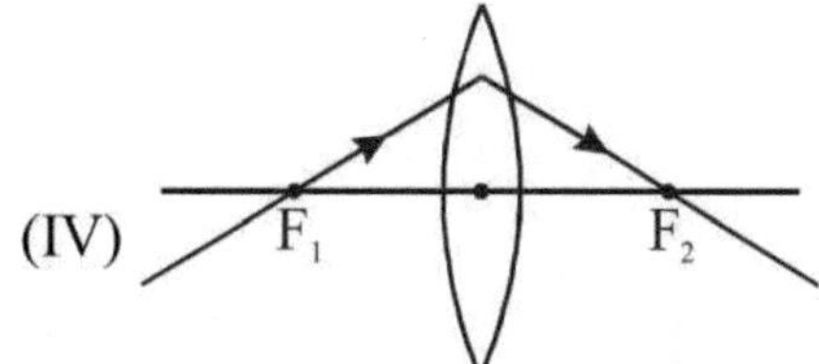

The diagrams showing the correct path of the ray after passing through the lens are

(A) II and III only (B) I and II only (C) I, II and III (D) I, II and IV

Q.5 Out of the five incident rays shown in the figure find the three rays that are obeying the laws of refraction and may be used for locating the position of image formed by a convex lens.

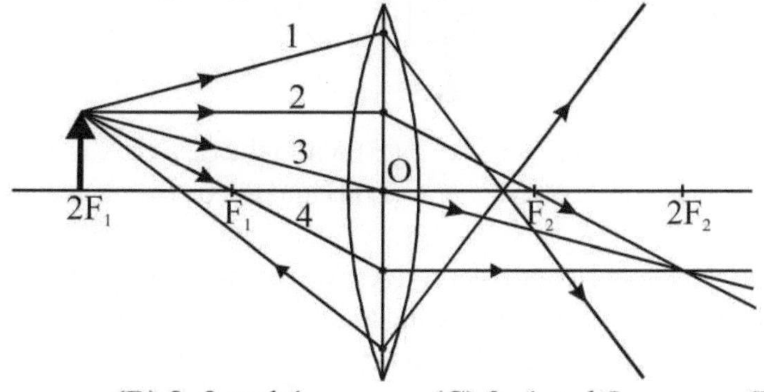

(A) 1, 2 and 3 (B) 2, 3 and 4 (C) 3, 4 and 5 (D) 1, 2 and 4

Q.6 What does the relationship $\angle i = \angle e$ mean ?

Q.7 Four students A, B, C and D carried out focal length of concave mirror as shown in four diagram :

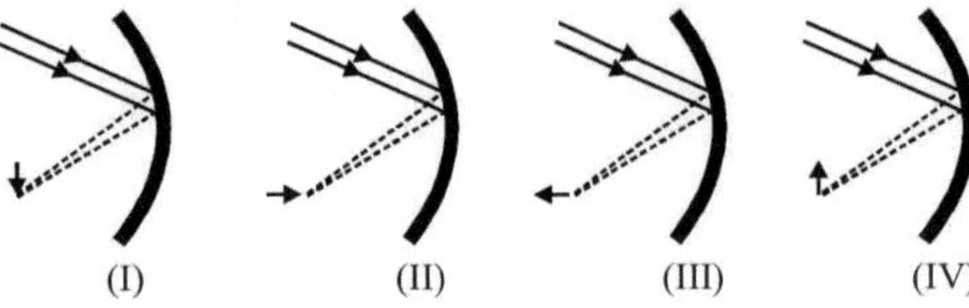

Correct diagram is :

(A) II (B) I (C) III (D) IV

Q.8 A student obtained a sharp image of the grill of a window on a screen, using a convex lens. For getting better results, the teacher suggested focusing of a distant tree instead of the grill. In which direction should the lens be moved for this purpose ?

(A) away from the screen (B) very far away from the screen

(C) behind the screen (D) towards the screen

Q.9 Parallel rays, from a distant tree, incident on the device X, forms its distinct image on a screen as shown. The diagram correctly showing the image of the tree on the screen, is diagram :

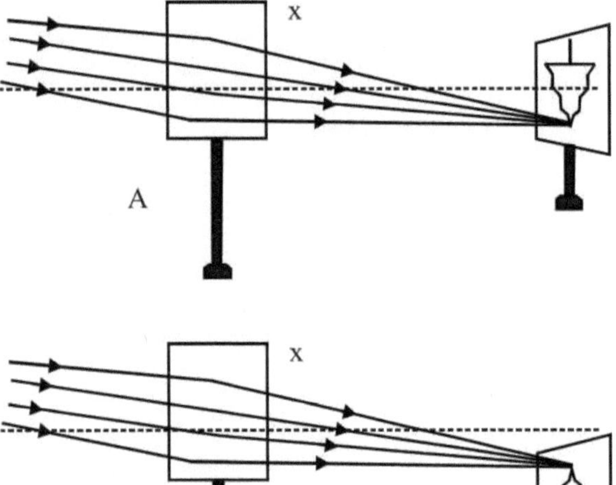

(A) A and the device X is convex lens (B) A and the device X is a concave mirror

(C) B and A the device X is convex lens (D) B and the device X is a concave mirror

Q.10 Three students measured the focal length of a convex lens using parallel rays from a distant object. All of them measured the distance between the lens and the inverted image on the screen.

Student A saw a sharp image on the screen and labelled the distance of f_1.

Student B saw a slightly larger blurred image on the screen and labelled the distance as f_2 .

Student C saw a slightly smaller blurred image on the screen and labelled the distance as f_3.

The relation between the three measurements would most likely be :

(A) $f_1 = f_2 = f_3$ (B) $f_1 < f_2$ and f_3 (C) $f_3 < f_1 < f_2$ (D) $f_1 < f_2$ and $f_1 = f_3$

Q.11 In an experiment to determine the focal length of a convex lens, a student obtained a sharp inverted image of a distant tree on the behind the lens. She then removed the screen and looked through the lens in the direction of the object. She will see :
(A) An inverted image of the tree at the focus of the lens
(B) No image as the screen has been removed
(C) A blurred image on the wall of the laboratory
(D) An erect image of the tree on the lens

Q.12 A ray of light is travelling from water to air, which figure shows correct refraction ?

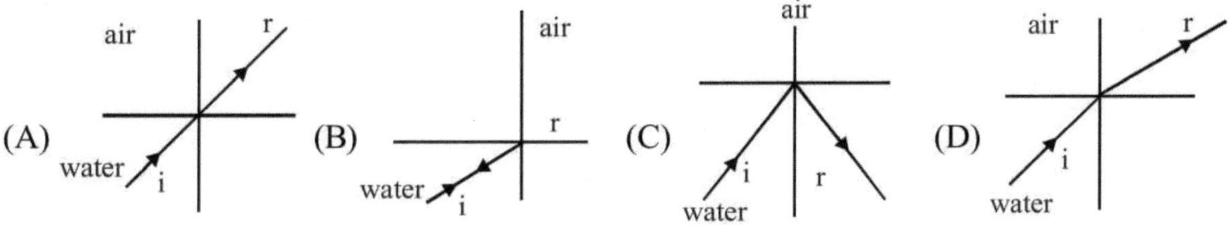

Q.13 Which characteristic of light remains unchanged on refraction ?
(A) velocity (B) frequency (C) refractive index (D) wavelength

Q.14 When ray of light enters glass from air, its wavelength :
(A) decreases (B) Increases (C) remains same (D) all of them

*****

CONCEPT APPLICATION LEVEL - III

SECTION-A

- **Fill in the blanks**

Q.1 A light wave of frequency 5×10^{14} Hz enters a medium of refractive index 1.5. In the medium the velocity of light wave is __________ and its wavelength is __________.

SECTION-B

- **Multiple choice question with one correct answers**

Q.1 When a ray of light enters a glass slab from air.
(A) Its wavelength decreases.
(B) Its wavelength increases.
(C) Its frequency decreases.
(D) Neither its wavelength nor its frequency changes.

Q.2 An eye specialist prescribe spectacles having combination of convex lens of focal length 40 cm in contact with a concave lens of focal length 25 cm. The power of this lens combination in diopters is
(A) +1.5 (B) –1.5 (C) +6.67 (D) –6.67

Q.3 A ray of light passes through four transparent media with refractive indices μ_1, μ_2, μ_3 and μ_4 as shown in the figure. The surfaces of all media are parallel. If the emergent ray CD is parallel to the incident ray AB, we must have

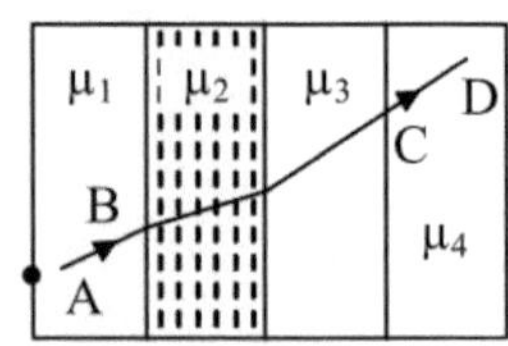

(A) $\mu_1 = \mu_2$ (B) $\mu_2 = \mu_3$ (C) $\mu_3 = \mu_4$ (D) $\mu_4 = \mu_1$

Q.4 A hollow double concave lens is made of very thin transparent material. It can be filled with air or either of two liquids L_1 or L_2 having refractive indices μ_1 and μ_2 respectively ($\mu_2 > \mu_1 > 1$). The lens will diverge a parallel beam of light if it is filled with
(A) Air and placed in air (B) Air and immersed in L_1
(C) L_1 and immersed in L_2 (D) L_2 and immersed in L_1

Q.5 A point object is placed at the centre of a glass sphere of radius 6 cm and refractive index 1.5. The distance of virtual image from the surface is
(A) 6 cm (B) 4 cm (C) 12 cm (D) 9 cm

Q.6 What is the relation between the refractive indices μ_1 and μ_2, if the behaviour of light ray is as shown in the figure.

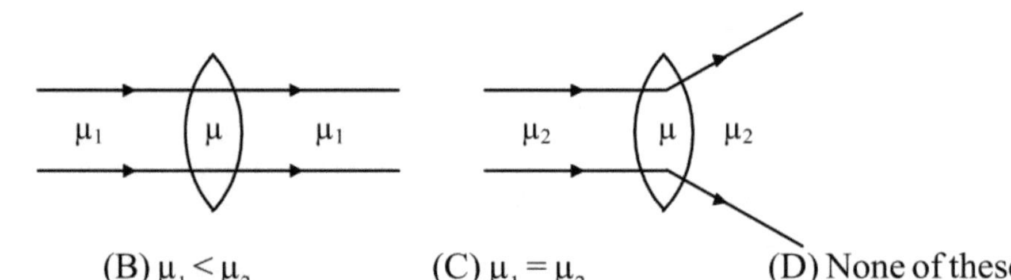

(A) $\mu_1 > \mu_2$ (B) $\mu_1 < \mu_2$ (C) $\mu_1 = \mu_2$ (D) None of these

Q.7 Which of the following lens can form image of an object on screen.
(A) Concave (B) Convex
(C) Both convex and concave (D) none of these

Q.8 To obtain a diminished image of an object, formed by a convex lens, where should the object must be placed?
(A) between F and 2F (B) At F
(C) between infinity and 2F (D) at 2F

Q.9. If object is placed between infinity and 2F of a convex lens, then image will form
(A) at F (B) between F and 2F (C) at 2 F (D) at infinity

Q.10 A convex lens A of focal length 20 cm and a concave lens B of focal length 5 cm are kept along the same axis with a distance 'd' between them. If a parallel beam of light falling on A leaves B as a parallel beam, then d is equal to
(A) 25 cm (B) 20 cm (C) 15 cm (D) 10 cm

Q.11 A thin rod of length f/3 is placed along the principal axis of a concave mirror of focal length f such that its image which is real and elongated, just touches the rod. The magnification is
(A) 2/3 (B) 3/2 (C) 3/5 (D) 5/3

Q.12 Two thin lenses, when in contact, produce a combination of power +10 diopters. When they are 0.25 m apart, the power reduces to +6 diopters. The focal length of the lenses are
(A) 0.125 m. 0.5 m (B) 0.25 m, 0.5 m (C) 0.25 m, 0.75 m (D) none of these

Q.13 A diminished image of an object is to be obtained on a screen 1.0 m from it. This can be achieved by appropriately placing.
(A) A convex lens of focal length more than 0.25 m.
(B) A convex mirror of suitable focal length.
(C) A convex lens of focal length less than 0.25 m.
(D) A concave lens of suitable focal length.

Q.14 An observer can see through a pin-hole the top end of a thin rod of height h, placed as shown in the figure. The beaker height is 3h and its radius h. When the beaker is filled with a liquid up to a height 2h, he can see the lower end of the rod. Then the refractive index of the liquid is

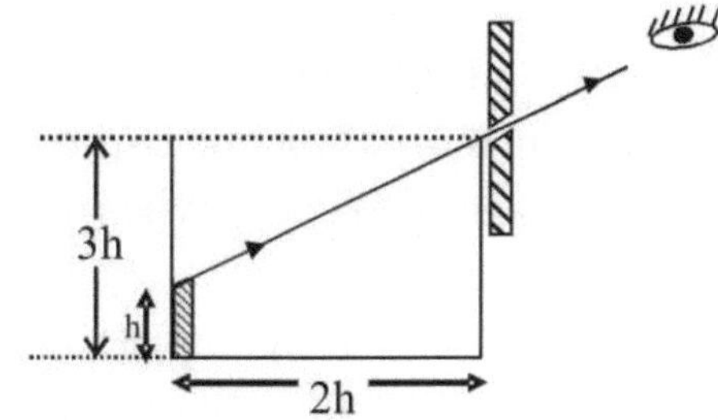

(A) $\frac{5}{2}$ (B) $\sqrt{\frac{5}{2}}$ (C) $\sqrt{\frac{3}{2}}$ (D) $\frac{3}{2}$

Q.15 Two plane mirrors A and B are aligned parallel to each other as shown in the figure. A light ray is incident at an angle 30° at a point just inside one end of A. The plane of incidence coincides with the plane of the figure. The maximum number of times the ray undergoes reflections (including the first one) before it emerges out is

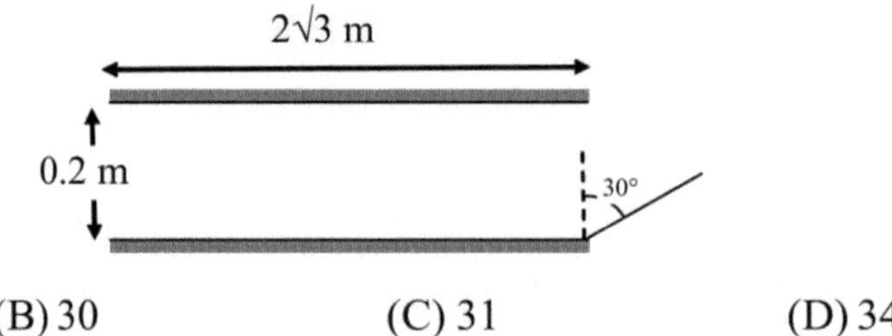

(A) 28 (B) 30 (C) 31 (D) 34

Q.16 The size of the image of an object, which is at infinity, as formed by a convex lens of focal length 30 cm is 2 cm. If a concave lens of focal length 20 cm is placed between the convex lens and the image at a distance of 26 cm from the convex lens, calculate the new size of the image.
(A) 1.25 cm (B) 1.67 cm (C) 1.05 cm (D) 2 cm

Q.17 A convex lens is in contact with concave lens. The magnitude of the ratio of their focal length is 2/3. Their equivalent focal length is 30 cm. What are their individual focal lengths?
(A) –15, 10 (B) –10, 15 (C) 75, 50 (D) –75, 50

Q.18 A short linear object of length 'b' lies along the axis of a concave mirror of focal length f at a distance u from the pole of the mirror. The size of the image is approximately equal to

(A) $b\left(\frac{u-f}{f}\right)^{1/2}$ (B) $b\left(\frac{f}{u-f}\right)^{1/2}$ (C) $b\left(\frac{u-f}{f}\right)$ (D) $b\left(\frac{f}{f-u}\right)^{2}$

Q.19 A concave mirror is placed on a horizontal table, with its axis directed vertically upwards. Let O be the pole of the mirror and C its centre of curvature. A point object is placed at C. It has a real image also located at C. If the mirror is now filled with water, the image will be
(A) real, and will remain at C
(B) real, and located at a point between C and ∞.
(C) virtual, and located at a point between C and O
(D) real, and located at a point between C and O.

SECTION-C

- **Multiple choice question with one or more than one correct answers**

Q.1 A converging lens is used to form an image on a screen. When the upper half of the lens is covered by an opaque screen.
(A) half the image will disappear (B) complete image will be formed
(C) intensity of the image will increase (D) intensity of the image will decrease

Q.2 Which of the following forms a virtual and erect image for all positions of the object?
(A) convex lens (B) concave lens (C) convex mirror (D) concave mirror

SECTION-D

- **Assertion & Reason**

Instructions: In the following questions as Assertion (A) is given followed by a Reason (R). Mark your responses from the following options.

(A) Both Assertion and Reason are true and Reason is the correct explanation of 'Assertion'

(B) Both Assertion and Reason are true and Reason is not the correct explanation of 'Assertion'

(C) Assertion is true but Reason is false

(D) Assertion is false but Reason is true

Q.1 **Assertion:** A ray of light entering from glass to air suffers from change in frequency.
Reason: Velocity of light in glass is less than that in air.

Q.2 **Assertion:** A plane mirror has unity magnification.
Reason: In the case of plane mirror the distance of image is equal to the distance of object.

Q.3 **Assertion:** Convex mirror is used as a driver's mirror.
Reason: Field view of a convex mirror is large.

Q.4 **Assertion:** Focal length of a lens remain same if it is cut across the axis along XX′.

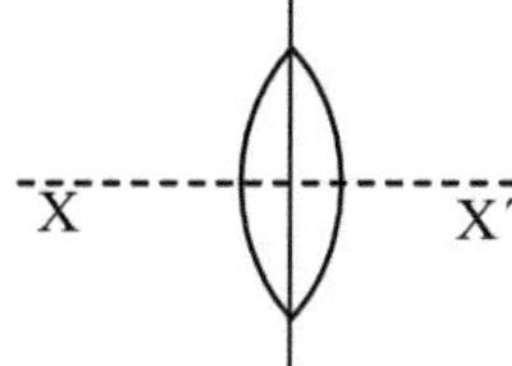

Reason: Both the refracting surfaces remain in contact if the lens is cut along $X - X'$ plane.

Q.5 **Assertion:** Power of a lens is indirectly proportional to its focal length.
Reason: Units of focal length and power of a lens are same.

SECTION-E

- **Comprehension**

An object O is placed in denser medium. A light ray OA travels from denser to rarer medium. Refracted ray AD appears to come from O′. O′ is image of the object O.

Given that: OC = 2m, $O'C = \frac{2}{\sqrt{3}}$ m and OB = 2m.

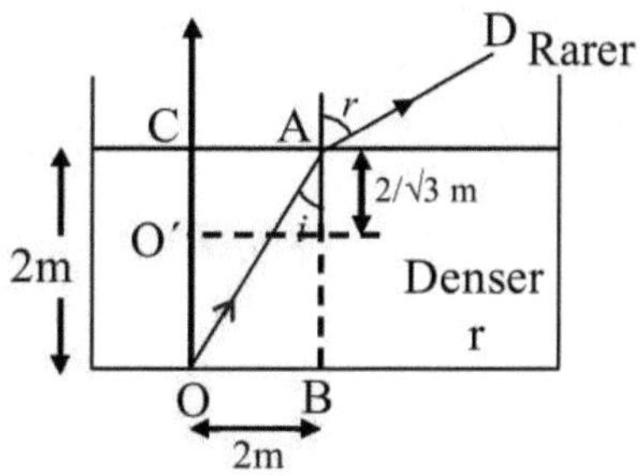

Q.1 Value of angle i is

(A) 60° (B) 45° (C) 30° (D) None of these

Q.2 Value of angle r is
(A) 60° (B) 45° (C) 30° (D) None of these

Q.3 Refractive index of denser medium w.r.t. rarer medium is
(A) $\frac{\sin i}{\sin r}$ (B) $\frac{\sin r}{\sin i}$ (C) $\frac{\sin (i-r)}{\sin r}$ (D) None of these

SECTION-F

- **Match the following (one to one)**
Column-I and **column-II** contains **four** entries each. Entries of column-I are to be matched with some entries of column-II. Only One entries of column-I may have the matching with the same entries of column-II and one entry of column-II Only one matching with entries of column-I

Q.1

	Column I		Column II
(A)	Law of reflection	(P)	1/focal length
(B)	Law of refraction	(Q)	$\angle i = \angle r$
(C)	Power of lens	(R)	$\frac{\sin i}{\sin r} = \text{constant}$
(D)	Absolute refractive index of glass	(S)	$\frac{\text{Speed of light in air}}{\text{Speed of light in glass}}$

SECTION-G

- **Match the following (one to many)**
Column-I and **column-II** contains **four** entries each. Entries of column-I are to be matched with some entries of column-II. One or more than one entries of column-I may have the matching with the same entries of column-II and one entry of column-II may have one or more than one matching with entries of column-I

Q.1

	Column I		Column II
(A)	Straight line which is normal to the mirror at its pole (P)	(P)	Will passes through principal focus (F)
(B)	A ray, parallel to the principal axis of concave mirror after reflection	(Q)	Focal length (f)
(C)	The distance between the pole and the principal focus of a mirror	(R)	Principal axis
(D)	A straight line passing through the pole (P) and the centre of curvature (c)	(S)	Half of radius of curvature (R)

SECTION-H

Q.1 Optical density of a medium depends on ___________ **[NSO 2010]**
(A) Density of the medium (B) thickness of the medium
(C) Velocity of light in that medium (D) None of these

Q.2 Figure shows a ray of light P striking a mirror AB. The mirror AB and the mirror CD make an angle of 120° with each other. The angle of reflection of ray P at CD is __________ **[NSO 2010]**

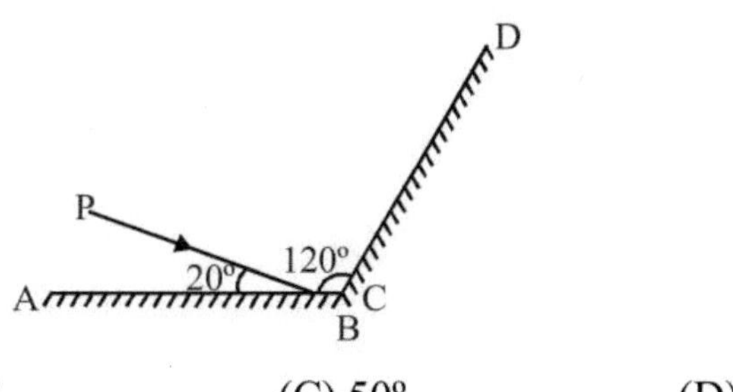

(A) 20° (B) 30° (C) 50° (D) 70°

Q.3 Two plane mirrors are placed parallel to each other at distance L apart. A point object O is placed betweeen them, at a distance $\frac{L}{3}$ from one mirror. Both mirrors form multiple images. The distance between any two images cannot be_________. **[NSO 2010]**

(A) $\frac{3L}{2}$ (B) $\frac{2L}{3}$ (C) 2L (D) None of these

Q.4 Which pairs of rays from the object in the drawing are used to construct the image location produced by the convex spherical mirror of focal length f and radius R? **[NSO 2010]**

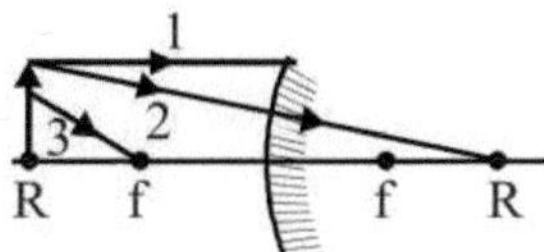

(A) 1 and 3 (B) 1 and 2 (C) 2 and 3 (D) any pair of rays of shown will work

Q.5 The diagram shows the paths of two rays of light from an object. The object is 10 cm in front of a lens as shown in the diagram. **[NSO 2010]**

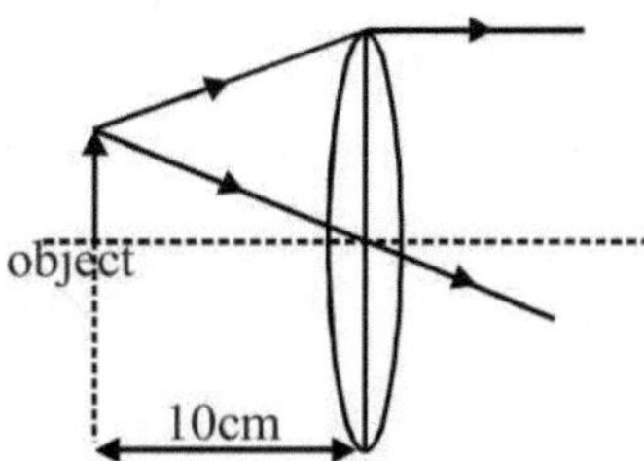

Which of the following statements is true about the given diagram ?
(A) The lens is converging and focal length of lens is greater than 10 cm.
(B) The lens is converging and focal length of lens is less than 10 cm.
(C) The lens is diverging and focal length of lens is greater than 10 cm.
(D) The lens is diverging and focal length of lens is less than 10 cm

Q.6 A fisherman is standing on the bank of a lake. To a fish under water, viewing obliquely the man looks **[NSO 2015]**
(A) Taller than what he actually is (B) Shorter than what he actually is
(C) The same height as he actually is (D) Depends on the obliquity

Q.7 A coordinate axis as shown in figure is kept in front of a converging lens at a distance 2f from it, where f is the focal length of the lens. Which of the following shows the approximate shape of the image ? Assume that X-axis is the principal axis of the lens. **[NSO 2015]**

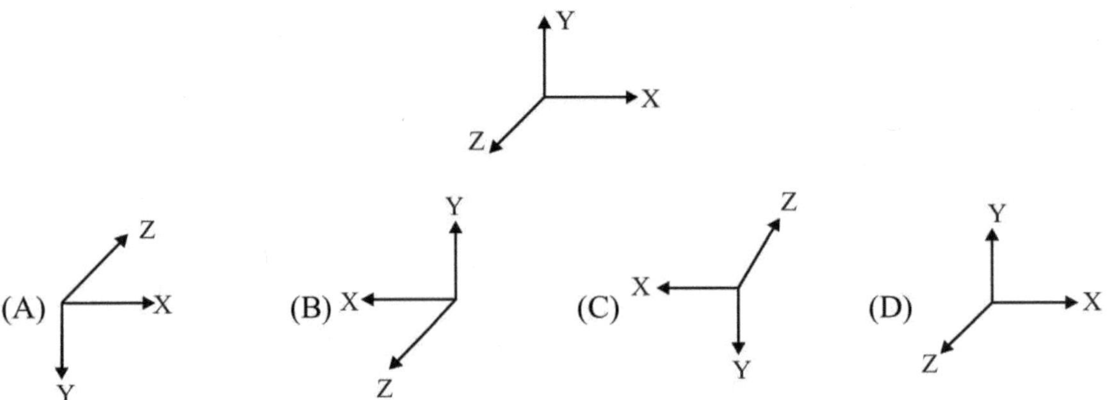

Q.8 Read the given statements and select the correct option. **[NSO 2015]**
Statement 1 : A concave mirror and a convex lens both have the same focal length in air. When they are submerged in water, they will still have the same focal length.
Statement 2 : The refractive index of water is greater than the refractive index of air.
(A) Both statements 1 and 2 are true and statement 2 is the correct explanantion of statement 1.
(B) Both statements 1 and 2 are true but statement 2 is not the correct explanation of statement 1.
(C) Statement 1 is true but statement 2 is false.
(D) Statement 1 is false but statement 2 is true.

Q.9 A concave mirror of focal length 10 cm is dipped in water as shown in the given figure.

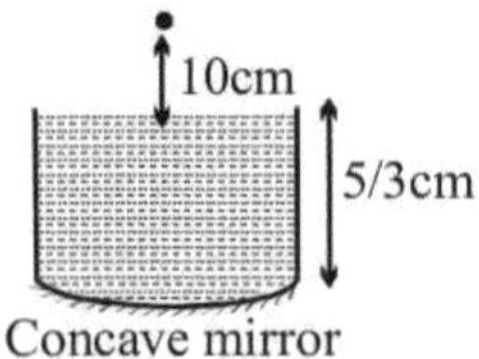

Given that the refractive index of water is $\frac{4}{3}$ and object S is placed on the principal axis of the concave mirror. The final image formed by the system is at **[NSO 2015]**

(A) $\frac{85}{4}$ cm from water surface (B) $\frac{85}{4}$ cm from mirror surface

(C) $\frac{94}{3}$ cm from water surface (D) $\frac{94}{3}$ cm from mirror suface.

SECTION-I

Q.1 The image formed by a concave mirror is observed to be real, inverted and larger than the object. Where should be the position of the object? **[NTSE 2016 Stage 1]**
(A) At the centre of curvature
(B) Between the principal focus and centre of curvature
(C) Beyond the centre of curvature
(D) Between the pole of the mirror and its principal focus.

Q.2 The path of ray of light in different media of refractive indices n_1, n_2, n_3 and n_4 is shown in figure. The velocity of light will be maximum in the medium whose refractive index is

[NTSE 2016 Stage 1]

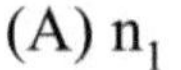

(A) n_1

(B) n_2

(C) n_3

(D) n_4

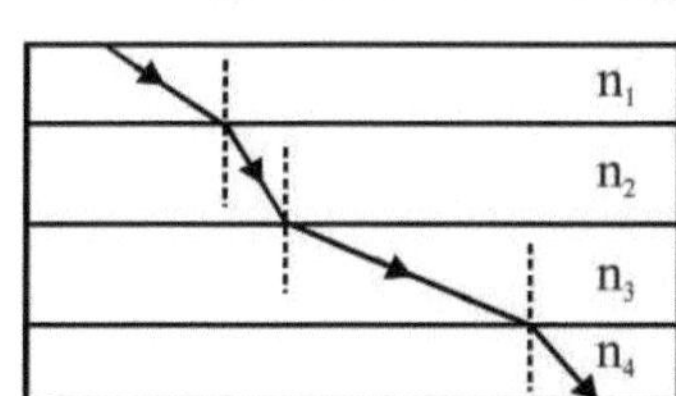

Q.3 A vessel is filled with oil as shown in the diagram. A ray of light from point O at the bottom of vessel is incident on the oil - air interface at point P and grazes the surface along PQ. The refractive index of the oil is close to – **[NTSE Stage II 2017]**

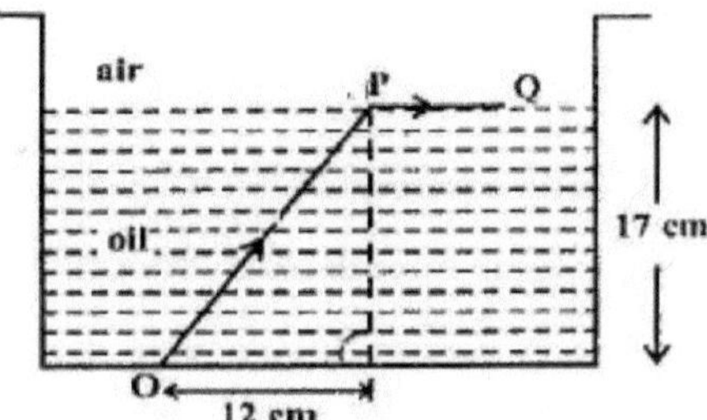

(A) 1.41 (B) 1.50 (C) 1.63 (D) 1.73

Q.4 The intensities of two interfering waves are I_1 and I_2. The best contrast in the interference pattern will be, when - **(Raj./ NTSE Stage-I/2005)**

(A) $I_1 = I_2$ (B) $I_1 >> I_2$ (C) $I_1 > I_2$ (D) I_1 or $I_2 = 0$

Q.5 In the given diagram the reflecting surface inside the box will be - **(Raj./ NTSE Stage-I/2005)**

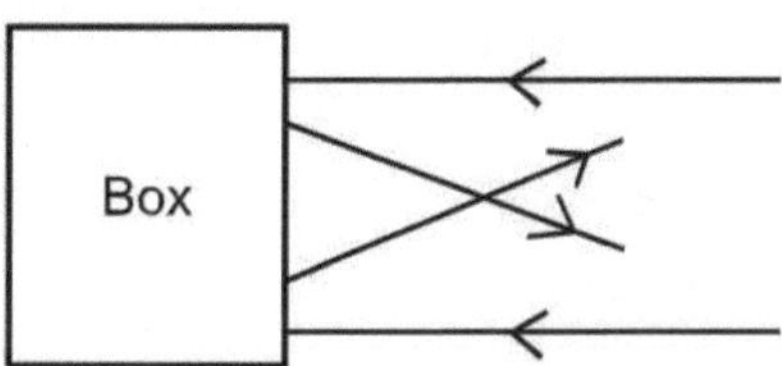

(A) Plane mirror (B) Concave mirror

(C) Convex mirror (D) Two inclined plane mirrors.

Q.6 On immersing a glass lens in water its focal length **(Raj./ NTSE Stage-I/2005)**

(A) will become zero (B) will decrease (C) will increase (D) will become infinite

Q.7 A point object is placed in the middle of two concave mirrors. The focal lengtth of each mirror is 10 cm. to obtain single image of point object, the distance between two mirrors in cm will be:

(Raj./ NTSE Stage-I/2006)

(A) 10 (B) 20 (C) 30 (D) 50

Q.8 If a ray of light is incident normally on the glass slab, then angle of refraction will be : **(Raj./ NTSE Stage-I/2006)**

(A) 0° (B) 45° (C) 60° (D) 90°

Q.9 While obtaining the image of a candle by a convex lens, if lower half portion of the lens is blackened to make it opaque completely, then the intensity of the image will be: **(Raj./ NTSE Stage-I/2007)**

(A) constant (B) decreased (C) increased (D) zero

Q.10 When a light wave of frequency 5×10^{14} Hz is passed through a medium of refractive index 1.5 then its wavelength will become: **(Raj./ NTSE Stage-I/2007)**

(A) 4000 Å (B) 4500Å (C) 6000Å (D) 9000Å

Q.11 The Lens used in the Camera is – **(Raj./ NTSE Stage-I/2007)**

(A) Convex Lens (B) Concave Lens (C) Biconvex Lens (D) Biconcave Lens

Q.12 An object in placed in front of a concave mirror of local length 'f' as shown in figure. Choose the correct shape of image. **(Haryana/ NTSE Stage-I/2013)**

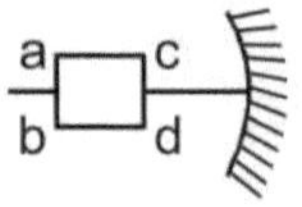

a 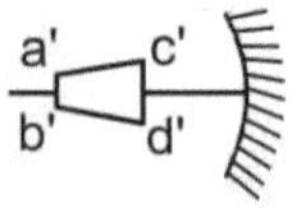 c
b d

(A) a' c' b' d' (B) 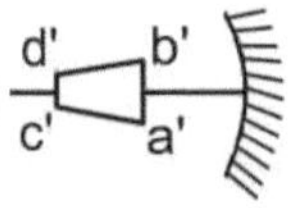 d' b' c' a' (C) 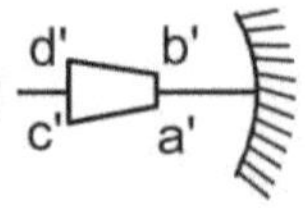 d' b' c' a' (D) a' c' b' d'

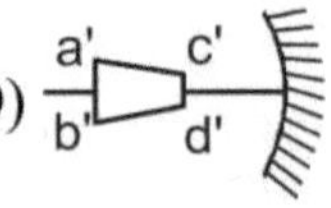

Q.13 Match the following **(Haryana/ NTSE Stage-I/2013)**

Column I	**Column II**
(i) Convex mirror, real object	p. Real image
(ii) Concave mirror, real object	q. Virtual image
(iii) Concave lens real object	r. Magnified image
(iv) Convex lens, real object	s. Diminished image

(A) (i)-q,s (ii) p,q,s (iii) q,r (iv)-p,q,r, s (B) (i)-q (ii) p,q,s (iii) q,r (iv)-p,q,r

(C) (i)-s (ii) p,q,s (iii) q,s (iv)-p,q,r,s (D) (i) q,s (ii) p,q,r,s (iii) q,s (iv)-p,q,r,s

Q.14 The minimum distance between an object and its real image in a convex lens is (f = focal length of the lens) **(West Bengal/ NTSE Stage-I/2013)**

(A) 2.5 f (B) 2f (C) 4f (D) f

Q.15 The frequency of light of wave length 5000 Å is **(West Bengal/ NTSE Stage-I/2013)**

(A) 1.5×10^5 Hz (B) 6×10 Hz (C) 6×10^{14} Hz (D) 7.5×10^{15} Hz

Q.16 The relation among u, v and f for a mirror is : **(Mizoram/ NTSE Stage-I/2013)**

(A) f = uv/(u + v) (B) v = fu(u + f) (C) u = fv(f + v) (D) all of these

Q.17 The correct relation between u, v and r for a mirror will be : (symbols represent traditional meaning) **(Raj./ NTSE Stage-I/2014)**

(A) $r = \frac{2uv}{u+v}$ (B) $r = \frac{uv}{2(u-v)}$ (C) $r = \frac{1}{u+v}$ (D) $\frac{1}{r} = \frac{1}{u} + \frac{1}{v}$

Q.18 White light is incident on the interface of glass and air as shown in the figure. If green light is just totally internally reflected then the emerging ray in air contains : **(Haryana./ NTSE Stage-I/2014)**

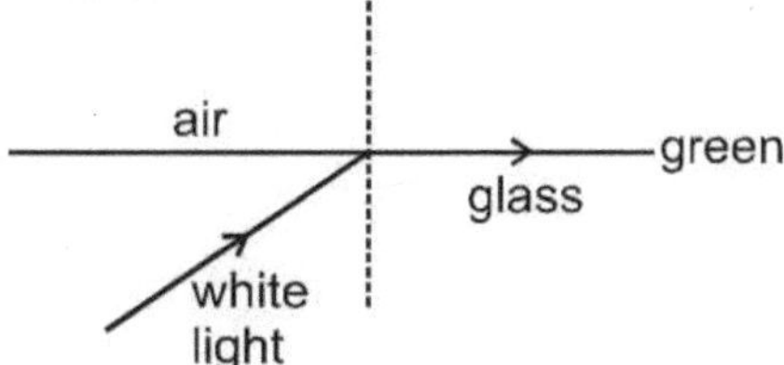

(A) Yellow, orange , red (B) Violet, indigo, blue
(C) All colours except green (D) All colours

Q.19 A concave mirror is placed in a horizontal table with its axis directed vertically upwards. Let O be pole of the mirror and C its centre of curvature. A point object is placed at C. It has a real image, also located at C. If the mirror is now filled with water, the image will be : **(Raj./ NTSE Stage-I/2014)**
(A) Real and located at a point between C and O.
(B) Real and will remain at C.
(C) Real and located at point between C and ∞ (infinity).
(D) Virtual and located at a point between C and O.

Q.20 If a lens of focal length 'f' is cut in two equal parts shown as :

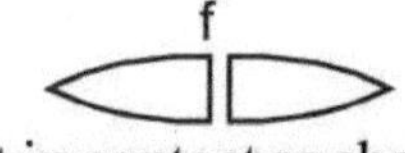

are put in contact as shown in figure (i) and (ii)

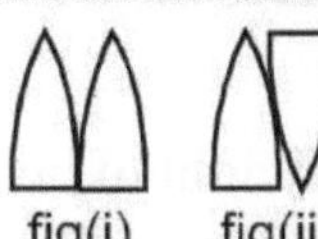

the resulting focal length of fig (i) and (ii) will be- **(Haryana/ NTSE Stage-I/2014)**
(A) f/2,0 (B) 0, f/2 (C) f,f (D) f/2, (infinity)

Q.21 The mirror used by a dentist to examine the teeth of a person is - **(M.P/ NTSE Stage-I/2014)**
(A) Convex (B) Concave (C) Plane (D) Plano convex

Q.22 For magnification in spherical mirrors object height is: **(MAHARASHTRA/ NTSE Stage-I/2014)**
(A) Negative (B) Positive
(C) For real images positive (D) For virtural image negative

Q.23 After refraction of light through a glass slab, incident ray and refracted are :
(MAHARASHTRA/ NTSE Stage-I/2014)
(A) Perpendicular (B) Parallel (C) In a straight line (D) (A) and (C)

Q.24 If sum of velocities of light in two media is 3.25×10^8 m/s and their difference is 0.75×10^8 m/s, find the refractive index of the second medium with respect to one :

(MAHARASHTRA/ NTSE Stage-I/2014)

(A) 1.25 (B) 1.6 (C) 1.5 (D) 1.3

Q.25 The ability of a lens to converge or diverge light rays depends on :

(MAHARASHTRA/ NTSE Stage-I/2014)

(A) Principal axis (B) Focal length (C) Object distance (D) Image distance

Q.26 The focal length of a concave mirror in air is f. If it is immersed in water $\left(n = \frac{4}{3}\right)$, then the focal length will be :

(Raj./ NTSE Stage-I/2015)

(A) f (B) $\frac{4}{3}$f (C) $\frac{3}{4}$f (D) 4f.

Q.27 A student was asked to draw a ray diagram for formation of image by a convex lens for the following positions of the object :

(Raj./ NTSE Stage-I/2015)

(1) Between F and 2F (2) At F
(3) At 2F (4) Between F and optical centre

The position for which virtual image can be formed among these is

(A) 2 (B) 1 (C) 3 (D) 4

Q.28 Amount of light entering into the camera depends upon: **(Delhi/ NTSE Stage-I/2014)**

(A) Focal length of objective lens
(B) Product of focal length & diameter of objective lens.
(C) Distance of objective from camera.
(D) Aperture setting of the camera.

Q.29 The resultant focal length of the lenses as shown in the figure is : **(Delhi/ NTSE Stage-I/2014)**

(A) 2t (B) $\frac{f}{2}$ (C) $\frac{f}{4}$ (D) f

Q.30 A man can see through a hole, the top end of a thin rod of height x, the height of beaker is 3x, If the beaker is filled with a liquid of refractive index μ upto height 2x, he can now see the lower end of rod. The value of μ is:

(Haryana/ NTSE Stage-I/2014)

3x
x
2x

(A) $\frac{5}{2}$ (B) $\sqrt{\left(\frac{5}{2}\right)}$ (C) $\sqrt{\frac{3}{2}}$ (D) $\frac{3}{2}$

Q.31 A glass prism of refractive index 3/2 is immersed in water of refractive index 4/3. A light beam incident normally on the face AB is totally reflected to reach the face BC if : **(Haryana/ NTSE Stage-I/2014)**

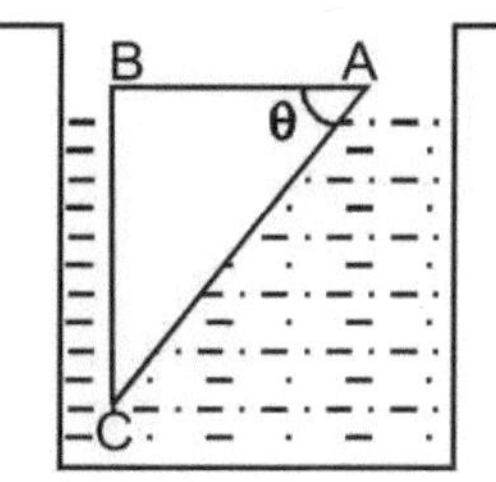

(A) $\sin\theta > \frac{8}{9}$ (B) $\frac{2}{3} < \sin\theta < \frac{8}{9}$ (C) $\sin\theta < \frac{2}{3}$ (D) $\sin\theta > \frac{3}{2}$

Q.32 If a part of a convex lens is covered, its focal length will : **(West Bengal/ NTSE Stage-I/2014)**
(A) Remain unchanged (B) Become twice
(C) Become half (D) Depend on the covered area

Q.33 The minimum distance between an object and its real image in a convex lens is :
(West Bengal/ NTSE Stage-I/2014)
(A) 2.5 times its focal length (B) 2 times its focal length
(C) 4 times its focal length (D) Equal to its focal length

Q.34 A convex lens forms a real image of a point object placed on its principal axis. If the upper half of the lens is cut **(Bihar/ NTSE Stage-I/2014)**
(A) The image will be shifted downwards (B) The image will be shifted upward
(C) The intensity of the image will decrease (D) None of the above

Q.35 A screen is placed at a distance 40 cm away from an illuminated object. A converging lens it placed between the source and screen and attempt is made to form an image on screen. If no position could be found. The focal length of the lens : **(Bihar/ NTSE Stage-I/2014)**
(A) Must be less than 10 cm (B) Must be greater than 20 cm
(C) Must not be greater than 20 cm (D) Must not be less than 10 cm

Q.36 Find the wrong statement related to convex lens: **(Maharashtra/ NTSE Stage-I/2015)**
(A) Two spherical surfaces bulging outward (B) Converging lens
(C) Positive focal length (D) Image is always virtual and diminished

Q.37 Velocity of light travelling from rarer medium to denser medium decreases by 30%. Find the refractive index of the denser medium with respect to rarer medium ? **(Maharashtra/ NTSE Stage-I/2015)**
(A) 1.35 (B) 1.5 (C) 1.4 (D) 1.428

Q.38 Object when placed at .... in front of concave mirror magnification of –1 is obtained.
(Maharashtra/ NTSE Stage-I/2015)
(A) Infinity (B) Centre of curvature
(C) Between focus and centre of curvature (D) Principal focus

ANSWERS

Try Yourself

1. (C)
2. (i) 7/9 m (ii) 2/9 (iii) Virtual, erect and diminished
3. $n_g = 3/2$
4. 1.32
5. 5/8
6. (i) $h_i = 5$ cm (ii) v = –10 cm (iii) virtual, erect & diminished (iv) –5 D
7. f = 25 cm, P = 4D

CONCEPT APPLICATION LEVEL - II

SECTION D

Q.1	D	Q.2	A	Q.3	D	Q.4	D	Q.5	C	Q.6	A	Q.7	D
Q.8	D	Q.9	B	Q.10	C								

SECTION G

Q.1 D Q.2 B Q.3 B Q.4 C Q.5 B

Q.6 It means that the incident ray and emergent ray are parallel to each other. Q.7 B

Q.8 D Q.9 A Q.10 A Q.11 A Q.12 D Q.13 B Q.14 A

CONCEPT APPLICATION LEVEL - III

SECTION-A

Q.1 2×10^8 m/s, 0.4×10^{-6} m

SECTION-B

Q.1	A	Q.2	B	Q.3	D	Q.4	C	Q.5	B	Q.6	B	Q.7	B
Q.8	C	Q.9.	B	Q.10	A	Q.11	B	Q.12	A	Q.13	C	Q.14	B
Q.15	C	Q.16	B	Q.17	A	Q.18	D	Q.19	D				

SECTION-C

Q.1 BD Q.2 BC

SECTION-D

Q.1 D Q.2 A Q.3 A Q.4 A Q.5 C

SECTION-E

Q.1 B Q.2 A Q.3 B

SECTION-F

Q.1 (A)-(Q), (B)-(R), (C)-(P), (D)-(S)

SECTION-G

Q.1 (A)-(R), (B)-(P), (C)-(Q,S), (D)-(P,R)

SECTION-H

Q.1	C	Q.2	C	Q.3	A	Q.4	B	Q.5	A	Q.6	A	Q.7	A
Q.8	D	Q.9	A										

SECTION-I

Q.1	B	Q.2	C	Q.3	D	Q.4	A	Q.5	B	Q.6	C	Q.7	B
Q.8	A	Q.9	B	Q.10	A	Q.11	A	Q.12	C	Q.13	D	Q.14	C
Q.15	C	Q.16	A	Q.17	A	Q.18	A	Q.19	A	Q.20	D	Q.21	B
Q.22	B	Q.23	B	Q.24	B	Q.25	B	Q.26	A	Q.27	D	Q.28	D
Q.29	B	Q.30	B	Q.31	A	Q.32	A	Q.33	C	Q.34	C	Q.35	D
Q.36	D	Q.37	D	Q.38	B								

5 HUMAN EYE AND THE COLOURFUL WORLD

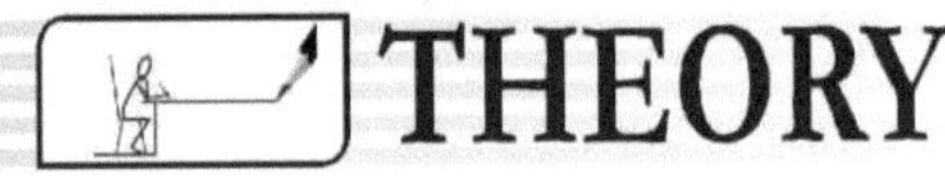

THEORY

5.1 INTRODUCTION

All of us have experienced how difficult it becomes when there is complete darkness and nothing can be seen! We are not talking about a scary movie here but we are talking about vision which is facilitated by our Eyes.

We know EYES makes it possible to see all the beautiful things around us, but ever wondered how? Why do some of you or your friends needs spectacles to see the black board in the class room or to read the book? Why do we squint when someone suddenly flashes a strong light on our face? How can things look bigger when kept under a plane glass like magnifying lens? Or how do we see various colours coming out of a pyramid shaped glass object called prism?

In this chapter we will try to find out all these answer and study one of the most sensitive organ of our body and how it works.

Knowledge Based Questions :

1. In a prism:
   (A) rays deviate towards the base of the prism.
   (B) rays deviate away from the base of the prism.
   (C) rays are reflected internally toward the vertex of the prism.
   (D) rays are diffracted around the prism.

2. Dispersion is:
   (A) bending of light toward the normal when it enters from a rarer medium to denser medium.
   (B) splitting of light into its component colours when it passes through a prism.
   (C) redistribution of energy of a beam of light when it passes through a slit.
   (D) bending of light around an obstacle when the size of the obstacle is comparable to the wavelength of the light.

3. The transparent membrane over the eye ball is called :
   (A) iris (B) cornea (C) pupil (D) retina

4. The muscles which control the thickness of the eye lens are called:
   (A) tendon muscles (B) ciliary muscles
   (C) bone marrow muscles (D) optic muscles

5. What controls the amount of light entering into the inner part of the eye?
   (A) Iris (B) Pupil (C) Cornea (D) Lens

6. The image formed by an astronomical telescope is :
(A) bigger than the actual size of the object. (B) smaller than the actual size of the object.
(C) double the size of the object. (D) none of the above.

7. Which colour suffers the least deviation when it passes through a prism?
(A) yellow (B) red (C) violet (D) green

8. When monochromatic light is passed through a prism it is :
(A) dispersed (B) polarised (C) diffracted (D) deviated

9. In an eye the focal length of the eye is changed by
(A) pupil (B) iris (C) ciliary muscles (D) retina

10. The least distance of distinct vision for a young adult with normal vision is
(A) 25 m (B) 2.5 cm (C) 25 cm (D) 2.5 m

5.2 HUMAN EYE

Human eye is a natural optical instrument which gives the sensation of vision. It forms an inverted, real image on a light sensitive surface called **the retina**. The vertical section of the human eyes is an optical system is shown in the given diagram. The main parts of human eye are as follows.

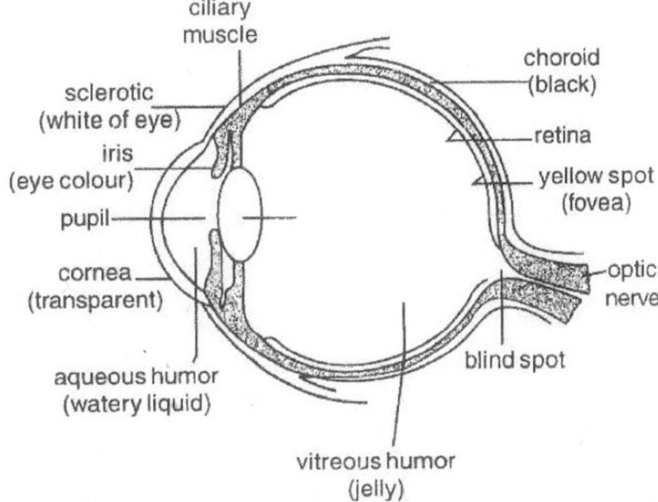

1. **Sclerotic :** It is the outer most covering of the eye. It consist of white tough fibrous tissues. **Its function is to protect the internal parts of the eye.**

2. **Cornea : (Window to the World)** It allows the light to enter into the eye ball. The front of the eye is sharply curved and is made of hard transparent membrane, known as cornea. It is a thin membrane covering the surface of eye - ball through which light enters. Maximum part of refraction occurs at cornea.

3. **Vitreous Humor :** It is a dense, jelly like fluid, slightly grey in colour, filling the posterior part of the eye ball. It has the following functions:
   (a) It prevents the eye ball from collapsing, due to the changes in the atmospheric pressure.
   (b) It partially helps in focussing the image clearly on the retina.

4. **Aqueous Humor:** It is a watery, saline fluid, filling the anterior portion of the eye. It has the following functions.
   (a) It prevents the anterior portion of the eye from collapsing, due to the changes in the atmospheric pressure.
   (b) When we wink our eyes, a tiny drop of the aqueous humor flows out from the side of the eye. Then it washes the eye and keeps the cornea moist. Otherwise, the cornea will shrivel and become opaque.

5. **Iris:** Behind the cornea there is an opaque coloured diaphragm known as iris. The colour of the eye depends on the colour of the iris. There is a circular hole in it, known as pupil. The action of iris is involuntary, so that, when radiating fibres contract, the pupil dilates.
   The light entering the eye is adapted by the pupil. The pupil dilates or contract depending upon the amount of light available.
   Its function is to control the amount of light entering the eye. This is achieved by the muscles present in the diaphragm. When the muscles contract, they increase the size of the pupil, thus allowing more light to enter the eye and vice versa.

6. **Eye Lens:** The eye lens is double convex lens or (bi-convex) and made of transparent and flexible tissues. It is behind the pupil and held by the muscles called ciliary muscles.
   It is a transparent, crystalline structure made up of many concentric layers. It is kept in its position by a strong elastic frame called the suspensory ligaments.
   The eye -lens helps to divide the eye chamber into two parts. The front chamber between the cornea and the eye-lens is called the anterior chamber and is filled with a fluid called the aqueous humor. Refractive index of aqueous humor is 1.337. The back chamber between the eye lens and the retina is called the posterior chamber and is filled with a jelly-like material called the vitreous humor. Refractive index of vitreous humor is also 1.337.

7. **Ciliary Muscles:** These muscles settle the position of the eye lens. They also control the focal length of the eye lens. These muscles together with suspensory ligaments control position of the eye lens.
   When these muscles contract, they decrease the focal length of the crystalline lens. Similarly, when these muscles relax, they increase the focal length of the crystalline lens.
   Its function is the alter the focal length of the crystalline lens, so that the image of the objects at various distances is clearly focussed on the retina.

8. **Retina:** There is a thin delicate membrane made of optical nerve fibers which covers most of the interior part of the eye. This is known as retina. Optical nerve spread throughout, end in the form of rods and cones to form the retina. At the centre of retina, there is a yellow spot which is most sensitive to the light. The yellow spot is a patch of about 2 mm in diameter spread over the retina. The center of the yellow spot is slightly depressed and is a portion of about 0.25 mm diameter known as fovea centralis which contains only cones.
   The spot where the optic nerves enters into the retina, there is no rod or cone and so this spot is insensitive to light. This is known as blind spot.

Fovea is depression in the center of the macula that contains only cones and constitutes the area of maximum visual acuity.

Macula : The macula is a very small area at the center of the retina. This is a thin layer of light-Sensitive tissue that lies at the back of the eye.

The inside surface of the rear part of the eyeball where the light entering the eye is focussed is called retina. **The surface of retina consists of about 125 million light - sensitive receptors. These receptors are of two types rods and cones shapes. When light falls on these receptors, they send electrical signals to the brain through optic nerve**.

9. **Choroid :** There is black membrane behind the retina composed of many blood vessels and lined internally with pigment cells, known as choroid. Its function is to darken the eye from inside and hence, prevent any internal reflection.

10. **Optical axis :**
The optical axis is the most direct line through the centre of cornea to the pupil, the lens and the retina. This is the line that draws sharpest focus when we look at an object
However this line intersects the retina below the fovea and is not the most light and color sensitive image

Optical axis
visual axis

11. **Visual axis :**
The visual axis draws a line from the center of the pupil to the fovea. This axis gives the best color vision but because it doesn't intersect the cornea and lens at their exact centers therefore image is not as clear as light passing through the optical axis.

Construction: The eye is nearly spherical in shape having a diameter of about 25 mm (1 inch). The walls of eyeball consists of two major layers. The outer covering is known as sclerotic layer. It is a tough, opaque white substance. It forms the white of the eye. The front of this coating forms a curved section known as cornea. The cornea protects the eye and helps in refraction of light. The second layer also called the inner layer is known as the choroid. It is black to prevent internal reflection and protects the light-sensitive parts of the eye.

Working of the Eye: The light rays coming from the object kept in front of us enter the pupil of the eye and fall on the eye lens. The eye-lens is a biconvex lens, so it converges the light rays and produces a real and inverted image of the object on the retina. The image formed on the retina is conveyed to the brain by the optic nerve and gives rise to the sensation of vision.

RODS AND CONES CELLS: The cells on the retina are of two shapes : rod-shaped and cone shaped. The rod cells of our retina respond to the intensity of light.

YELLOW SPOT: The most sensitive point on the retina is called the yellow spot. It is situated at the centre of the retina and is lightly raised. It has a little depression called fovea-centralis, which is extremely sensitive to light. Its function is to form an extremely clear image.

BLIND SPOT: The least sensitive point is known as the blind spot. There are no rods and cones at the point where optic nerves leave the eyeball to go to the brain.

Knowledge Enhancer

Colour perception of Animals :

Different animals have different colour perception due to different structure of rod shaped cells and cone shaped cells. For example, bees have some cone-shaped cells that are sensitive to ultraviolet. Therefore bees can see objects in ultraviolet light and can perceive colours which we cannot do.

Human beings cannot see in ultraviolet light as their retina do not have cone-shaped cells that are sensitive to ultraviolet light.

The retina of chicks have mostly cone shaped cells and only a few rod shaped cells. As rod shaped cells are sensitive to bright light only therefore, chicks wake up with sunrise and sleep in their resting place by the sunset.

Visual impairment means that the eye does not work properly. Visual impairment occurs when any part of an eye involved in the transmission of light like cornea, pupil, eye lens, vitreous humor or the part of eye responsible for the conversion of light into electrical impulse or signal like retina of the part of eye responsible for carrying electrical impulses to the brain like optic nerve is damaged.

What happens when we enter a dim lit room from the region of very bright light?

When we enter a room with dim – light from the region of very bright light, we do not see anything in the room. This is because of the following facts. In a very bright light, the iris contracts the pupil so that less light enter the eye. When we enter the dim – light room, the iris takes some time to expand the pupil or increase the size of the pupil so that more light enters the eye to make the things in the room visible.

Accommodation of an eye: A normal eye can see the near and far off objects clearly if the sharp images of these objects are formed on the retina. Since the distance between the eye lens and retina is fixed (i.e v = constant), so to see the object different position from the eye lens the focal length of the lens has to be changed accordingly to form the sharp images of these objects.

$$\because \qquad -\frac{1}{u}+\frac{1}{v}=\frac{1}{f}$$

If the object to be seen is far off (i.e. at infinity), then the sharp image of this object can be formed on the retina of the eye by increasing the focal length of the eye lens.

The focal length of a lens increases if its thickness decreases. Thus, to decrease the thickness of the eye lens and hence to increase its focal length, ciliary muscles are completely relaxed. Now the parallel beam of light coming from the far off object is focussed on the retina and hence the object is seen clearly.

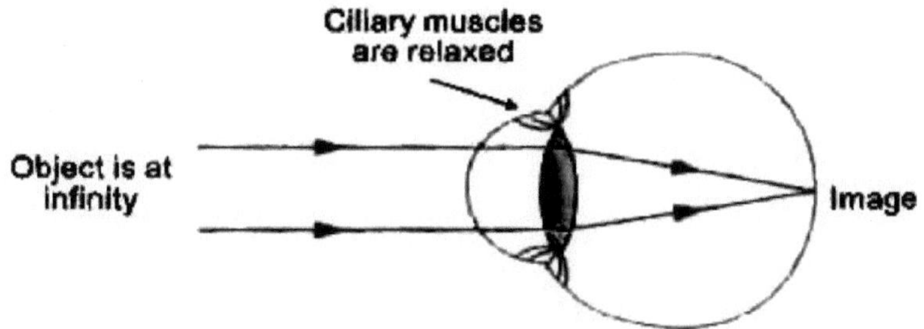

If the object to be seen is close to the eye i.e., near the eye, then the sharp image of this object can be formed on the retina of the eye by decreasing the focal length of the eye lens. The focal length of a lens decreases if its thickness increases. Thus to increase the thickness of the eye lens and hence to decrease its focal length, ciliary muscles contract. Now the beam of light coming from the near object is focussed by the lens on the retina. Hence the object is seen clearly (Figure)

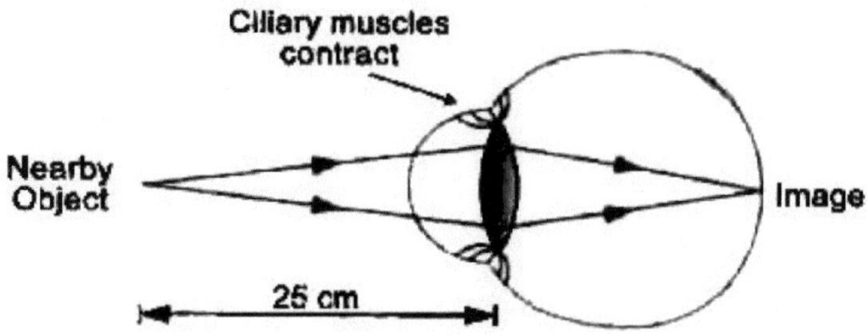

Conclusion: Thus, we observe that the focal length of the eye lens is adjusted automatically by the action of ciliary muscles such that a sharp image of the object at different positions from the eye are formed on the retina. This process is known as accommodation of an eye.

Least distance of distinct vision for a normal eye of different age groups.

Babies = 7 cm

Adult = 25 cm

Person of age 55 years and above = 100 cm.

However in our discussion we are concerned with a normal eye of an adult so least distance of distinct vision is taken as 25 cm.

Power of Accommodation: For a normal eye, the near point is 25 cm from the eye lens i.e. u = –25 cm. The distance of the retina (screen) from the eye lens is about 2.5 cm i.e., v = 2.5 cm. Now using

$$\frac{1}{f} = -\frac{1}{u} + \frac{1}{v}$$

we get $\frac{1}{f} = -\frac{1}{(-25)} + \frac{1}{2.5} = \frac{1}{f} = \frac{1}{25} + \frac{1}{2.5} = \frac{11}{25}\ cm^{-1}$

$\therefore$ Power of eye lens, $P = \frac{100}{f(\text{in cm})} = 100 \times \frac{11}{25} = 44\ D$

The far point of the normal eye is at infinity i.e., $u = -\infty$, Since image is formed at the retina, so $v = 2.5$ cm

$$\therefore \quad \frac{1}{f} = -\frac{1}{u} + \frac{1}{v} = \frac{10}{25}\ \text{cm}^{-1}$$

Hence, power of eye - lens, $P = \frac{100}{f} = 100 \times \frac{10}{25} = 40$ D

Thus we find that the maximum variation in the power of eye lens = 44 D – 40 D = 4D
Therefore, for a normal eye, the power of accommodation is about 4 diopter (D)

5.2.1 Advantage of Having Two Eyes in Humans

1. A single human eye has a horizontal field of view of 150°. However, with two eyes, separated by few centimeters, the horizontal field of view increases to 180°. Furthermore, the ability to detect faint objects is enhanced with two eyes.
2. The two eyes separated by few centimeters, in the front portion of head, no doubt limits the field of view to 180°. However, this positioning increases our ability to judge the depth, a phenomenon called **steropsis**.

With one eye, the world is two dimensional and flat, much the same, as you see images or television screen or a movie. With both eyes open, the world takes on a third dimension of depth. As our eyes are separated by few centimeters, each eye receives an image which is slightly different. When our brain combines these images into one, the sensation of depth is produced.
Here, it is interesting to note that most of the animals and birds have two eyes, placed almost diametrically on their head. Thus, animals or birds have almost 360° view. However, they do not have sensation of depth.

ACCOMMODATION OF EYE

The process by which the ciliary muscles alter the focal length of the crystalline lens, so as to focus nearer or far-off objects clearly on the retina is called the accommodation of the eye.

POWER OF ACCOMMODATION

The human eye in its normal condition, can enable us to see objects from a nearby distance D up to objects at far off or 'infinite distance'. This becomes possible because of the **ability of the ciliary muscles to alter the focal length of the eye lens and thus make it bring into sharp focus the images of objects at varying distances right on the retina. We call this ability a 'power' of the eye or its power of accommodation**.

NEAR POINT AND FAR POINT

There is a limit to the power of accommodation of the eye. A normal eye can see any object which is at a distance of 25 cm to infinity by using its power of accommodation. **The point nearest to the eye at which an object is visible distinctly is called the near point of the eye. It is 25 cm for a normal eye. The maximum distance upto which the normal eye can see the things clearly is called the far point of the eye. It is infinity for a normal eye**.

RANGE OF VISION

The distance between the near point and far point of an eye is known as range of vision. For a normal eye, the range of vision is 25 cm to infinity.

PERSISTENCE OF VISION

The image formed on the retina of the eye does not fade away instantaneously, when the object is removed from the sight. The impression (or sensation) of the object remains on the retina for about (1/16)th of a second, even after the object is removed from the sight. This continuance of the sensation of eye is called the persistence of vision.

Let a sequence of still pictures be taken by a moving camera. If the sequence of these still pictures is projected on a screen at a rate of 24 images or more per second then the successive impressions of the image on the screen appear to blend or an image (or a scene) on the screen appears just before the impression of previous image on the retina is lost. Hence, the sequence of images blend into one another giving the impression of a moving picture. This principle is used in motion picture projection or in cinematography.

Illustration 1

How does the change in curvature of the eye lens help us to see the distant as well as nearer objects clearly?

Solution

When we have to see the distant objects, the ciliary muscles relax and thus the eye lens become thin, resulting in a larger focal length. On the other hand, to see the nearby objects, the ciliary muscles contract thus making the eye lens thicker in the centre. This decreases the focal length of the eye lens, thus making it possible to see the nearby object clearly.

Try yourself

1. What is the relation between the size of the pupil and the intensity of light entering an eye?
2. What is the focus region for an image in a person with normal eye vision?

5.3 DEFECTS OF VISION AND THEIR CORRECTION

The common defects of vision are as follows:

1. Myopia or short – sightedness
2. Hypermetropia or long – sightedness
3. Astigmatism
4. Presbyopia

5.3.1 Myopia or short – sightedness

A person suffering from myopia or short – sightedness can see nearby objects clearly but cannot see the far away objects clearly. In this case the image is formed in front of the retina.

The defect is due to the following reasons:

(i) Eye ball is larger than the normal.

(ii) The maximum focal length (due to excessive curvature of the cornea) of the lens is insufficient to produce clearly formed image on the retina.

Correction: This defect can be corrected by using a **concave (diverging)** lens. So a man suffering from this defect wears spectacles of concave lens with sufficient focal length. Due to this lens, rays coming from infinite, diverge and seem to come from the far point of the defective eye. So the final image is formed at retina.

Focal length and power of concave lens used to correct short – sightedness: If the focal length of the lens be f and d be the far point of defective eye. Then from the expression,

$$\frac{1}{v}-\frac{1}{u}=\frac{1}{f}$$

Here $u=\infty$ and $v=-d$

$$-\frac{1}{d}-\frac{1}{\infty}=\frac{1}{f} \Rightarrow \frac{1}{-d}=\frac{1}{f}$$

$$\boxed{f=-d}$$

A shortsighted person therefore should use a divergent lens of focal length equal to his far point. If 'd' is measured in meter, then the power of lens is

$$P=\frac{1}{f}\text{ dioptre}$$

With the use of extra lens, the near point of the defective eye also increases.

(i) Figure shows a defective short sighted eye when the image of a far off object is formed in front of the retina.

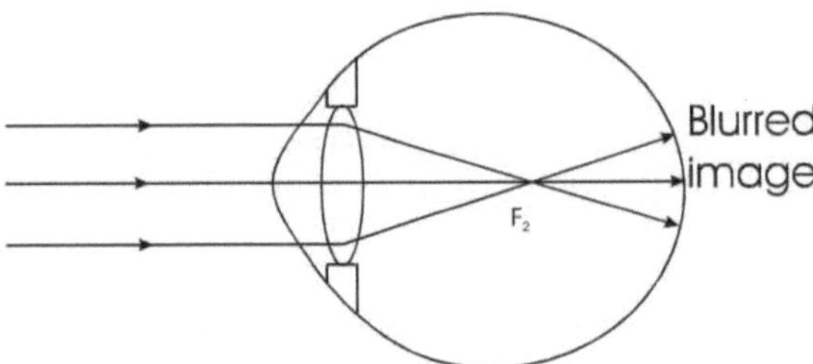

(ii) Figure Shows a defective short sighted eye when the object is situated at the far point of clear vision.

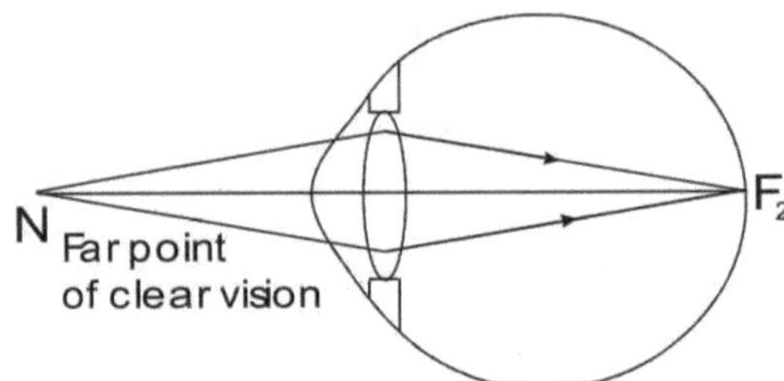

(iii) Figure shows a corrected short, sighted eye when image of a distant object is formed at the far point of clear vision.

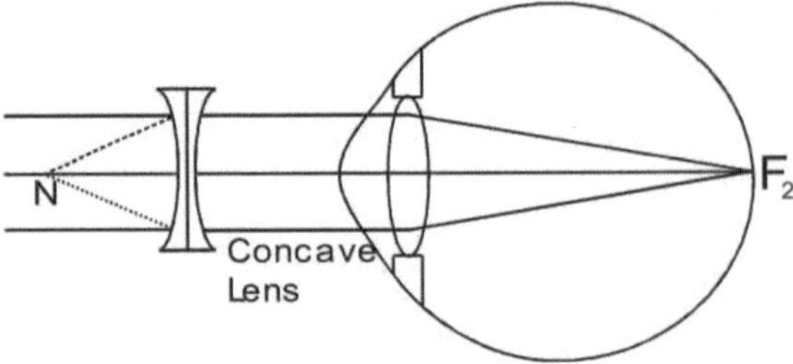

Image of far off object is formed at point N where the eye can see clearly.

Knowledge Enhancer

Let a nearsighted person can see upto a maximum distance x and wants to see upto a distance y then $u = -y$; $v = -x$; $f = ?$

$$\therefore \quad \frac{1}{f} = \frac{1}{v} - \frac{1}{u} = \frac{1}{-x} - \left[-\frac{1}{y}\right] = \frac{1}{y} - \frac{1}{x} = \frac{x-y}{xy}$$

$$\therefore \quad f = \frac{xy}{x-y} \text{ and } P = \frac{x-y}{xy}$$

Short-Sightedness or Myopia

A person suffering from this defect can see the nearer objects clearly, but cannot see the far-off objects clearly.

Causes:

(i) The focal length of eye lens becomes too small.

(ii) Some times the eye ball gets elongated and therefore the image of far-off objects are formed in front of the retina.

Correction :

A Short sighted person can see clearly to some distance. Beyond this distance the images get blurred. The farthest point from which a short sighted person can see clearly is called far off point of clear vision. To enable such a person see the objects situated at infinity, we must use some lens, so that the image of the object is formed, at the far off point. Generally, the lens used is a concave lens and its focal length depends upon the degree of abnormality in the eye.

5.3.2 Hypermetropia or long – sightedness

A person suffering from hypermetropia or long – sightedness can see distant object clearly but cannot see nearby objects clearly. In this case the image is formed behind the retina.

The defect is due to the following reasons:

(i) Either the eye ball is too small.

(ii) The minimum focal length of the eye lens is more.

Correction: This defect can be corrected by using a convex lens of suitable focal length. So a man suffering from this defect wear spectacles of convex lens with sufficient focal length. The convex lens of spectacles reduces the divergence of rays of light entering the eye, and final image is formed at retina.

Focal length and power of a convex lens used to correct long – sightedness : If the object is placed at O' (Near point of a normal eye) then the lens forms its image at O the near point of the defective eye. Let 'D' be the least distance of distinct vision for the normal eye and 'd' the least distance of distinct vision for the defective eye.

Then for extra lens $u = -D$ and $v = -d$

Therefore from the lens equation $\frac{1}{v} - \frac{1}{u} = \frac{1}{f}$

We have, $-\frac{1}{d} - \frac{1}{-D} = \frac{1}{f} \Rightarrow -\frac{1}{d} + \frac{1}{D} = \frac{1}{f}$

$\therefore \quad \frac{1}{f} = \frac{d-D}{dD} \Rightarrow \boxed{f = \frac{dD}{d-D}}$

If D is 25 cm then $\boxed{f = \frac{25d}{d-25} \text{cm}}$

$\therefore$ d > 25 cm therefore f is positive and the lens is convex

In meter $f = \frac{d}{4(d-25)}$ and power $= \frac{4(d-25)}{d}$ dioptre

(i) Figure 1 shows a defective long sighted eye when the object is situated at the least distance of distinct vision. In this case, the image is formed behind the retina.

(ii) Figure 2 shows a defective long sighted eye when the object is situated at the near point of clear vision and its image is clearly formed on the retina.

(iii) Figure 3 Shows a corrected long sighted eye when the convex lens forms the image at the near point of the defective eye.

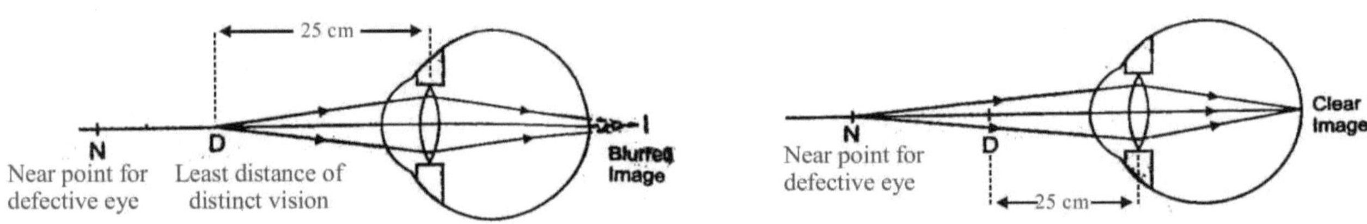

Figure 1 Figure 2

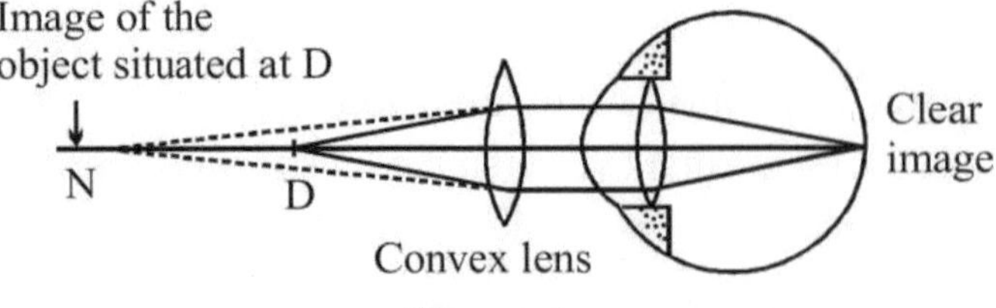

Figure 3

LONG SIGHTEDNESS OR HYPERMETROPIA

A person suffering from this defect can see far off objects clearly, but cannot see clearly the objects situated at a distance of 25 cm or at the least distance of distinct vision.

Causes:(i) The minimum focal length of eye lens is too large.

(ii) Due to some reason, the eye ball becomes smaller in size and hence, the image of the object, situated at 25 cm or at the least distance of distinct vision, is formed behind the retina.

Correction: A long sighted person can see a near object clearly only if it is held at some distance away from the least distance of distinct vision. This minimum distance from which a person can see clearly is called the near distance of clear vision. To enable such a person to see from a distance of 25 cm, a lens must be used, such that it forms the image of the object at the near point of defective eye distance of clear vision. Generally, the lens used is convex lens of suitable focal length.

Knowledge Enhancer

Let the farsighted eye can see a minimum distance y (i.e. near point of the eye). If the eye is to see clearly an object at the distance of distinct vision (i.e. at 25 cm), then the image of the object should form at a distance of y.

$\therefore$ $u = -25$ cm; $v = -y$; $f = ?$

By lens formula,

$$\frac{1}{f}=\frac{1}{v}-\frac{1}{u}=\frac{1}{-y}-\left[-\frac{1}{25}\right];\ \frac{1}{f}=\frac{1}{25}-\frac{1}{y}=\frac{y-25}{25y}$$

$$\therefore \quad \text{Power of lens} = \frac{100(y-25)}{25y} = \frac{4(y-25)}{y}$$

5.3.3 Astigmatism

This defect arises due to different sections of cornea having different radii of curvature. One section of cornea may be more sharply curved than the other. The man cannot focus on both horizontal and vertical line simultaneously.

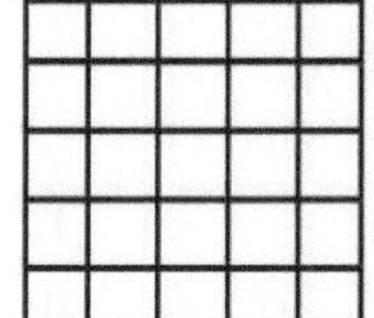
Normal wire gauge

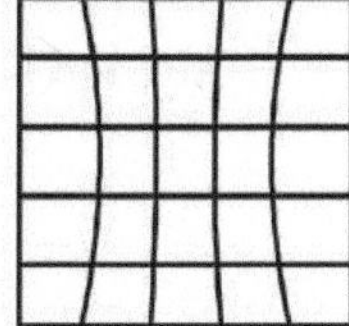
Wire gauge with Distorted vertical lines

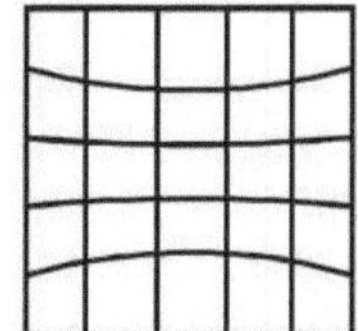
Wire gauge with distorted Horizontal lines

For remedy a cylindrical lens with the axis of the cylindrical lens parallel to the correct axis of the cornea, is used.

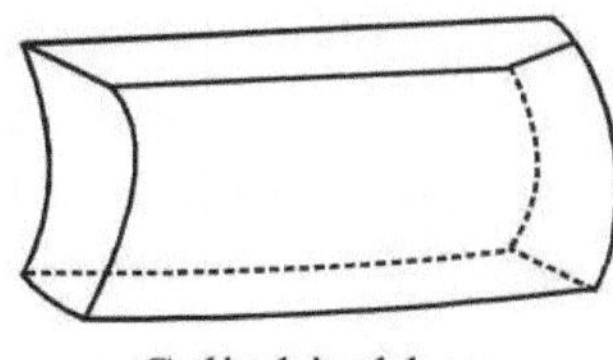
Cylindrical lens

If along with astigmatism, myopia or hypermetropia is also associated, which is generally very common, then for the complete remedy of the defect, sphero–cylindrical (or compound) lens are used.

Eye with this defect is unable to see the lines in different axes but at the same distance with same clarity. It occurs due to irregular curvature of cornea / by birth or arises due to some injury. Horizontal and vertical lines can't be seen simultaneously with this defective eye. Objects in one direction get well focussed and in perpendicular direction remain blurred.

Correction: In this case, the spectacles are cylindrical lenses of suitable focal length.

5.3.4 Presbyopia

PRESBYOPIA : It is purely an old age problem due to which the person cannot see near by an object clearly. In other words, Presbyopia is old age hypermetropia.

Cause

In old age, the ciliary muscles become stiff, and hence, they do not contract. This they are unable to make the crystalline lens thicker, with the result that the focal length of the crystalline lens does not decrease as desired. Thus, the image of the object situated at the least distance of distinct vision is formed behind the retina.

Correction : Same as in the case of hypermetropia

Note : Some times a person who already had myopia at younger age, may suffer from presbyopia at old age. Such persons overcome this by using bifocal lens as shown :

Concave lens

Convex lens

Bifocal Lens

To rectify long sightedness, glasses fitted with convex lenses are used and for short sightedness, glasses fitted with concave lenses are used.

Defect	Description	Cause	Remedy
Myopia or short sightedness	Eye can see distinctly only to the near object. Far - point of eye comes closer than infinity.	Focal length of eye lens decreases. Rays from ∞ focus at a point in front of the retina.	Using a concave lens of focal length = distance of far point from defective eye.
Hypermetropia or far sightedness	Eye can see distinctly the far off objects. Near point of eye shifts away from the eye.	Focal length of eye lens increases. Rays from near point focus at a point at the back of retina.	Using a convex lens of focal length (f) where $\frac{1}{f}=\frac{1}{v}-\frac{1}{u}$ f, v ,u having usual meaning.
Astigmatism	Object gets focused in one direction but out of focus in perpendicular.	Cornea is not spherical but has a higher curvature at one plane.	By prescribing cylindrical lens in place of spherical.
Presbyopia	Image of nearby objects appears blurred. Power of accommodation of the eye decreases.	Decreasing effectiveness of the ciliary muscles and loss of flexiblity of the lens with age.	By using a converging lens for reading and other intericate work.

Do you know that our eyes can live even after our death?

By donating our eyes, after we die, we can light the life of two blind persons. About 5 million people in developing countries are blind and most of them can be cured. Their blindness is due to cornea turning opaque, due to some disease or bad hygiene.

The opaque cornea can be removed and in its place healthy cornea from the donated eye can be transplanted. This allows the light to enter in the eye ball, and hence, the person can see. An eye bank collects, evaluates and distributes the donated eyes. All donated eyes are checked using strict medical standards. Those donated eyes found unsuitable for transplantation are used for valuable medical research.

What should be kept in mind while donating eyes?

- Eyes must be removed within 4-6 hours after death. Nearest eye bank should be informed immediately.
- Eye bank team removes eyes at the home of deceased or the hospital in which death occurs.
- Removal of eyes takes 10-15 minutes. It does not lead to disfigurement of the deceased.
- Eye donors can belong to any age group or sex. Even the people who wear spectacles or are operated for cataract can donate eyes. People suffering from diabetes, hypertension, asthma can also donate their eyes.
- People who were infected with AIDS, Hepatitis B and C, rabies, tetanus, cholera, acute leukaemia, meningitis, encephalitis, cannot donate eyes.

5.3.5 Other Problems of the Eye

Colour - Blindness :

The retina of our eye has large number of light sensitive cells having shapes of rods and cones. The rod-shaped cells respond to the intensity of light with different degrees of brightness and darkness whereas the cone shaped cells respond to colours. In dim light rods are sensitive, but cones are sensitive only in bright light. The cones are sensitive to red, green and blue colours of light to different extents.

Due to genetic disorder, some persons do not possess some cone-shaped cells that respond to certain specific colours only. Such persons cannot distinguish between certain colours but can see well otherwise. Such person are said to have colour-blindness. Driving licenses are generally not issued to persons having colour-blindness.

Phorias :

Phorias is the defect and it can be corrected using spectacles with prismatic lenses.

Phorias is a condition when a viewer sees two individual images using both eyes, instead of one image that a normal person sees i.e. merged by our brain.

If both eyes are affected, a misconvergence occurs, meaning the images by both eyes need to be repositioned individually in order to get a single image.

This is done with the help of prismatic eye glasses.

Cataract :

A common problem in old age is cataract, which gradually reduces the amount of light reaching the retina. The crystalline lens of the eye is made of proteins that are arranged in a regular pattern, which makes the lens transparent. When a group of these protein molecules get lumped in a region, it becomes opaque, and we say that a cataract has developed in the region. Gradually the cataract grows, and finally, the whole lens becomes opaque. And as the cataract grows, the ability of the person to see diminishes.

Correction for cataract :

To restore vision, the affected lens is surgically removed, and an artificial lens is placed in its place. There are two methods to remove the cataract. In the first method cataract is removed by surgery and the patient has to use thick glasses. Due to it the objects appear larger and field of view is decreased. The second method is modern one in which an artificial lens is implanted in the patient's eye, which is called intraocular lens. After the removal of cataract the artificial lens is implanted in front of thin membrane. Surgical cut is minimum in this method, thick glasses are not required and field of view is increased.

Apart from the common defects described above, a person may develop other problems that hinder clear vision. For example, looking at the sun with naked eyes during a solar eclipse can damage the retina.

Knowledge Enhancer

Contact lens

A contact lens is a small lens which is worn directly on the cornea. It has one clear advantage over spectacles. When a person wearing spectacles looks through the corner of the eye, the cornea and the centre of the lens are not in line. As a result, the peripheral view gets distorted. Since a contact lens moves with the cornea, this problem does not arise. Apart from this, some people may prefer contact lenses for cosmetic reasons.

Illustration 2

The distance between the eye lens and retina is fixed. Then, how is the eye lens said to have adjustable focal length.

Solution

As per the lens formula, we have $\frac{1}{v} - \frac{1}{u} = \frac{1}{f}$. In the eye, the distance between the eye lens of retina, called image. Distance 'v' is fixed. Therefore, eye lens adjusts its focal length 'f' for different object distances 'u'. Eye lens adjusts its focal length by changing its thickness. To see different distant objects, the eye lens changes its shape. This is why it is said that the eye lens has adjustable focal length.

Try yourself

3. A boy uses spectacles of focal length 50 cm. Name the defect of vision he is suffering from. Compute the power of this lens.
4. A person can see things clearly only upto 3 m. Prescribe a lens for his spectacles so that he can see clearly upto 12 m.

5.4 ANGULAR MAGNIFICATION

Angular magnification is defined as the ratio of the angle subtended by the image at the eye to the angle subtended by the object at the eye of the observer. Thus,

$$M_0 = \frac{\text{angle subtended by the image at the eye.}}{\text{angle subtended by the object at the eye.}}$$

$$\boxed{M_0 = \frac{\beta}{\alpha}}$$

This is also known as the **magnifying power**.

Thus, the magnifying power is the factor by which the image on the retina can be enlarged by using the microscope.

5.4.1 Simple Microscope

It is a convex lens of small focal length, with a handle to hold. To see a small object by this instrument, the lens is moved towards the object till the object comes in between the focus and optical centre of the lens. So a virtual, erect and magnified image is formed. This is the principle of simple microscope. It is used in spectacles and by watch repairers.

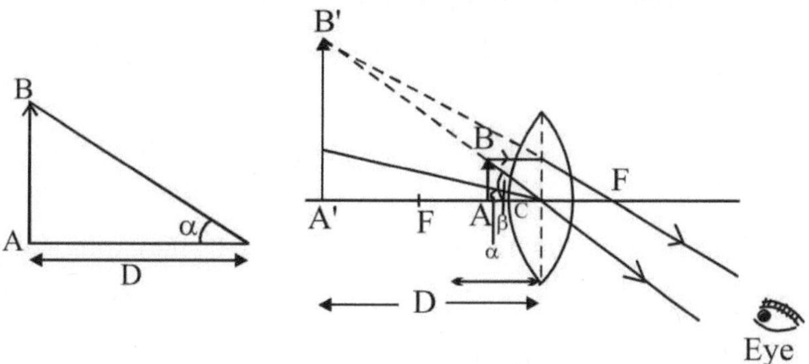

Magnifying Power : The ratio of the size of image and object is called the magnifying power. Magnifying power of a simple microscope is given by following formula –

(i) When final image is formed at near point distance D :

$M = 1 + D/f$

D is the least distance of distinct vision which is 25 cm and f is the focal length of the convex lens.

(ii) When final image is formed at infinity

$M = D/f$

(iii) Magnifying power is inversely proportional to the focal length of lens.

(iv) The magnifying power of a simple microscope is maximum when the image is formed at the least distance of distinct vision (D).

5.4.2 Compound Microscope

This instrument is used to view very small objects like structure of bacteria after considerable magnification.

Construction: It consists of a cylindrical metal tube with a convex lens of small aperture and short focal length fixed at one end of it. This lens is always towards the object and is called the objective. At the other end of the tube another smaller tube is fitted. At the outer end of this tube a convex lens E is fixed which has aperture and focal length greater than that of objective. This lens is directed towards the eye and is called eye piece. The tube as a whole can be moved in or out with the help of rack and pinion arrangement.

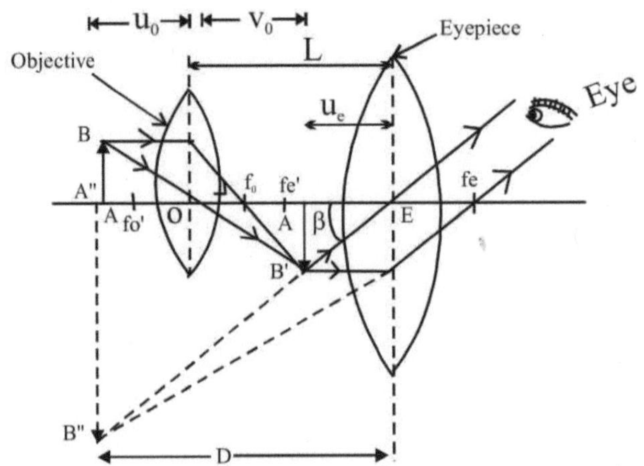

Working: AB is an object which is placed in front of the objective at a distance slightly greater than the focal length of the objective lens. A real, inverted and magnified image A'B' of the object AB is formed on the other side of the lens. It acts as the object for the eye piece. The position of eye piece is so adjusted that A'B' lies between its focus (F_e) and optical centre (E). A virtual, erect and magnified image A"B" of the object A'B' is formed. It is clear that magnification of the object is achieved by both the lenses- objective and eye piece. Hence the final image will be highly magnified.

Magnifying power of a compound microscope

The magnifying power of a compound microscope is the ratio between the final size of the virtual image to the actual size of the object.

$$\text{Magnifying power } m = \frac{\text{Final size of the image seen through the microscope}}{\text{Actual size of the object}}$$

Mathematically, magnifying power of a microscope is given by the expression below, whose derivation is beyond the scope of this book.

$$\text{Magnifying power} \quad \boxed{\mathbf{m = \frac{D \times L}{f_0 \times f_e}}}$$

where D = Least distance of distinct vision (25 cm for a normal eye)

L = Distance between the objective lens and the eye piece or total length of the microscope tubes (in cm)

f_0 = focal length of the objective lens (in cm)

f_e = focal length of the eye piece (in cm)

5.4.3 Astronomical Telescope

Far off objects like planets, stars, aeroplanes etc. appears small and blurred, although being very large in size, due to their large distance from the eye. The instrument which is used to view these objects clearly and enlarged, is called telescope.

Telescopes are of two types-

(A) Astronomical Refracting Telescope (B) Newton's Reflecting Telescope

Astronomical Refracting Telescope: It is used to view astronomical bodies. An inverted, virtual and enlarged image is formed by it.

Construction : It consists of a long cylindrical metal tube with a convex lens of large focal length and large aperture fixed at one end of it. This lens is called objective (O). At the other end of the tube a smaller tube is fitted which can be moved in or out with the help of rack and pinion arrangement.

Magnification : $m = \frac{f_0}{f_e}$ **Lenght of telescope** = $f_0 + f_e$

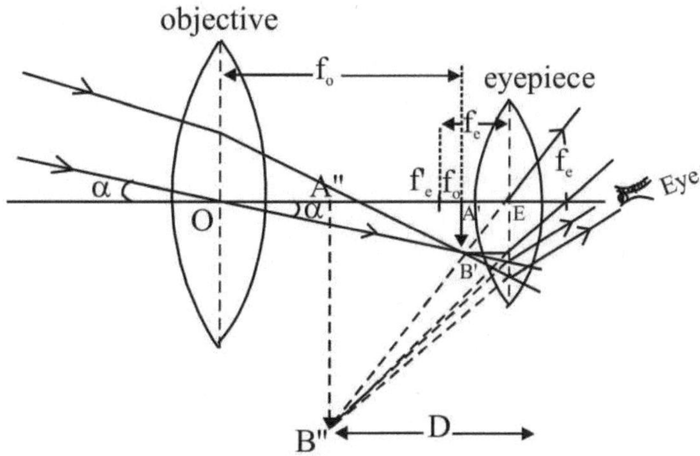

A convex lens of small aperture and short focal length is fixed at the outer end of the smaller tube, which is called eye piece (E).

Working: Image formation of a distant object AB by telescope is shown in Figure. A real, inverted and diminished image A'B' of the object AB is formed by the lens O on the other side of the lens at the principal focus F_o. This image acts as the object for the eye piece. The eye piece is so adjusted that the image A'B' lies between the principal focus (F_e) and optical centre (E) of the eye piece. An erect image of A'B' but virtual, inverted and magnified image of the distant object AB is obtained by the eye piece.

Illustration 3 **A telescope has an objective of focal length 140 cm and an eye piece of focal length 5 cm. Find**

(i) **The magnification of the telescope for viewing distant objects for normal adjustment.**

(ii) **Sepration between the objective lens and the eye piece.**

Solution Objective of focal length, $f_0 = 140$ cm

Eyepiece of focal length, $f_e = 5$ cm

(i) The magnification of the telescope

$$m = \frac{f_0}{f_e} = \frac{140}{5} = 28$$

(ii) Separation between the object lens and the eye piece,

$L = f_0 + f_e = 140 + 5$

$= 145 \text{ cm} = 1.45 \text{ m}$

5.5 REFRACTION OF LIGHT THROUGH A PRISM

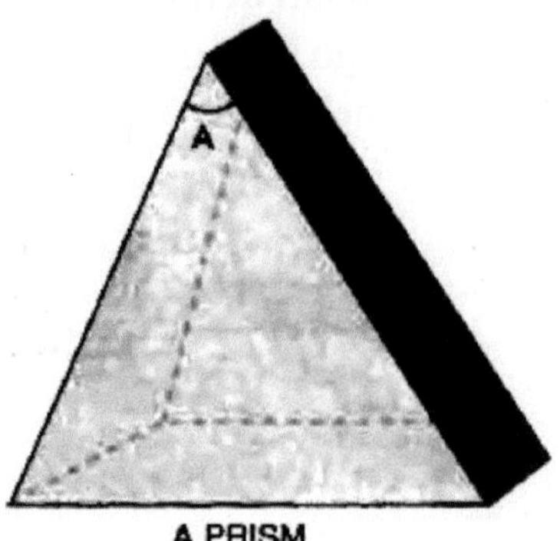

Prism is a homogenous transparent refracting medium bounded by at least two non – parallel surfaces inclined at some angle. It is made of glass and having three rectangular faces and two triangular faces. A commonly used prism is shown in figure. The two non – parallel plane surface participating in the refraction of light are called refracting surfaces. **The angle between two non – parallel refracting surfaces is called angle of prism or refracting angle. It is denoted by A.**

PRACTICAL LEARNING

1. **Find Angle of deviation (The angle between the incident ray and emergent ray is called angle of deviation.) of a ray of light passing through the prism.**

Procedure:

(i) Place a glass prism on a sheet of white paper.

(ii) Mark its boundary with H.B. pencil.

(iii) Now fix two pins at points B and C as shown in figure.

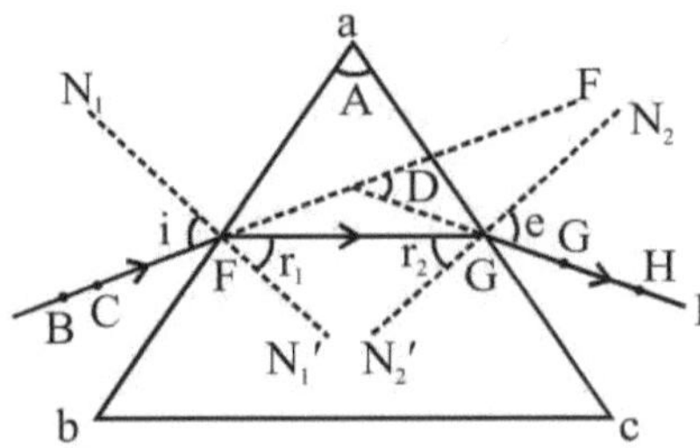

(iv) Look through the refracting face ac and fix two pins at H and I such that the pins H and I and the images of pins B and C lie in a straight line.

(v) Now remove the prism and all pins.

(vi) Join the points B and C and extend this line so that it touches the refracting surface ab at point E.

(vii) Also join the points H and I and extend this line so that it touches the refracting surface ab at point E.

(viii) Also join points E and G.

(ix) Draw perpendiculars $N_1 N'_1$ and $N_2 N'_2$ on the refracting surface ab at point E and on the refracting surface ac at point G respectively.

(x) $\angle N_1EC = \angle$ i angle of incident and the ray BCE is the incident ray.

(xi) $\angle N_2GH = \angle$ e angle of emergence and the ray GHI is the emergent ray.

(xii) Produce the emergent ray GHI backward so that it intersects the incident ray produces forward at point J.

(xiii) $\angle$ FJG = $\angle$ D, Angle of deviation of the incident ray of light passing through the prism.

Thus, angle of deviation of a ray of light is defined as the angle between the directions of incident ray of light and the emergent ray of light.

5.5.1 Dispersion of white light through a glass prism

Q. What is Dispersion?

Ans. Spliting of white light into seven colours is called dispersion.

When white light passes through a glass prism, we get a band of seven colours on the white screen as shown in figure. The colour obtained on the screen are violet, indigo blue, green, yellow, orange and red. These colours can be remembered as VIBGYOR.

From this observation, we can conclude that white light is a mixture of seven colours. The phenomenon of spliting white light into seven colours is known as dispersion.

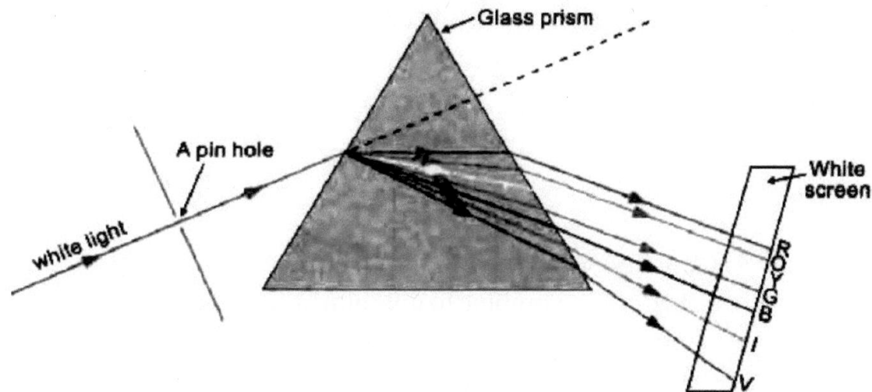

Note: The spliting of white light into seven colours when it passes through a prism was investigated by **Sir Issac Newton, a great physicist**.

Composition of white light: White light is a mixture of seven colours i.e. violet, indigo, blue, green, yellow, orange and red. Every colour has its own characteristic wavelength. Different colours with their wavelengths are given below in the Table.

S No	Colour	Wavelength
1	Red	7900 Å
2	Orange	6000 Å
3	Yellow	5800 Å
4	Green	5400 Å
5	Blue	4800 Å
6	Indigo	4500 Å
7	Violet	4000 Å

CAUSE OF DISPERSION:

White light consists of seven colours: **red, orange, yellow, green, blue, indigo** and **violet**. Each colour has its own wavelength. The wavelength of red colour is the longest and the wavelength of violet colour is the shortest. The speed of light or colour depends upon the wavelength. If wavelength of a colour is large, the speed of the colour is also large. Thus, each colour of light travels with different speed in a given medium. The speed of red colour is more than the speed of orange in a medium. The speed of orange colour is more that the speed of yellow colour and so on. Therefore, the speed of red colour is a medium is the highest and the speed of violet colour is the least. **Hence, all colours of white light are refracted by different amounts while passing through the glass prism. Therefore when a white light passes through a glass prism, different constituent colours come out the prism at different angles. This gives rise to the dispersion of white light.**

PRACTICAL LEARNING

2. **Newton's Disc :**

White color light consists of seven colors. This can be proved by newtons disc experiment.

A circular disc of cardboard is painted with coloured radial bands order of these colors & their respective widths are the same as in spectrum of sunlight. On rotating the disc rapidly about its centre, all the colours blend and a sensation of almost white light is produced on the retina due to persistence of vision.

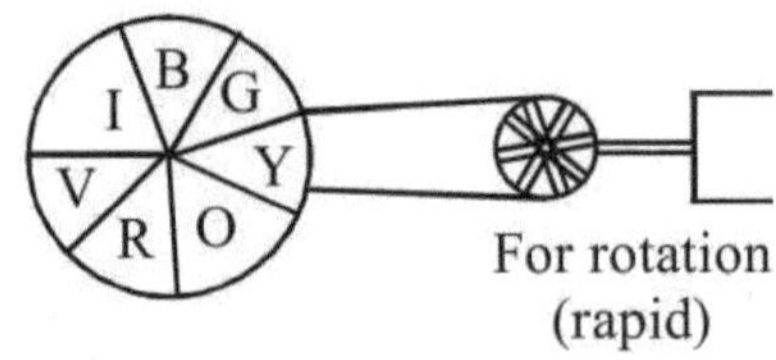

Conclusion :

Seven colors combine to give almost white color but not perfectly white because pigment colours instead of spectrum colours, the disc will not appear perfect white but give dull appearance.

Pigment colours are impare, thus the disc appears greyish instead of perfect white.

3. **Investigate dispersion of white light in a glass prism**

(i) Place a thick card board having a small hole in it in front of a glass prism.

(ii) Allow sunlight to fall on the card board. The hole in the card board allows a beam of white light to fall on the prism.

(iii) Place a white screen at some distance away from the prism.

(iv) Rotate the prism slowly until a band of seven colours is observed on the white screen.

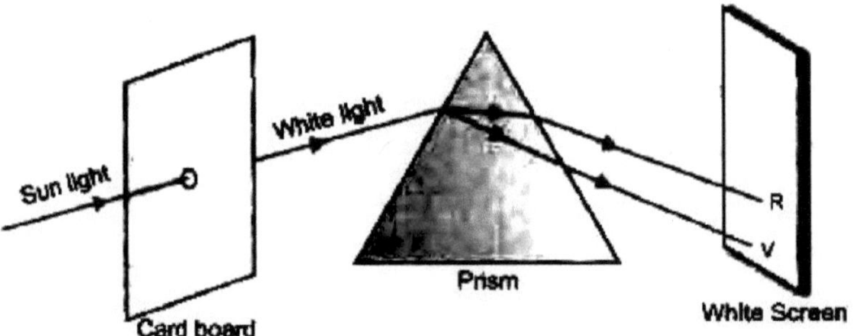

Conclusion: When a beam of white light falls on a glass prism, white light splits into its constituent colours (i.e. seven colours). This phenomenon of splitting white light into seven colours by a glass prism is known as dispersion of white light.

4. **Show that a glass prism splits colours of white light passing through it and does not produce any colour by itself.**

Apparatus required: Two glass prisms, two cards boards each having fine hole at its centre, a white screen.

Procedure:

(i) Place a card board X in front of a prism A. A ray of white light coming from the hole in the card board X is made to fall on the prism A.

(ii) Now place another card board Y in between two prisms A and B as shown in figure.

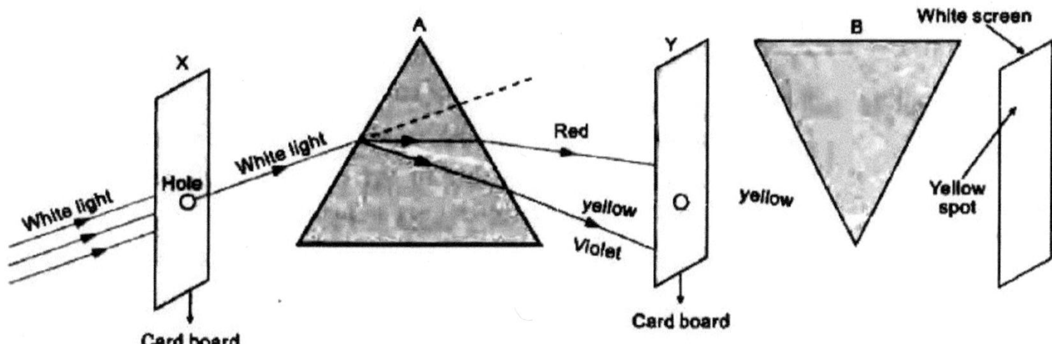

(iii) White light splits into its seven colours when passes through the prism A.

(iv) Now card board Y is adjusted in such a way that only yellow colour passes through the hole of this card board.

(v) Yellow colour passing through the hole of the card board Y falls on the prism B.

(vi) A beam of light passing through prism B is obtained on the white screen.

(vii) It is found that only yellow spot is obtained on the screen.

Conclusion: This activity shows that a glass prism splits colours of white light passing through it and the prism does not produce any colour by itself.

5. Achromatic combination

Show that the colours of white light splitted by a glass prism can be recombined to get white light by another glass prism (Recombination of the spectrum of white light)

Newton took two exactly similar prism i.e. the prisms were of the same material and had the same refracting angle.

He passed white light through a slit and allowed it to fall on the prism A. He obtained a spectrum on the white screen. Now he interposed prism B in an inverted position as shown in the Figure. He found that a patch of white light is formed on the white screen.

Apparatus required: Two glass prism made of same kind of glass, a card board having a fine hole at its centre, a white screen.

Procedure:

(i) Place a card board in front of prism A. A ray of white light coming from the hole of the card board falls on the prism A (Figure)

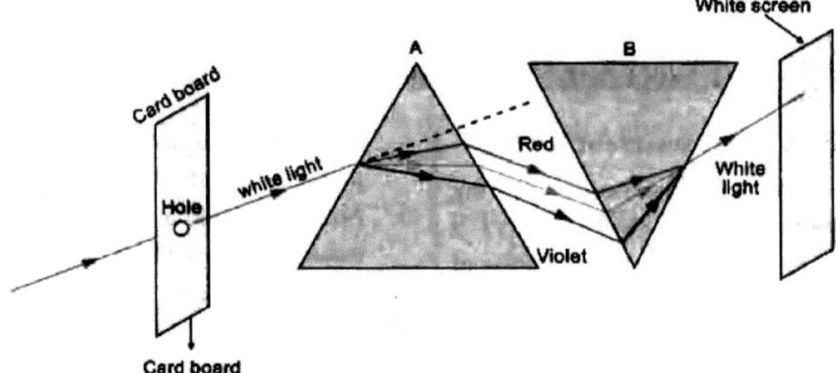

(ii) White light splits into seven colours by prism A is made to fall on another glass prism B placed with its base upward. Since prism A disperses white light, so it is known as dispersing prism.

(iii) The prism B deviates colour of light towards its base. The various colours recombines at the opposite face of glass prism B.

(iv) The light received on the white screen placed in front of prism B is white. Since the prism B recombines the colours of light to produce white light, so glass prism B is known as recombination prism.

This activity was initially performed by the great scientist Issac Newton.

Knowledge Enhancer

In figure, ABC is the principal section of the prism. For drawing ray diagrams only principal section is used Refraction of light through an equilateral glass prism is shown below :

EF — Incident ray
FG — Refracted ray
GJ — Emergent ray
$\angle A$ — Angle of prism
$\angle i$ — Angle of incidence
$\angle r$ — Angle of refraction
$\angle e$ — Angle of emergence
$\angle D$ — Angle of deviation

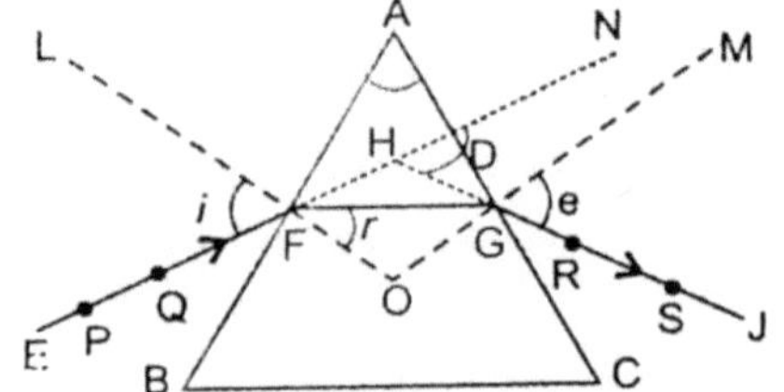

Refraction of light through an equilateral glass prism

(i) Angle of deviation - The angle between the incident ray and emergent ray is called angle of deviation.

(ii) Angle of prism : The angle of a prism or the refracting angle of a prism is the angle between the plane on which light is incident and the plane from which light emerges.

(iii) Angle of incidence - It is the angle that the incident ray makes with the normal to the plane where the ray first strikes the prism.

(iv) Angle of Emergence - It is the angle made between the emergent ray and the normal to the plane from which the ray emerges out.

Illustration 4

What happens to a light ray that obliquely falls on the transparent side of a prism?

Solution

Light ray is partially reflected and partially refracted at the refracting surface where the light ray strikes. The refracted light ray bends towards the base of the prism and finally suffers second refraction at the opposite surface from where it emerges out of the prism.

Try Yourself

5. Why do the constituents of white light have a different angle of refraction at prism interface?
6. Which colours of white light bend the least and most when passing through a prism?

5.5.2 The Prism Equation

Let ABC be the principal section of the prism with base BC and angle of the prism at A as shown in figure.

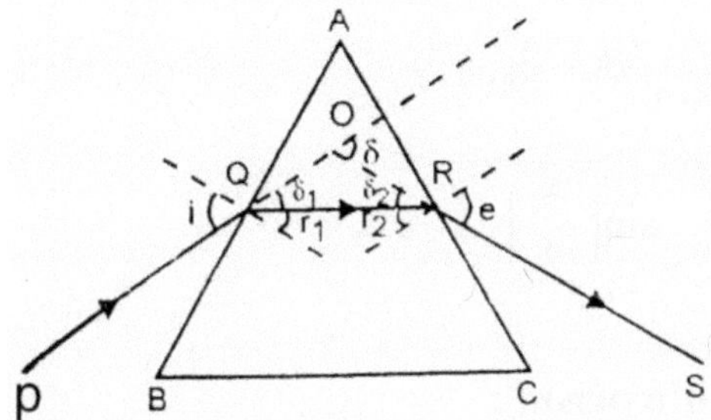

The incident ray PQ after suffering refraction at a front face AB goes along QR, and finally emerges on the second refracting surface AC along RS. In this process the light ray deviates from its original path by an angle δ.

Let i, r_1, δ_1 be the angle of incidence, angle of refraction and angle of deviation respectively at the first face AB. Let e, r_2 and δ_2 be the angle of emergence, angle of incidence and angle of deviation respectively at the second face.

From $\Delta OQR = \delta = \delta_1 + \delta_2$

$$\delta = (i - r_1) + (e - r_2)$$

$$\delta = i + e - (r_1 + r_2) \qquad \text{...(i)}$$

From ΔAQR

$$\angle QAR + \angle AQR + \angle ARQ = 180^\circ,\ A + (90 - r_1) + (90 - r_2) = 180^\circ$$

$$A = r_1 + r_2 \qquad \text{...(ii)}$$

Substituting this value in equation (i),

$$\delta = i + e - A \qquad \text{...(iii)}$$

$$A + \delta = i + e$$

$$\mathbf{i + e = A + \delta} \qquad \text{...(iv)}$$

This is the prism Equation.

Angle of minimum deviation

The angle 'e' is determined by the angle of incidence 'i'. Thus, the angle of deviation 'δ' is also determined by :

(i) For a particular value of angle of incidence, the angle of deviation is minimum. In this situation, the ray passes symmetrically through the prism.

Hence for minimum deviation i = e and if i = e we can get $r_1 = r_2$.

From eqn. (iii), we have

$$\delta_m = i + i - A$$

$$i = \left(\frac{A + \delta_m}{2}\right) \quad \text{....(v)}$$

From eqn. (ii), we have

$$A = r + r$$

$$r = A/2$$

Using snell's law,

$$\mu = \frac{\sin i}{\sin r} = \frac{\sin\left(\frac{A + \delta_m}{2}\right)}{\sin\left(\frac{A}{2}\right)} \quad \text{....(vi)}$$

Deviation produced by a thin prism :

According to the prism equation,

$$A + \delta = i + e$$

$$\delta = i + e - A \quad \text{....(vii)}$$

Using snell's law at face AB

i & r are very small

$$\mu = \frac{\sin i}{\sin r} = \frac{i}{r_1} \quad \therefore\ i = \mu r_1$$

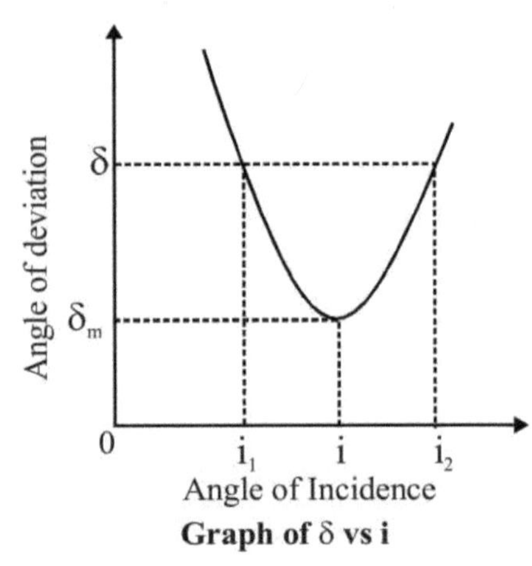

Graph of δ vs i

Similarly, $e = \mu r_2$

Substituting these values in eqn. (vii)

$$\delta = \mu r_1 + \mu r_2 - A$$

$$\delta = \mu(r_1 + r_2) - A \quad \text{....(using eqn. (iv))}$$

$$\delta = \mu A - A$$

$$\delta = (\mu - 1) A$$

Hence deviation produced by a thin prism is independent of the angle of incidence.

Illustration 4

If a thin prism given a deviation of 3° for violet colour, deviation of 2.5° for red colour, Then find deviation for mean colour of light . $\mu_v = 1.60$, $\mu_r = 1.50$

Solution

Using the formula -

$$\delta = (\mu - 1)A$$
$$\delta v = (\mu_v - 1)A$$
$$3 = (1.60 - 1)A$$
$$\Rightarrow \quad A = 3/0.60 = 5^\circ$$

Also , $$\mu = \frac{\mu_v + \mu_r}{2} = \frac{1.60 + 1.50}{2} = 1.55$$

$$\delta = (\mu - 1)A$$
$$\delta = 0.55 \times 5^\circ = (2.75)^\circ$$

Try Yourself:

7. A prism of refractive index 3/2 is placed in water of refractive index 4/3. If the prism angle is 60°, calculate the angle of minimum deviation in water.
8. A ray of light passes symmetrically through a glass prism ($\mu = 1.5$) of angle 60°. Calculate angle of incidence.

5.5.3 Dispersion of light in Nature

You must have seen a beautiful rainbow in the sky after rainfall. This rainbow is formed due to the dispersion of sunlight. When sunlight falls on the water drops suspended in the atmosphere after rainfall, rainbow is formed due to the dispersion of sun light. The waterdrops suspended in air (or atmosphere) act as prisms.

<u>Rainbow</u> : Rainbow is the example of dispersion of sunlight. The formation of rainbow after rainfall is shown in figure.

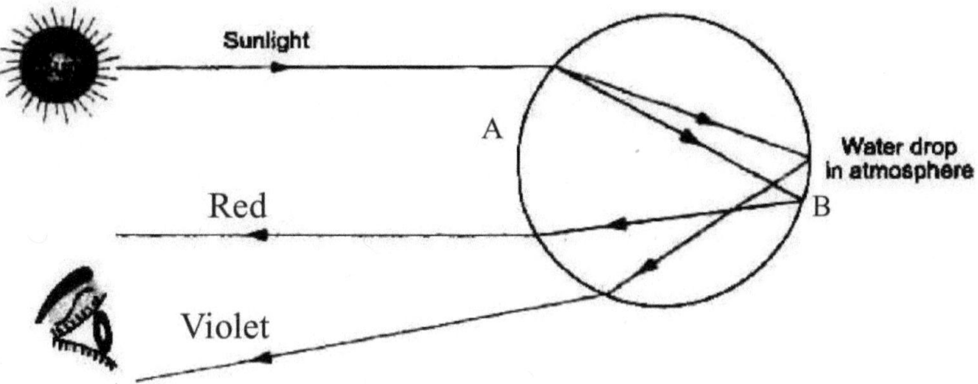

When sunlight falls on a water drop suspended in air, then the sunlight is refracted. The refracted sunlight splits (or dispersed) into its constituent colour (i.e. seven colours). Thus water drop suspended in air behave as a glass prism. The red colour deviates the least and the violet colour deviates the most. Different colours of refracted sunlight fall upon the opposite face of the water drop. Now each colour is partly reflected back into the drop. The reflected colours on reaching the lower surface of water drop are refracted again into the air. Thus, we get a spectrum of seven colours, which is known as rainbow.

Rainbow is one of the most beautiful example of spectrum formed due to the dispersion of light in nature. ***The rainbow is produced due to the dispersion of sunlight by tiny droplets of water suspended in air, just after the rain*.**

You can also see rainbow on a bright sunny day, in the mist created by a waterfall or a water fountain. **Rainbow is always formed in the direction opposite to that of the sun**. For example, if the sun is towards west, the rainbow is formed on the eastern horizon.

Conditions for Observing a Rainbow:

Rainbow is observed during a rainfall or after the rainfall or when we look at a water fountain provided the sun is at the back of the observer.

Knowledge Enhancer

FORMATION OF RAINBOW

Rainbow is one of the most beautiful example of spectrum formed due to the dispersion of light in nature. The rainbow is produced due to the dispersion of sunlight by tiny droplets of water suspended in air, just after the rain.

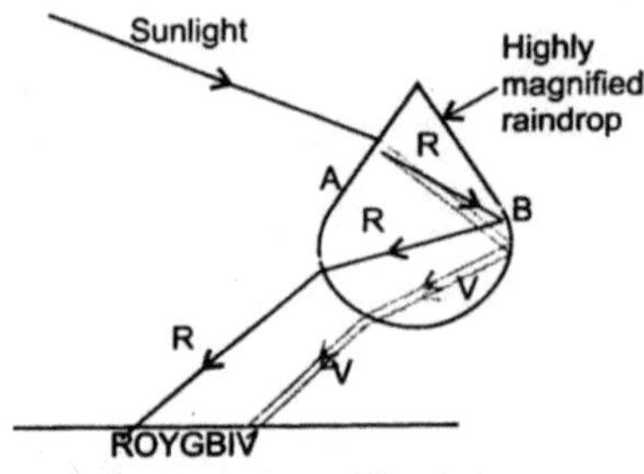

Formation of rainbow

The suspended tiny droplets of water act as innumerable small prisms. When the sunlight is incident on the side A of the tiny droplet of water, it gets refracted as well as dispersed. The dispersed rays on striking the surface B of the tiny water drop suffer total internal reflection, and hence, moves on towards surface A. At the surface A, the ray further suffer refraction and emerge out in the form of band of colours in the form of a circular arc along the horizon. The red colour appears on the upper arc of rainbow and violet colour on the innermost arc.

Illustration 5

What happens to a white light ray when it passes through two prisms kept in inverted position with respect to each other?

Solution

A white light ray, on passing through two prism kept in inverted position with respect to each other, emerges as a white light.

Try Yourself

9. When & where do you see a rainbow?

5.6 TOTAL INTERNAL REFLECTION

5.6.1 Definition

It is the phenomenon of reflection of light totally back into a denser medium as it travels from denser medium to meet the interface with rarer medium at an angle greater than critical angle 'C'. As shown in fig. when a ray of light starting from point O in denser medium goes to a rarer medium, it bends away from the normal and angle of refraction $\angle r$ increases as angle of incidence $\angle i$ goes on increasing. Normal ray OP ($\angle i = 0$, $\therefore$ $\angle r = 0$) goes undeviated along PQ and for oblique rays at A, B $\angle r > \angle i$. At point C, $\angle i = \angle c$, critical angle for which refracted ray goes along CR_3, i.e. along XX' and $\angle r = 90°$ in rarer medium.

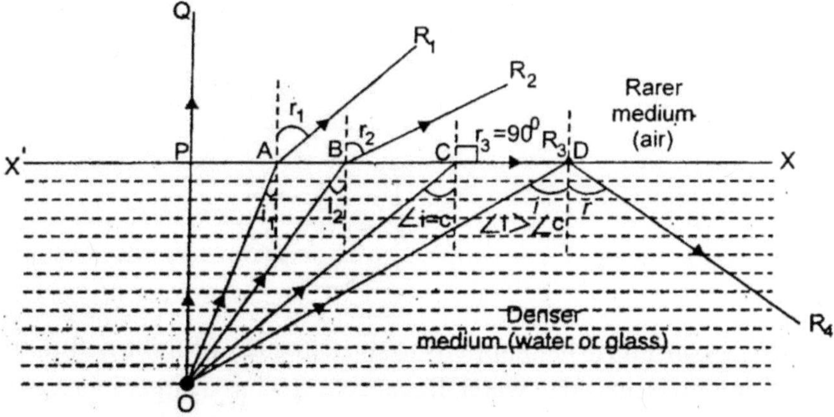

At point D, $\angle i > \angle c$, and ray, instead of suffering refraction, undergoes reflection totally back along DR_4, in denser medium. **Hence beyond C, rays suffer "Total Internal Reflection."**.

Necessary Conditions for total internal reflection to occur

(i) The rays of light must travel from denser to rarer medium.

(ii) The angle of incidence $\angle i$ in the denser medium must be greater than the critical angle i_C, for the given pair of media.

5.6.2 Definition of Critical Angle (i_C)

It is that angle of incidence in the denser medium for which angle of refraction in the rarer medium is 90°.

5.6.3 Relation Between Critical Angle and Refractive Index

In above figure, for refraction at C, the light ray is travelling from denser medium to rarer medium.

∴ Refractive index of air w.r.t. denser medium :

$$^{med}\mu_{air} = \frac{\sin i_C}{\sin 90°} \quad \text{or} \quad ^{med}\mu_{air} = \frac{\sin i_C}{1}$$

$$^{air}\mu_{med} = \frac{1}{\sin i_C} \quad \text{or} \quad i_C = \sin^{-1}\left(\frac{1}{\mu}\right)$$

APPLICATIONS OF TIR

1. **Sparkling of diamond:** A diamond sparkles because, when it is held in a certain way, the intensity of the light coming from it is greatly enhanced. Fig. helps to explain that this enhancement is related to total internal reflection. Part of the drawing shows a ray of light striking a bottom face of the diamond at an angle of incidence exceeding the critical angle, the ray is totally reflected back into the diamond, eventually exiting the top surface to give the diamond its sparkle. The critical angle is **24.4°**. The value is so small, therefore the index of refraction of diamond is large compared to that of air.

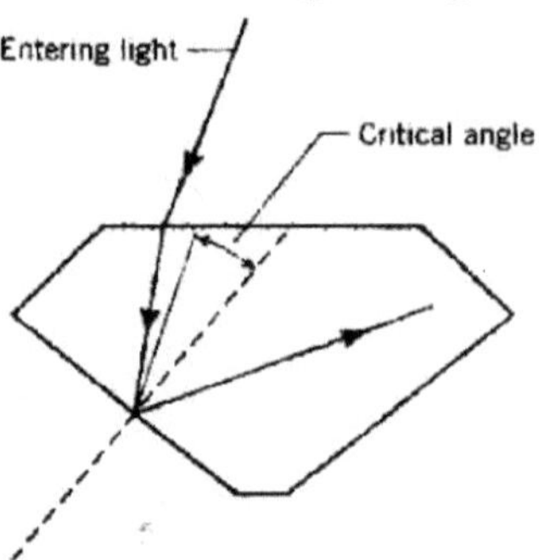

Now consider what happens to the same ray of light within the diamond when the diamond is placed in water. Because water has a larger index of refraction than air, the critical angle increases to 33.3°. Therefore, only this part of the light is reflected back into the diamond, and the remainder escapes into the water. Consequently, less light exits from the top of the diamond, causing it to lose much of its brilliance.

2. **Optical fibre :** Take a thin solid wire (called strand) made up of glass or quartz, etc. Coat it from outside with some material whose μ is less than that of glass or quartz, etc. Now, because it is thin, hence whichever ray of light enter it from one of its ends, will strike the inside surface at some angle which will definitely be greater than the critical angle. Hence, it will suffer total interned reflection again and again until it comes out from the other end. This is the principle on which optical fibres work. Hence in effect, light can travel axially within an optical fibre, although the axis of fibre may be flexible having bent or wavy profile.

A bundle of optical fibres is called a light pipe and is able to send image of an extended object from one end to another by picking up images of small-small parts of the object and sending them likewise to the other end.

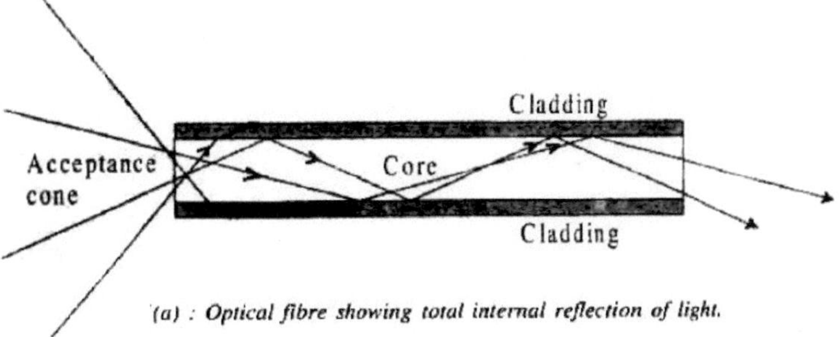

(a) : Optical fibre showing total internal reflection of light.

Use of Optical fibres :

(a) For medical examination inside the stomach, intestines etc., called endoscopy.

(b) The recent trend is to send even electrical signal through optical fibres, by converting them into electromagnetic radiations/light waves.

3. **Mirage : It is an optical illusion, in which inverted image of a distant object can be seen, as it reflected from a pond or a lake in hot regions due to continuous atmospheric refraction and total internal reflection**. In deserts, because of intense heat, the layers of air, near the surface of the earth get heated so soon that the density adjustment does not take place, hence the densities and refractive indices of the layers immediately above the sand are lower than those of the layers higher up. The rays of light from a distant object, after passing through layers, which are gradually less refracting, bend more and more away from normal, till they fall on a layer at an angle, greater than the critical angle and it gets totally reflected. These reflected rays then travel up and undergo a series of refractions, but in a direction opposite to those in first case, they now pass through layers which are gradually more and more refracting, till they reach the eye of the observer, who sees an image of the object, as though reflected from the surface of a lake of water.

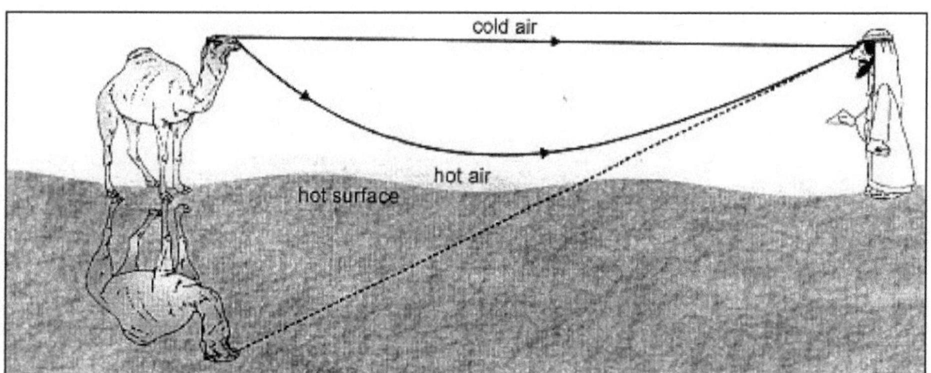

4. **Looming : It is an optical illusion in which inverted image of a distant object can be seen, as if reflected from a pond or lake or sometimes as if suspended in the atmosphere in cold regions due to continuous atmospheric refraction and total internal refection**. Looming is observed in very cold regions caused by the total internal reflection of light coming from the ship or any other object.

In cold region, air above water is cold (denser) whereas above it, it is hot (rarer). So when light ray from the object travels from cold to warm air (denser to rarer) it undergoes continuous atmospheric refraction, and causes total internal reflections in downward directions due to which we see objects hanging up in sky.

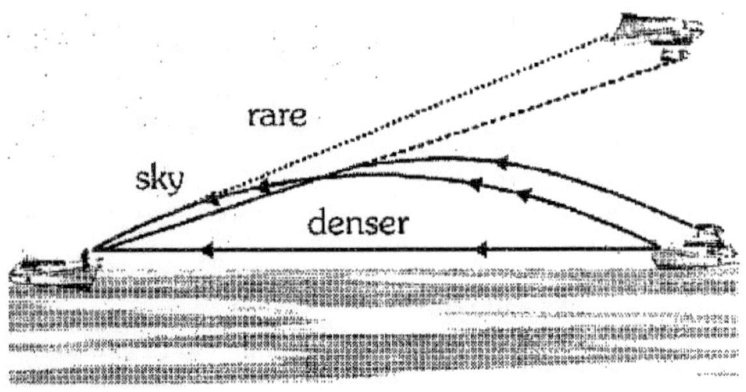

Illustration 6

Considered a right angled isosceles prism ABC , What should be the minimum refractive index of glass so that ray PQ incident normally on the face AB is totally internally reflected by the face BC. Given critical angle of glass $C_g = 41°48'$.

Solution

Let the ray PQ, be incident normally on face AB.

(i.e. $\angle i = 0°$ for face AB)

$\therefore$ It will go undeviated along QO ($\because \angle r = 0°$)

Now, for isosceles ΔA, $A = 90°$, and $\angle B = \angle C = 45°$

$\therefore$ The ray PQO falls at an angle of 45° on face BC :

$\therefore$ $\angle i_1 = 45$ (at face BC)

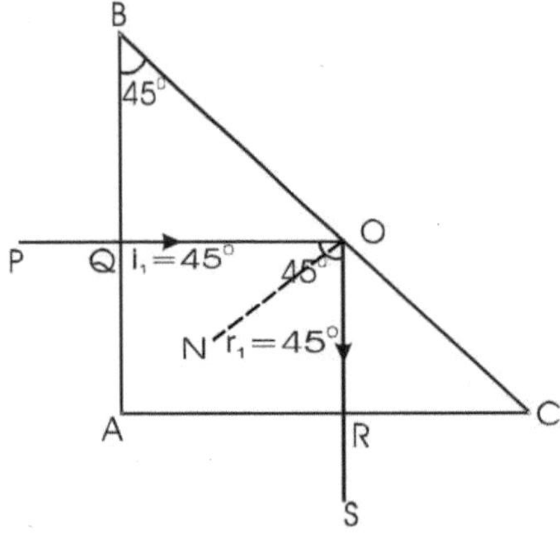

Now, Cg (Critical angle of glass) = 41°48'

$\therefore$ $\angle i_1 > \angle Cg$.

Hence the ray PQO suffers total internal reflection at O and will go along ORS.

(i.e., $\angle r_1 = 45°$)

Now, $^{a}\mu_g = \dfrac{1}{SinC} = \dfrac{1}{Sin45^0} = \sqrt{2} = 1.414$

$\therefore$ Minimum refractive index of glass for total internal reflection 1.414.

Illustration 7

A laser beam is directed at an angle θ, to the normal of one side of a rectangular block to fused quartz. Part of the light striking the side of the block passes into the block and strikes an adjacent face. For what angle θ will the laser beam be totally reflected in the block?

Solution

Snell's law gives for the refraction into the block

$$(1.00)\sin\theta = n_2 \sin\theta_2.$$

If the beam is totally internally reflected at the adjacent face, the incident angle on that face must be at least.

$$\theta_c = \sin^{-1}\left(\frac{1.000}{1.458}\right) = 43.30°$$

Since the block is rectangular, $\theta_2 + \theta_c = 90°$ so θ_2 is less than 46.70° for the internal reflection of occur.

$$\sin\theta = (1.458)\sin 46.70° = 1.06.$$

The sine function cannot be greater than one, so the angle, θ, which will produce the internal reflection must be less than or equal to 90°. That is, all incident angles will cause the light to be totally internally reflected at the adjacent face as long as the light strikes that faces.

Try Yourself

10. The critical angle of a liquid is 30°. Find its refractive index?
11. Calculate the critical angle for diamond when ray of light is travelling from diamond to air $\mu_{diamond} = 2.42$

5.6.4 Secondary Rainbow

The secondary rainbow is formed when the sunlight suffer two total internal reflection as well as dispersion from water droplets suspended in the atmosphere. The colour pattern is just reverse of that in the primary rainbow, i.e. violet colour on the outer edge and red colour on the inner edge of the rainbow. It is seen at an angle 52°-55° with the line joining the sun and the observer, when the sun is at the back of the observer. The primary rainbow is found to be more intense than the secondary rainbow.

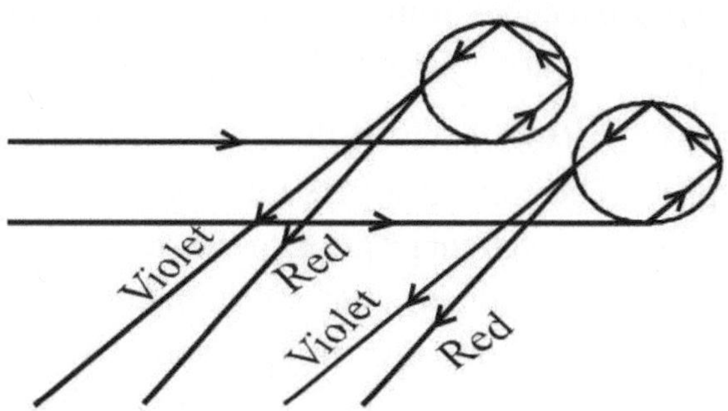

5.7 ATMOSPHERIC REFRACTION

It is the deviation of light from a straight line as it passes through the atmosphere due to the variation in air density as a function of altitude. Atmospheric refraction can make distant objects appear to shimmer or ripple. Atmospheric refraction causes astronomical objects to appear higher in the sky than they are in reality. The situation gets worse when the atmospheric refraction is not homogenous, when there is turbulence in the air for example. This is the cause of twinkling of the stars and deformation of the shape of the sun at sunset and sunrise.

5.7.1 Common Phenomenon of Atmospheric Refraction of Light

1. **Twinkling of Stars:** Light emitted by stars passes through the atmosphere of the earth before reaching our eyes. The atmosphere of the earth is not uniform but consists of many layers of different densities. The layers close to the surface of the earth are optically denser. As we go higher and higher, the density of layers and refractive index decreases progressively. As the light form a star enters the upper – most layer of the atmosphere, it bends towards the normal as it enters the next layer. This process continues till the light enters our eyes. So due to refraction of light, the apparent position of the star is different from the actual position of the star (Figure)

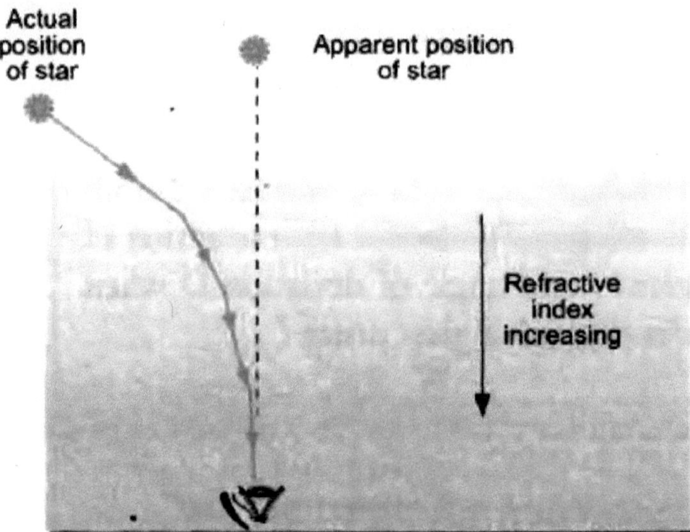

Moreover, the different layers of the atmosphere are moveable and the temperature and the density of layers of atmosphere changes continuously. Hence, the apparent position of the star changes continuously. **The change in the apparent position of the star leads to the twinkling of a star**.

Note: Planets do not twinkle : Planets are very close to the earth as compared to the stars. So the intensity of light we receive from the planets is very large. Therefore, the variation in the brightness of the planets is not detected. Hence planets do not twinkle.

When light from a far distant star enters the atmosphere of the earth. It passes through rarer to denser air atmosphere. Therefore, it suffers atmospheric refraction and light bends towards the normal. This changes the apparent position of the star for a person viewing it from the earth's surface. Further, air molecules are in a state of continuous random motion. The random motion of air molecules keeps changing the refractive index in various atmospheric regions. This continuously changes the apparent position of a star for a person viewing it from earth's surface, making it twinkle.

2 **Advance Sunrise and Delayed Sunset : We can see the sun for few minutes even after it has actually set :** We can see the sun for few minutes even after it has actually set; Actual sun sets when it is below horizon in the evening. The rays of light from the sun below the horizon reach our eyes because of refraction of light. These rays appear to come from the apparent position of the sun which is above the horizon as shown in figure. Hence we can see the sun for few minutes (about **2 minutes**) even after it has actually set. Similarly, the sun can be seen about **2 minutes** before it actually rises. Thus, we gain **4 minutes** of additional daylight each day.

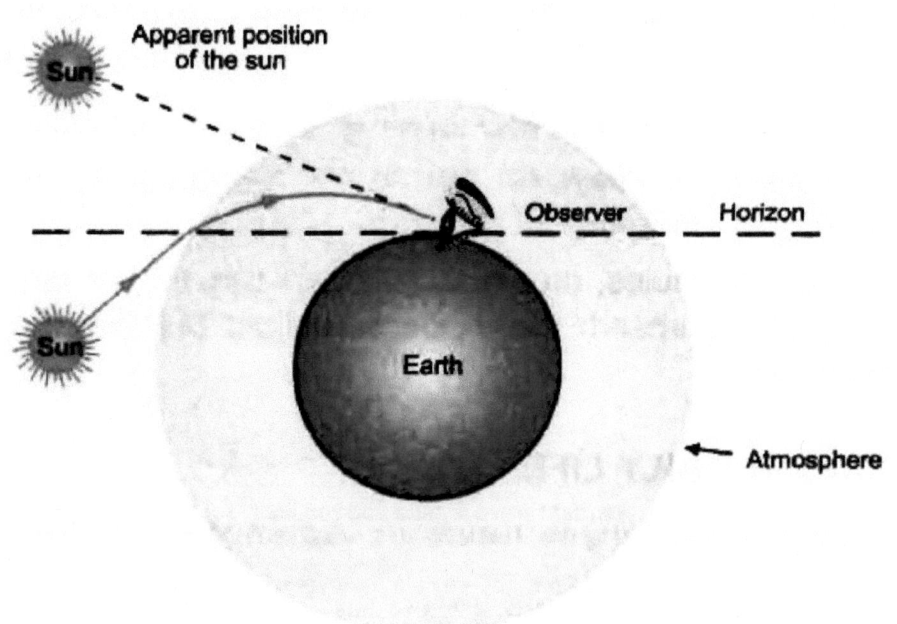

A diagram showing the atmospheric refraction of sun's rays causing apparent early sunrise and late sunset is shown in figure.

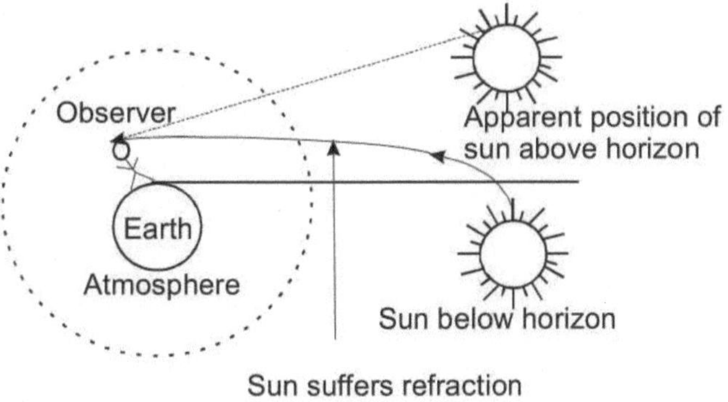

5.8 SCATTERING OF LIGHT

This is the phenomenon in which light is deflected from its path due to its interaction with the particles of the medium through which it passes . Basically, the scattering process involves the absorption of light by the molecules followed by its re-radiation in different directions.

Scattering represents basically change in the direction of light. As sunlight travels through the earth's atmosphere, it gets scattered by the large number of molecules and numerous small particles present in atmosphere.

If A = amplitude of incident light
λ = wavelength of incident light
V = volume of the scattering particle
a = amplitude of scattered light at a distance r from the scattering particle

$$a = \frac{AV}{r\lambda^2}$$

As intensity of scattered light (I_s) varies directly as square of amplitude of scattered light (A^2) therefore

$$I_s \propto \frac{1}{\lambda^4}$$

intensity of scattered light varies as the fourth power of the wavelength of incident light. Important factor in scattering is relative size of the wavelength of light (λ) and the scatterer (of typical size, say x)

For $x << \lambda$ Rayleigh's scattering is valid i.e. when size of scatterer is much smaller than wavelength of light $I_s \alpha \frac{1}{\lambda^4}$ this is called **elastic scattering**

For $x >> \lambda$ Rayleigh scattering is not valid and all wavelengths are scattered nearly equally. This is called **inelastic scattering**

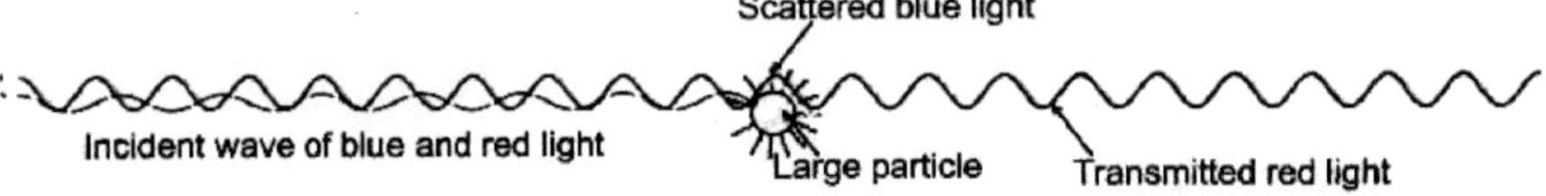

Figure shows a large particle whose diameter is greater than the wavelength of the blue light, but smaller than the wavelength of red light. Now, when a mixture of red and blue light is made incident on such a particle, then the blue light is absorbed by the particles and then transmitted in all possible directions, i.e., the blue light is scattered. The red light, however, continues moving straight as it is not absorbed or scattered.

Now, if your eyes receives scattered blue light, then the particle will appear blue in colour to you.

When the white sunlight enters the atmosphere of earth, the particle size is smallest. Thus, the violet light which has the smallest wavelength in white light scatters.

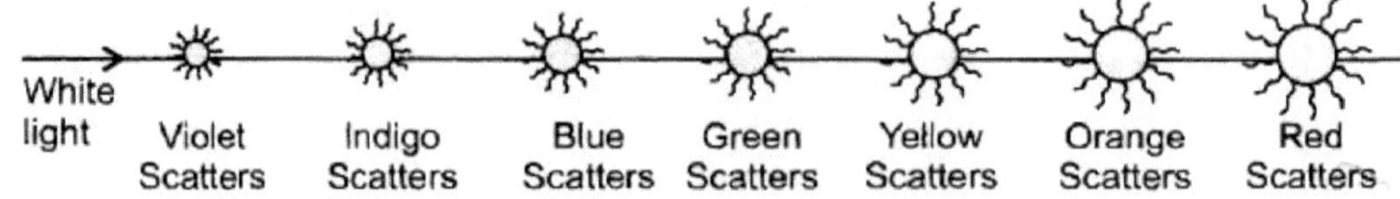

From the above statement it does not imply, that all the violet waves present in sunlight scatter. Instead it means that if **only a particular ray, which strikes a particle, whose diameter is greater than the wavelength of violet light gets scattered**. From this it follows that quite a large number of rays of white sunlight will reach us without scattering.

As the white light continues its journey through the atmosphere, the number and particle size present in the air increase. This results in the scattering of indigo and blue wavelengths. If the white light travels through longer distance through atmosphere, as during sunset or sunrise than even yellow, orange and red scatter. The red light has wavelength 1.8 times the wavelength of violet light, and hence, scatters last of all.

5.8.1 Tyndall effect

The earth's atmosphere is a heterogeneous mixture of minute particles. These particles include smoke, tiny water droplets, suspended particles of dust and molecules of air. When a beam of light strikes such fine particles, the path of the beam becomes visible. The light reaches us, after being reflected diffusely by these particles. **The phenomenon of scattering of light by the colloidal particles gives rise to Tyndall effect**. This phenomenon is seen when a fine beam of sunlight enters a smoke-filled room through a small hole. Thus, scattering of light makes the particles visible. Tyndall effect can also be observed when sunlight passes through a canopy of a dense forest. Here, tiny water droplets in the mist scatter light.

5.8.2 Some Common Phenomena of atmospheric scattering (Applications in Daily Life)

Some phenomena occurring in nature are explained on the basis of scattering of light.

(i) **Sky would appear black in daytime if earth had no atmosphere:** If earth had no atmosphere, then there would be no gas present in the atmosphere. Since there is no scatterer in the atmosphere of the earth, so there will be no scattering of light. Hence, the sky would appear dark as there is not scattering of light.

When the earth had no atmosphere, sunlight would be visible only if we look directly at the sun. Even stars will be seen in day time in the absence of the earth atmosphere.

(ii) **Why is the colour of clear sky blue?**

Blue colour of sky is due to scattering of sunlight, light from the sun, while travelling through earth's atmosphere, gets scattered by large number of molecules in the earth's atmosphere.

As $x << \lambda$ Rayleigh's scattering is valid.

The intensity of scattered light varies inversely as the fourth power of wavelength of light.

As blue color has a shorter wavelength than red. therefore blue color is scattered much more strongly. Hence the sky looks blue.

(iii) **Why sunset and sunrise are Red?**

At the time of sunrise or sunset, the position of the sun is very far away from us. The sunlight travels longer distance through the atmosphere of the earth before reaching our eyes. Scattering of blue light is more than the scattering of red light. As a result of this, more red light reaches our eyes than any other colour. Hence sunset and sunrise appear red.

During noon, the sun is overhead and sunlight travels less distance through the earth's atmosphere to reach our eyes. In this case, the scattering of almost all colours is very small. Hence the sun appears white.

However, as the sun rises up the horizon, the distance travelled by sunlight in the atmosphere decreases and hence, yellow, orange or red light are not scattered. Thus, sky appears blue & the sunlight yellowish.

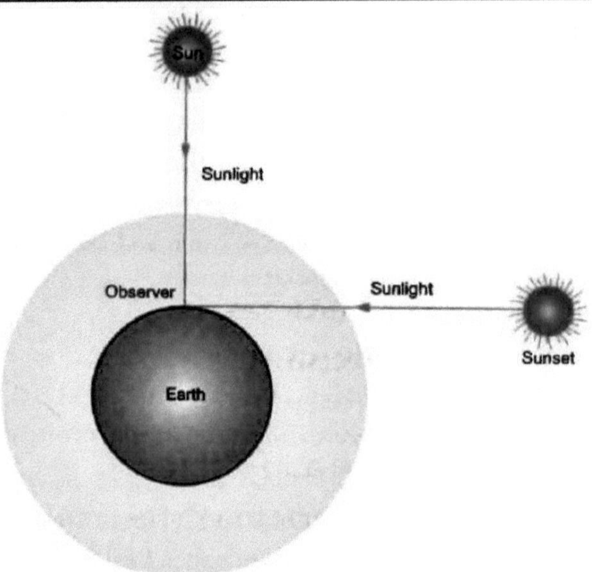

(iv) Why clouds are white?

The clouds are at much lower height. They are seen due to scattering of light from lower parts of the atmosphere which contains large dust particles water droplets ice particles etc.

In this case size of scatterer $x >> \lambda$ Therefore all wavelengths are scattered nearly equally

All colours scattered equally merge to give us the sensation of white. Hence clouds generally appear white. **"This is termed as mie scattering".**

(v) Danger Signals are of red colour?

When light falls on the signal, all colours are scattered much more than that of red colour. So the red colour suffering least scattering remains confined around the signal, which in turn illuminates the signal significantly. Thus the danger signals can be seen from very far off distances. Moreover, among all colours, red light is scattered least by smoke or fog. Hence, red signals are visible even through the smoke or fog.

Note : The red light has largest wavelength among the spectral colours, and hence, is least scattered. Thus, red light can easily pass through for mist or smoke without getting scattered, and hence, is visible from long distance. Thus it is used as universal danger signal.

Illustration 8

Why does the sky appears dark instead of blue to an astronaut?

Solution

In space no particles are present. Thus, no scattering of light takes place. Hence, the sky appears dark as light by its own nature is invisible, but produces us the sensation of vision.

CONCEPT MAP

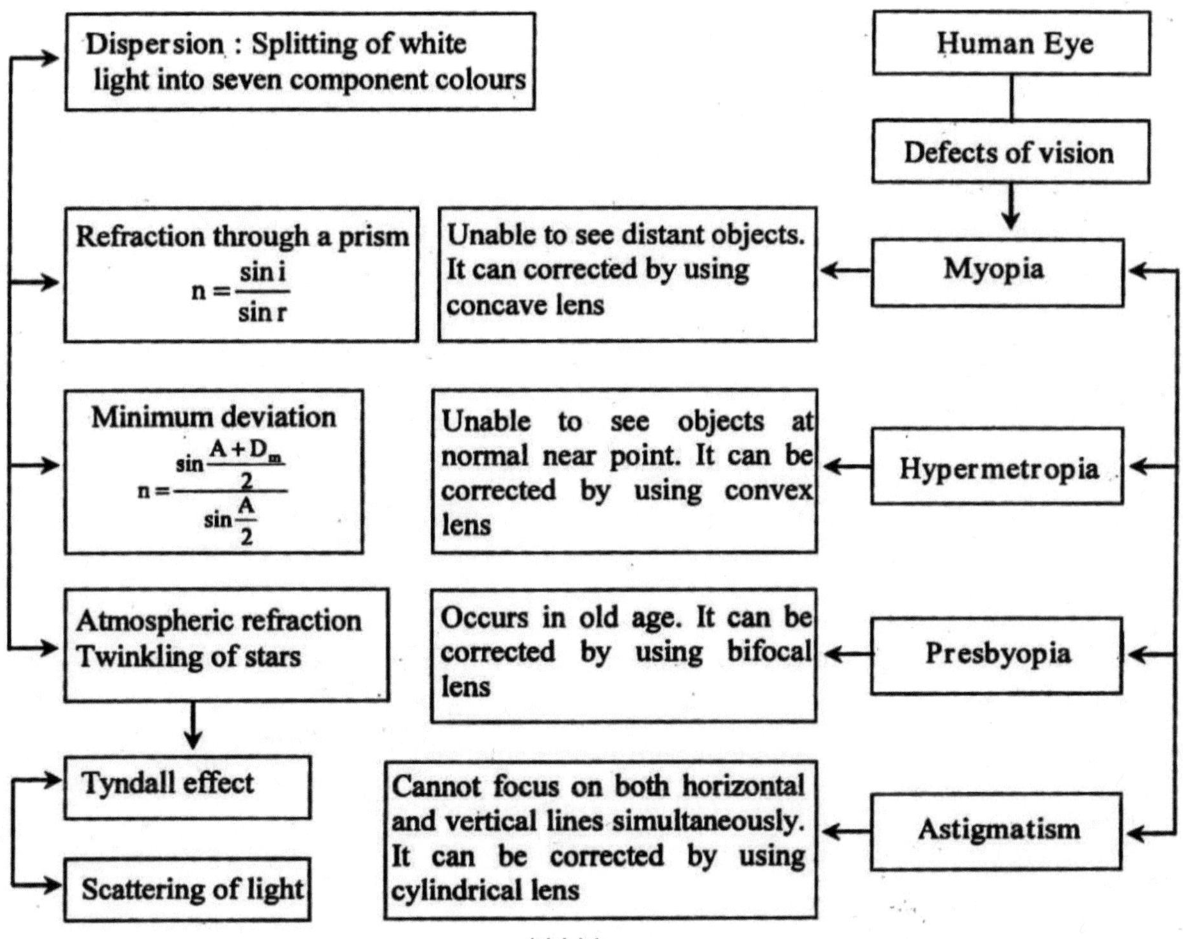
Dispersion : Splitting of white light into seven component colours
Human Eye
Defects of vision
Refraction through a prism
$n = \frac{\sin i}{\sin r}$
Unable to see distant objects. It can corrected by using concave lens
Myopia
Minimum deviation
$n = \frac{\sin \frac{A + D_m}{2}}{\sin \frac{A}{2}}$
Unable to see objects at normal near point. It can be corrected by using convex lens
Hypermetropia
Atmospheric refraction Twinkling of stars
Occurs in old age. It can be corrected by using bifocal lens
Presbyopia
Tyndall effect
Scattering of light
Cannot focus on both horizontal and vertical lines simultaneously. It can be corrected by using cylindrical lens
Astigmatism

*****

LET US RECAPITULATE

- Human eye is just like a camera.
- **Parts of human eye are:** Cornea, Iris, Lens Ciliary muscles Retina and Optic nerve.
- **Cornea** is the aperture or window of an eye. It allows light to enter in the eye
- **Iris** controls the amount of light entering the eye through pupil.
- Lens of the human eye focuses light on the retina of eye to make the image of an object.
- **Ciliary muscles** increases or decreases the focal length of the eye lens
- **Retina** acts as the screen or film to obtain the image of an object
- **Optic nerve** carries signal to the brain from interpretation.
- **Accommodation of an eye** is the ability of eye lens to change its focal length to form a sharp images of objects at different position from the eye on the retina of the eye.
- **Near point** is the nearest position of an object from human eye so that its sharp image is formed on the retina.
- **Near point** of a normal person is 25 cm.
- **Far point** is the farthest position of an object from a human eye so that the sharp image of the object is formed on the retina.
- **Range of vision** is the distance between the near point and the far point of an eye.
- Power of accommodation of a normal human eye is about 4 dioptre.
- **Defective eye:** The eye which is unable to see the objects clearly is known as defective eye.
- Common defects in a human eye are:
  (i) **Hypermetropia** or long – sightedness or far – sightedness.
  (ii) **Myopia** or short – sightedness or near – sightedness
  (iii) **Presbyopia** and
  (iv) **Astigmatism**
- **Hypermetropia:** A human eye which can see distant objects clearly but cannot see clearly the near by objects is said to be suffered with a defect called hypermetropia.
- **Cause of hypermetropia:** It is due to (i) the increase of the focal length of the eye lens and (ii) the decrease in the size of eye ball.
- Hypermetropia can be corrected by using a convex lens of suitable focal length.
- **Myopia:** A human eye which can see near object clearly but cannot see clearly the distant objects is said to be suffered with a defect called Myopia.
- **Cause of Myopia:** It is due to (i) the enlargement of the eye ball and (ii) the excessive curvature of the cornea.
- Myopia can be corrected by using a concave lens of suitable focal length.
- **Astigmatism:** A human eye which cannot focus on both horizontal and vertical lines simultaneously suffers from astigmatism.

- Astigmatism can be corrected by using a cylindrical lens.
- **Cataract:** A human eye in which a opaque membrane is formed over the eye lens suffers from cataract
- Cataract can be corrected by performing surgery.
- **Prism** is a homogeneous transparent refracting medium bounded by at least two non – parallel suffers inclined at some angle.
- **Angle of prism:** The angle between two non parallel refracting surfaces is called angle of prism.
- **Angle of deviation:** The angle between the directions of incident ray or light and the emergent ray of light is called angle of deviation of the ray of light passing through the prism.
- **Dispersion of white light:** The phenomenon of splitting white light into seven colours when it passes through a glass prism is called dispersion of white light.
- **Spectrum:** A band of seven colours of white light is called spectrum.
- **Red colour deviates the least** while passing through a glass prism.
- **Violet colour deviates the most** while passing through a glass prism.
- Glass prism splits the colours of white light passing through it and does not produce any colour by itself
- Rainbow is the example of dispersion of sun light.
- Rainbow is formed by tiny drops of water suspended in the atmosphere
- **Atmospheric refraction:** The refraction of light taking place in the atmosphere is known as atmospheric refraction
- Twinkling of stars takes place due to atmospheric refraction of light emitted by the stars.
- The sun can be seen for few minutes even after it has actually set due to refraction of light
- When light falls on tiny particles, this light is absorbed by these particles. Then these particles re – emit light in all directions. This process is known as **scattering of light**.
- Intensity of scattered light, $I \propto \frac{1}{\lambda^4}$, if size of scatterer is small as compared to the wavelength of light.
- In a clear atmosphere of the earth, colours of small wavelength like violet, and blue are scattered more than red colour
- In a polluted atmosphere of the earth (containing dust and smoke particles), the scattering of colours of higher wavelength is more than the scattering colours of smaller wavelengths.
- Blue colour of sky, greenish – blue colour of sea water, red colour of sunset and sunrise and white colour of clouds are due to scattering of light.

CONCEPT APPLICATION LEVEL - I [NCERT Questions]

MULTIPLE CHOICE QUESTIONS:

Q.1 **Human eye can focus objects at different distance by adjusting the focal length of the eye lens. This is due to**

(A) presbyopia **(B) near sightedness**

(C) accommodation **(D) far sightedness** **Ans.(C)**

Q.2 **Human eye forms the image of an object at its.**

(A) cornea **(B) iris** **(C) pupil** **(D) retina** **Ans. (D)**

Q.3 **The least distance of distinct vision for a young adult with normal vision is about?**

(A) 25 m **(B) 2.5 cm** **(C) 25 cm** **(D) 50 cm** **Ans.(C)**

Q.4 **The change in focal length of an eye lens is caused by the action of**

(A) pupil **(B) retina** **(C) ciliary muscle** **(D) iris** **Ans.(C)**

Q.5 **A person needs a lens of power – 5.5 diopters for correcting distant vision. For correcting his near vision, he needs a lens of power + 1.5 diopter. What is the focal length of the lens required for correcting (i) distant vision and (ii) near vision?**

Ans. (A) $f=\frac{1}{P}=-\frac{1}{5.5}=-0.18\,m=-18.0\,cm$

(B) $f=\frac{1}{P}=\frac{1}{1.5}=0.67\,m=67.0\,cm$

Q.6 **The far point of a myopic person is 80cm in front the eye. What is the nature and power of the lens required to correct the problem?**

Ans. $\frac{1}{f}=-\frac{1}{d}=-\frac{1}{80\,cm}$ or $f=-80$ cm

$\therefore$ $Power=\frac{100}{f}=-\frac{100}{80}=-1.25D$

The lens is concave lens.

Q.7 Make a diagram to show how hypermetropia is corrected. The near point of a hypermetropic eye is 1 m. What is the power of the lens required to correct this defect? Assume that the near point of the normal eye is 25 cm

Ans.

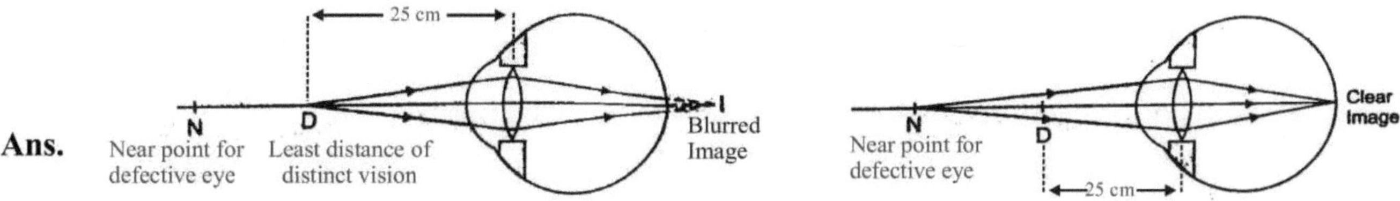

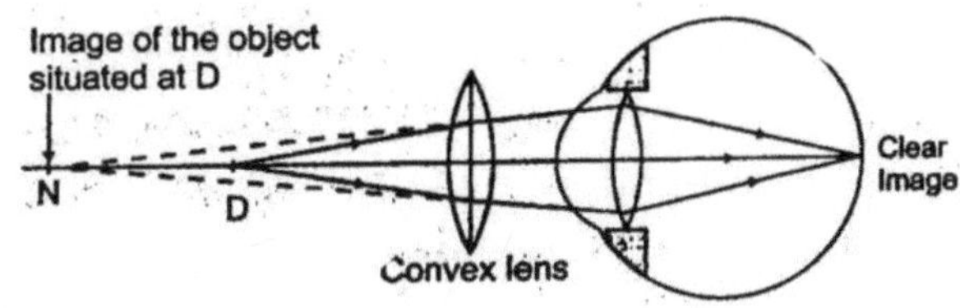

$$\frac{1}{f} = \frac{1}{-100} + \frac{1}{(d)} = \frac{1}{25} - \frac{1}{100} = \frac{3}{100} \quad \text{or} \quad f = \frac{100}{3}\text{ cm},$$

$$\therefore \quad \text{Power} = \frac{100}{f} = +3.0\text{ D}$$

Q.8 Why is a normal eye not able to see clearly the objects placed closer than 25 cm?

Ans. The nearest position of an object from normal human eye so that its sharp image is formed on retina is 25 cm. If the object is placed at a distance less than 25 cm, then the blurred image of the object is formed on retina as the focal length of eye lens cannot by decreased below a certain limit. Hence, eye cannot see it clearly.

Q.9 What happens to the image distance in the eye when we increase the distance of an object from the eye?

Ans. The image distance remains the same in the eye because the eye has the ability to change the focal length of its lens to make the image always on the retina when the object distance increase from the eye.

Q.10 Why do stars twinkle?

Ans. Light emitted by stars passes through the atmosphere of the earth before reaching our eyes. The atmosphere of the earth is not uniform but consists of many layers of different densities. The layers close to the surface of the earth are optically denser. As we go higher and higher, the density of layers and refractive index decreases progressively. As the light form a star enters the upper – most layer of the atmosphere, it bends towards the normal as it enters the next layer. This process continues till the light enters our eyes. So due to refraction of light, the apparent position of the star is different from the actual position of the star. The different layers of the atmosphere are movable and the temperature and the density of layers of atmosphere changes continuously. Hence, the apparent position of the star changes continuously. **The change in the apparent position of the star leads to the twinkling of a star**.

Q.11 Explain why the planets do not twinkle?

Ans. Planets are very close to the earth as compared to the stars. So the intensity of light we receive from the planets is very large. Therefore, the variation in the brightness of the planets is not detected. Hence planets do not twinkle.

Q.12 Why does the sun appear red early in the morning?

Ans. The sunlight travels longer distance through the atmosphere of the earth before reaching our eyes. Scattering of blue light is more than the scattering of red light. As a result of this, more red light reaches our eyes than any other colour. Hence sunset and sunrise appears red.

Q.13 Why does the sky appear dark instead of blue to an astronaut?

Ans. The blue colour of sky is due to the scattering of sunlight. The scattering of sunlight in the atmosphere is due to the presence of atoms and molecules of gas, droplets and dust particles. When the astronaut is in space, then there is no atmosphere (or atoms and molecules of gases, droplets and dust particles) around him. Therefore sunlight does not scatter and hence sky appears dark.

Q.14 What is meant by power of accommodation of the eye?

Ans. The ability of the eye lens to adjust its focal length is called accommodation of the eye. Power of accommodation of an eye is defined as the maximum variation in the power or focal length of the eye lens.

Q.15 A person with a myopic eye cannot see objects beyond 1.2 m distinctly. What should be the type of the corrective lens used to restore proper vision?

Ans. Concave lens of focal length given by

$$\frac{1}{f} = \frac{1}{d} = -\frac{1}{1.2\,\text{m}}$$

or $$f = -1.2\text{ m}$$

or $$P = \frac{1}{f} = \frac{-1}{1.2} = -0.83\,\text{D}$$

Q.16 What is the far point and near point of the human eye with normal vision?

Ans. The farthest position of an object from the human eye so that its sharp image is formed on the retina is at infinite distance from the eye.

The nearest position of an object from a human eye so that its sharp image is formed on the retina is at 25 cm from the eye.

Q.17 A student has difficulty in reading the black board while sitting in the last row. What could be the defect the child is suffering from? How can it be corrected?

Ans. Near sighted or myopia. This defect can be corrected by using concave lens of suitable focal length.

CONCEPT APPLICATION LEVEL - II

SECTION A
VERY SHORT ANSWER QUESTIONS

Q.1 Name the outermost part of human eye?

Ans. Cornea

Q.2 Write the function of iris in the human eye.

Ans. Iris controls the amount of light entering the eye by controlling the size of the pupil.

Q.3 Name the part of human eye which acts as a screen to obtain the image of an object?

Ans. Retina

Q.4 Name two common defects of vision.

Ans. (i) Myopia (ii) Hypermetropia

Q.5 What is hypermetropia or far – sightedness?

Ans. A human eye which can see distant objects clearly but cannot see the near objects clearly is said to be suffered with a defect called hypermetropia or far sightedness.

Q.6 Name the type of a lens used to correct hypermetropic eye.

Ans. Convex lens

Q.7 What is Myopia or near – sightedness?

Ans. A human eye which can see near objects clearly but cannot see the distant objects clearly is said to be suffered with a defect called myopia or near – sightedness.

Q.8 Name a type of a lens used to correct myopic eyes?

Ans. Concave lens.

Q.9 What is a presbyopia (a defect of vision)?

Ans. A human eye which cannot see the near objects clearly after a certain age is said to be suffered with a defect called presbyopia.

Q.10 How is a cataract caused in a human eye?

Ans. Cataract is caused due to the formation of an opaque membrane over the eye lens.

Q.11 How can cataract be corrected?

Ans. By performing surgery to replace the affected eye lens with an artificial lens.

Q.12 Name the phenomenon occurring in nature due to dispersion of light?

Ans. Rainbow

Q.13 How is the intensity of scattered light depend on the wavelength of incident light?

Ans. $I \propto \frac{1}{\lambda^4}$ (Only for elastic scattering)

Q.14 Out of the blue and red light, which is scattered most by the atmosphere of the earth?

Ans. Blue light

Q.15 What is Tyndall Effect?

Ans. The phenomenon of scattering of light by dust, smoke and water droplets suspended in air is known as Tyndall effect.

Q.16 State two reasons due to which myopia may be caused?

Ans. This defect arises due to either by (i) the elongation of the eye ball or (ii) the excessive curvature of the cornea.

Q.17 What is the difference between images produced by a telescope and binoculars?

Ans. The image produced by telescope does not give perception of depth whereas the image produced by binoculars produces 3-dimensional image with increased field of view and intensity.

Q.18 Which liquids fills the space between cornea and eye lens & the space between eye lens and the retina?

Ans. Aqueous humor and vitreous humor respectively.

Q.19 Sometimes you see a person reading the newspaper by placing it very close to his eyes. Which defect is he suffering from.

Ans. Short signtedness or myopia.

Q.20 How can a person suffering from astigmatism along with myopia or hypermetropia be corrected?

Ans. Sphero-cylindrical lens (compound lens).

Q.21 What part of the eye can be donated after death?

Ans. The cornea from dead body is removed within 6 hours of the death and transplanted in the eyes of the blind person with opaque cornea.

Q.22 Why do we observe wavering or flickering of the objects near a fire on a very hot day?

Ans. Due to refraction, air above air is lighter than cold air above it.

$\mu_{\text{hot air}} < \mu_{\text{cold air}}$

$\therefore$ Wavering is the effect of atmospheric refraction.

Q.23 Why is blind spot termed so?

Ans. Because the image formed at this point is not sent to the brain.

Q.24 What is the number of receptors contained in the retina?

Ans. Its more than 125 million receptors.

Q.25 Chicken can see only in bright light. What type of cells are present in its retina?

Ans. Its retina has more cone cells than rod cells. In the morning the first ray of light is observed easily.

Q.26 Name the defect that can not be corrected with use of spectacle?

Ans. Colour blindness.

Q.27 Which part of human eye helps in the perception of colours ?

Ans. The retina of the human eye has a large number of cone-shaped and rod shaped cells. The rods respond to the intensity of light and the cones to the colours. These helps us to perceive colours.

Q.28 Give the condition required to achieve a larger magnification of a small object by a compound microscope ?

Ans. To achieve a larger magnification of small object, both the objective and the eyepiece of a compound should have smaller focal length. Magnification of the order of 1000 is possible with very good design of the microscopes such as in the oil-immersion type of microscopes.

SECTION B
CONCEPTUAL QUESTIONS

Q.1 Copy the following diagram on your answer sheet after showing the refracted rays of light from eye lens, assuming the eye is a normal human eye?

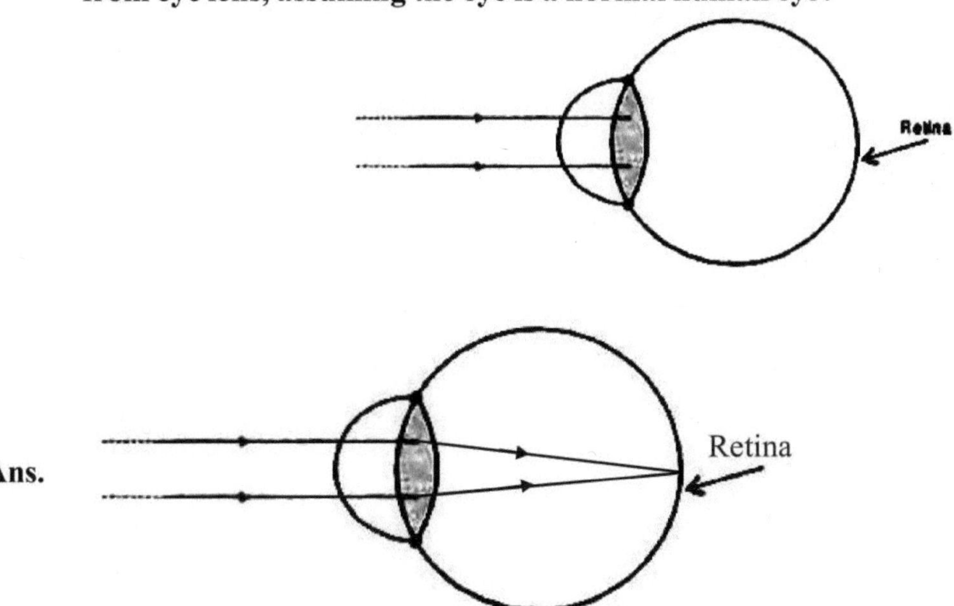

Q.2 Copy the following diagram on your answer sheet showing the different colours on the white screen.

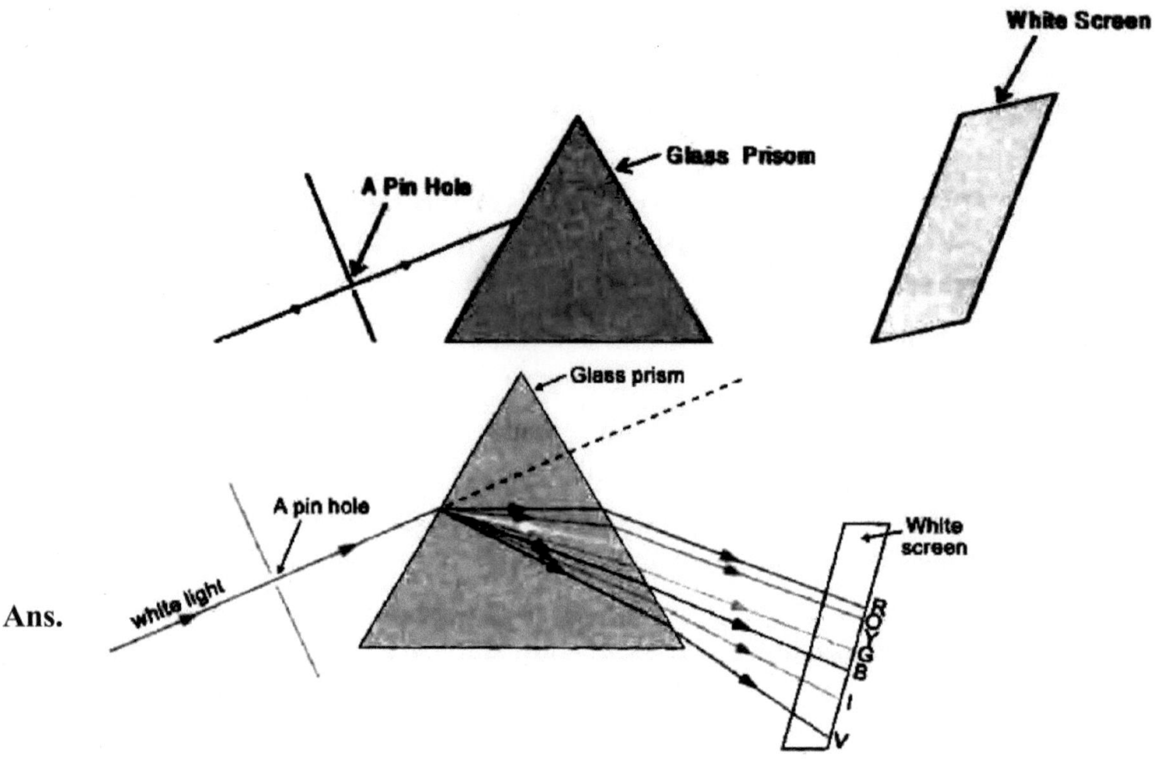

Ans.

Q.3 The ciliary muscle of a normal eye are in their (i) most relaxed (ii) most contracted state. In which of the two cases is the focal length of the eye – lens more?

Ans. The focal length of eye – lens is more when the ciliary muscles of a normal eye are in their most relaxed state.

Q.4 Why do we have two eyes instead of one eye ?

Ans. Two eyes are better than one eye because (i) the field of view with two eyes is more than with one eye (ii) two eyes view three dimensional picture of an object (i.e. the length, breadth and depth or height of an object) where as one eye gives only two dimensional picture of an object.

Q.5 When white light passes through a glass, seven colours namely red, orange, yellow, green, blue, indigo and violet are seen on the white screen. All these colours have different angles of deviation. Explain why?

Ans. Speed of colour in a medium depends upon its wavelength. All the colours have different wavelength. The red colour has the longest wavelength and violet colour has the least wavelength. Therefore, red colour has the highest speed in the glass prism and the violet colour has the lowest speed in the glass prism. Hence, all colours of white light are refracted by different amounts while passing the glass prism. Therefore, all the colours have different angles of deviations.

Q.6 On a sunny day stand at a certain distance from a fountain of a water the position of the sun is at your back. What do you observe? Explain the reason of your observation?

Ans. We observe a rainbow. The droplets of water behave as glass prism. When sun light falls on these drops, dispersion of light takes place. Hence, rainbow is seen.

Q.7 What happens to the power of the eye lens in case of myopia and hypermetropia?

Ans. In myopia, it increases because eye lens thickeness increases, focal length decreases $P \propto \frac{1}{F}$

$\therefore$ power increases. In hypermetropia, it decreases because eye lens thickness decreases, focal length increases and power decreases.

Q.8 What are the factors on which deviation produced by a prism depend?

Ans. (i) Angle of the incidence
(ii) Angle of the prism
(iii) Nature of material of the prism
(iv) Color of light being used i.e. wavelength of incident light

Q.9 What are rod shaped and cone shaped cells. How do they help us in seeing color?

Ans. Cone cells are light sensitive cells and retina has a large number of such cells. These respond to the colors i.e. in perceiving different colours. Rod shaped cells are sensitive to the intensity of light.

Q.10 A prism causes dispersion of white light while a rectangular slab doesn't. Explain?

Ans. In prism, the refraction of light takes place at two slant surfaces. The dispersion of white light occurs at the first surface of prism where its constituent color are deviated through different angles. At the second surface they suffer only refraction and they get further seperated.
In a rectangular glass block the refraction takes place at two parallel surfaces. Constituent colour on refraction, but these colour on suffering refraction of the second surface emerge out in form of a parallel beam, which give an impression of white light.

Q.11 Arrange in the order of : [Yellow, Green, Blue, Red]
(i) Increasing order of their wavelength
(ii) Increasing order of their frequency

Sol. (i) Blue, Green, Yellow, Red
(ii) Red, Yellow, Green, Blue

V I B G Y O R
"wavelength Increases" →
← "frequency Increases"

Q.12 State rayleigh's law and the condition for which it can be followed?

Ans. Intensity (I) $\propto \dfrac{1}{(\text{wavelength})^4}$

$$I \propto \frac{1}{\lambda^4}$$

Condition:

If 'a' is the diameter of the particle & 'λ' is the wavelength of the incident ray then, Rayleigh's law can only be followed if

$$a << \lambda$$

Q.13 Differentiate between a microscope and a telescope based on its use.

Ans. A microscope is an optical instrument which is used to see the finer details of tiny objects and a telescope is used for viewing distant objects clearly.

Q.14 How is the length of the telescope tube related to the distance between the objective and the eyepiece of the telescope ? How can the magnification of the telescope be increased ?

Ans. The length of the telescope tube is equal to the distance between the objective and eyepiece of the telescope. In order to increase the magnification of the telescope, the objective must have a large focal length and the eye piece a small focal length.

Q.15 What is phorias ?

Ans. This is a defect of eye. With this defect, the eye sees two images of one object. This defect is due to lack of balance among the muscle which hold the two eye in their axes. This lack of balance produces cross eyes. It is remedied by using prismatic lenses.

Q.16 Why is eye lens of telescope smaller than objective lens ?

Sol. The eye lens of telescope is smaller than its objective lens to sharpen the image which is obtained using telescope.

Q.17 How does the eye adjust itself to deal with light of varying intensity ?

Ans. The amount of light entering the eye is controlled by the pupil if the intensity of the outside light is low then the pupil expand to allow more light to enter the eye. If the outside intensity is high, then the pupil contracts so that less light enters the eye.

Q.18 Which phenomenon of vision is made use of in cinematography ? Explain briefly how it is used.

Sol. Persistence of vision is made use of in cinematography. It is the ability of an eye to continue to see the image of an object for a very short duration even after the removal of the object. We are able to see the movie pictures in a cinema due to the persistance of vision.

SECTION C

NUMERICALS PROBLEMS

Q.1 If the concave lens of focal length (f = 1.5m) used to restore the proper vision, then what is the power of lens.

Ans. The concave lens of focal length f used to restore the proper vision $f = -1.5$ m

$$\therefore \quad \text{Power of lens, } P = \frac{1}{f} = -\frac{1}{1.5} = -0.67 \text{ D}$$

Q.2 A young boy can adjust the power of his eye-lens between 50 D & 60 D. His far point is infinity.

(a) What is the distance of his retina from the eye-lens ?

(b) What is his near point?

Ans. (a) When the eye is fully relaxed, its focal length is largest and the power of the eye lens is minimum. This power is 50 D according to the given data. The focal length is 1/50 m = 2cm. As the far point is at infinity, the parallel rays coming from infinity are focused on the retina in the fully relaxed condition. Hence, the distance of the retina from the lens equal to the focal length which is 2 cm.

(b) When the eye is focused at the near point, the power is maximum which is 60D. The focal length in this case is f= $\frac{1}{60}$ m = 5/3 cm. The image is formed on the retina and thus v= 2cm. We have,

$$\frac{1}{v}-\frac{1}{u}=\frac{1}{f}, \quad \text{or} \quad \frac{1}{u}=\frac{1}{v}-\frac{1}{f}=\frac{1}{2}-\frac{3}{5} \quad \text{or } u=-10 \text{ cm}$$

The near point is at 10 cm.

Q.3 A person cannot see objects clearly beyond 50 cm. Find the power of the lens to correct the vision.

Ans. Here v = –50 cm, u = ∞. Hence using $\frac{1}{f}=\frac{1}{v}-\frac{1}{u}$.

We find f = –50 cm = – 0.50 m.

So power of the lens is $P=\frac{1}{-0.50 \text{ m}}=-2\text{D}$

Q.4 A myopic person having far point 80 cm uses spectacles of power –1.0 D. How far can he see clearly?

Ans. Use $\frac{1}{v}-\frac{1}{u}=\frac{1}{f}$. Here v = –80 cm; f = –100 cm

Hence $\frac{1}{-80}-\frac{1}{u}=\frac{1}{-100}$

or $-\frac{1}{u}=-\frac{1}{100}+\frac{1}{80}=\frac{-80+100}{80\times 100}$. This gives u = –400 cm = –4 m

Q.5 In an equilateral prism, i= 30° and deviation is 37°. What are the angles marked as A, e and f?

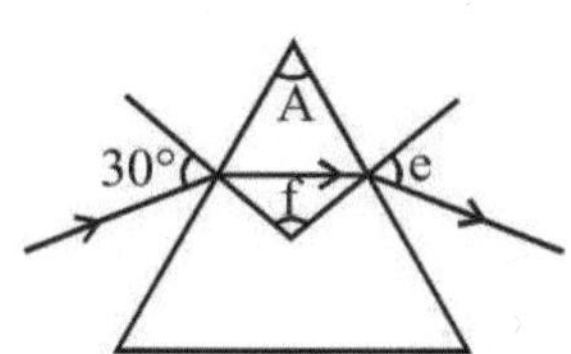

Sol. A = 60° → Equilateral prism

i = 30° δ = 37°

By prism eq. i + e = A + δ

⇒ e = 67°

Also, A + f = 180°

⇒ f = 120°

Q.6 A person having a myopic eye used the concave lens of focal length 50 cm. What is the power of the lens.

Ans. The formula for the power of lens in power (P)

$$f = 0.5 m$$

$$P = \frac{1}{f}$$

$$P = \frac{1}{0.5} = 2 \text{ dioptre.}$$

Q.7 A 52 year old near-sighted person wears eye glass of power of –5.5D for distance viewing. His doctor prescribes a correction of +1.5D in the near-vision section of his bi-focals this measured relative to the main parts of the lens

(i) What is the focal length of his distance viewing part of the lens.

(ii) What is the focal length of the near vision section of the lens.

Ans. (i) Focal length of lens for distance

viewing $F_1 = \frac{1}{P_1} = \frac{1}{-5.5}$

$= -0.182$ m

$= -18.2$ cm

(ii) Focal length for near vision

$$F_2 = \frac{1}{P_2} = \frac{1}{1.5}$$

$= 0.667$ m $= 66.7$ cm

SECTION D
PREVIOUS YEAR VERY SHORT ANSWER QUESTIONS
(1 MARKS QUESTIONS)

Q.1 What is the nature of the image formed at the retina of human eye ? (C.B.S.E. 2011)

Ans. Real and inverted image.

Q.2 Write the function of iris in the human eye? (CBSE. 2007 (Delhi), 2015, 2016)

Ans. Iris controls the size of the pupil.

Q.3 Name the part of human eye which acts as a screen to obtain the image of an object. (C.B.S.E. 2012, 2014)

Ans. Retina

Q.4 What is the function of pupil in human eye? (C.B.S.E. 2011, 2012)

Ans. It controls and regulates the light entering the eye.

Q.5 Name the part of human eye that is 'A thin membrane through which light enters the eye'. (C.B.S.E. 2011)

Ans. Cornea

Q.6 Name the part of human eye that is 'A dark muscular diaphragm that controls the size of the pupil'. (CB.S.E. 2011)

Ans. Iris

Q.7 How does the focal length of eye lens change when we shift looking from a distant to a nearby object? (C.B.S.E. smaple Paper 2010)

Ans. Focal length of eye lens decreases.

Q.8 Mention the value of range of vision for normal eye. (C.B.S.E. 2014, 2016)

Ans. Range of vision for normal eye is 25 cm to infinity.

Q.9 Mention the value of near point for normal eye. (C.B.S.E. 2014, 2015)

Ans. 25 cm

Q.10 Mention the value of far point for normal eye. (C.B.S.E. 2014, 2015)

Ans. Infinity.

Q.11 Name the ability of eye lens of eye lens to adjust its focal length. (C.B.S.E. 2014)

Ans. Accommodation.

Q.12 Name two common defects of vision. (CBSE 2015, 2016)

Ans. (i) Myopia (ii) Hypermetropia

Q.13 Name the type of a lens used to correct myopic eye.

Ans. Concave lens.

Q.14 State the type of corrective lens which is required by a person who can neither clearly see objects placed at the near point nor at infinity. (C.B.S.E. 2014)

Ans. Bi-focal lens.

Q.15 What is dispersion of light ? (C.B.S.E. 2012, 2015, C.B.S.E. (Foreign) 2016)

Ans. The phenomenon of splitting white light into seven colours when it passes through a glass prism is called dispersion of light.

Q.16 Draw a diagram showing refraction of a ray of light through a glass prism and mark the angle of deviation.

Ans.

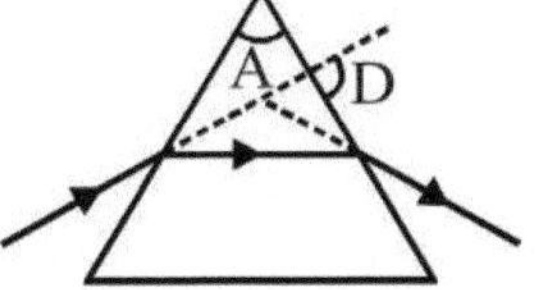

Q.17 Name the three phenomenon of light responsible for the formation of rainbow in the sky. (C.B.S.E. 2012)

Ans. (I) Refraction, (ii) dispersion and (iii) internal reflection of light.

Q.18 Name the part of human eye that helps in changing the focal length of the eye lens. (C.B.S.E. 2011

OR

Name the part of responsible for the power of accomondation of the human eye. (C.B.S.E. 2012)

Ans. Ciliary Muscles

Q.19 Light of two colours A and B pass through a glass prism. 'A' deviates more than B from its path of incidence. Which colour has a higher speed in the prism ? (C.B.S.E. 2011)

Ans. Colour B has higher speed than that of colour A.

Q.20 Name the colours that suffer maximum and minimum deviation respectively while passing through a prism. (C.B.S.E. 2014)

Ans. Red colour suffer minimum deviation and violet colour suffer maximum deviation.

Q.21 What is Tyndall effect ? (C.B.S.E. 2012, 2015)

Ans. The phenomenon of scattering of light by dust, smoke and water droplets suspended in air is know as Tyndall effect.

Q.22 A short sighted person cannot see clearly beyond 2 m. Calculate the power of less required to correct his vision. (C.B.S.E. 2011)

Ans. Here, d = 2m

The concave lens of focal length f = – d is needed to correct his vision

$\therefore \quad f = -d = -2\text{ m}$

$\therefore \quad \text{Power of lens, } P = \frac{1}{f} = -\frac{1}{2} = -0.5\text{ D.}$

Q.23 Copy the following diagram on your answer sheet showing the formation of image, assuming the given eye is a myopic eye OR (C.B.S.E. 2011)
Draw ray diagram showing myopic eye.

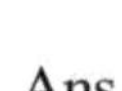

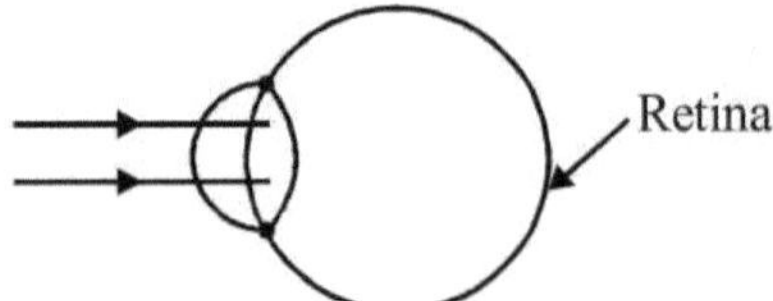

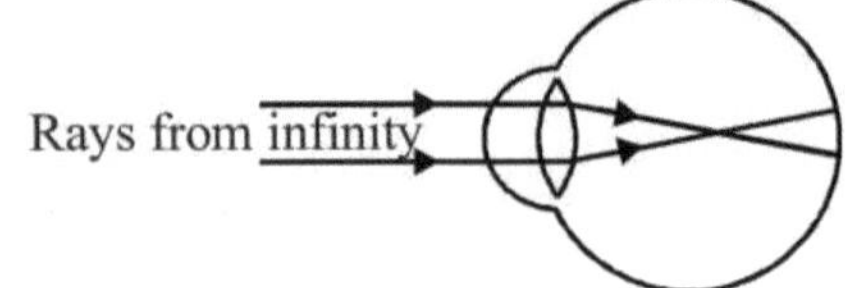

Q.24 Name the component of white light that deviates (i) the least and (ii) the most while passing through a glass prism. (C.B.S.E. 2011, 2012, 2014, 2015, 2016)

Ans. (i) red colour (ii) violet colour

Q.25 A person is advised to wear spectacles with concave lenses. What type of defect of vision is he suffering from ? (C.B.S.E. 2012)

Ans. Myopia

Q.26 What is meant by scattering of light ? (C.B.S.E. 2014, 2015, 2016)

Ans. Scattering represents basically change in the direction of light.

As sunlight travels through the earth's atmosphere, it gets scattered by the large number of molecules and numerous small particles present in atmosphere.

Q.27 Name the component of white light that has the greatest wavelength. (C.B.S.E. 2014, 2015, 2016)

Ans. Red colour

Q.28 Name the part of our eyes that helps us to focus near and distant objects in quick succession. (C.B.S.E. 2010)

Sol. Ciliary muscle

SECTION E
PREVIOUS YEAR SHORT ANSWER QUESTIONS
(2 AND 3 MARKS QUESTIONS)

Q.1 Why do we observe the seven colours when white light passes through a glass prism ? Which component of white light deviates the least ? (C.B.S.E. 2011, 2012)

Ans. White light is a mixture of seven colours. The speed of different colours of white light is different in glass prism. So when white light passes through a glass prism, it splits into seven colours. Red colour deviates the least.

Q.2 When we enter a dim-lit room from a bright light, we are not able to see the object in the room for some time. Explain, why ? (C.B.S.E. 2011, 2016)

Ans. In a bright light, the iris contracts the pupil of an eye to allow less light to enter the eye. When, we enter the dim-lit room iris takes time to expand the pupil of an eye to allow more light to enter the eye so that the visible image of the object lying in the room are formed on the retina of the eye.

Q.3 A convex lens made of glass forms a sharp image on the screen for a particular position of an object with respect to the lens. A human eye lens is also a convex lens but it can form sharp images on the retina of eye for differnt positions of the objects. Explain why ? (C.B.S.E. 2010)

Ans. A convex lens made up of glass has a fixed focal length and hence it forms a sharp image on the screen for a particular position of an object. However, the focal length of human eye lens can be changed by the action of ciliary muscles. In other words, human eye lens has the ability to change its focal length to form sharp images of objects at different positions. This process is known as accommodation of eye.

Q.4 An old person is unable to see clearly nearby object as well as distant objects.
(i) What defect of vision is he suffering from ?
(ii) What kind of lens will be required to see clearly the nearby as well as distant objects ? Give reasons ? (C.B.S.E. 2012, 2014)

Ans. (i) Presbyopia
(ii) This defect is corrected by using bi-focal lens. A bi-focal lens consists of a concave lens which forms the upper surface of lens and a convex lens which forms the lower surface of the lens. The upper surface enables the person to see distant object clearly and the lower surface helps the person to see the near objects clearly.

Q.5 How is normal eye able to see distinctly distant as well as nearer objects ? What is the distance of distinct vision ? (C.B.S.E. 2012)

Ans. Eye has the ability known as accommodation of eye to see distant as well as nearer objects clearly. When object is far away, the focal length of lens is increased due to the relaxed ciliary muscles. Hence sharp image of object is formed on the retina of eye. When object is nearer to the eye, the focal length of lens is decreased due to the contraction of ciliary muscles and hence sharp image of the object is formed on the retina of eye. The distance of distict vision is 25 cm.

Q.6 Why do different colour get separated when white light passes through prism ? How can we recombine the components of white light after a prism has separated them ? Explain with the help of figure. (C.B.S.E. 2012)

Ans. Different colours have different speeds in glass prism. Due to this fact, different colours get separated while passing through the prism.

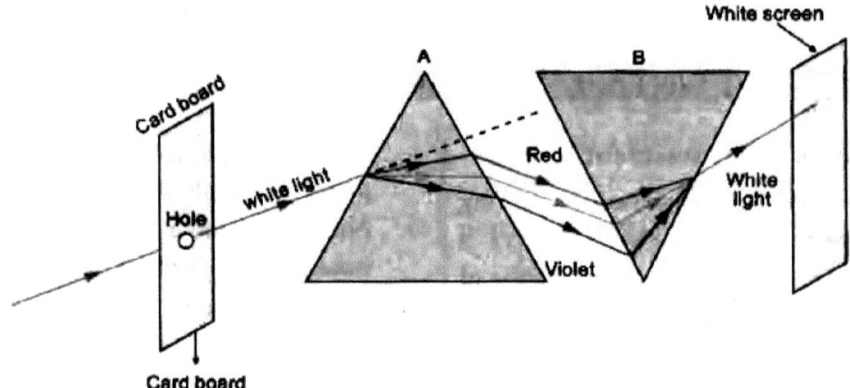

Q.7 What would have been the colour of sky if the earth had no atmosphere ? Given reason for your answer. (C.B.S.E. 2012)

Ans. If the earth has no atmosphere, the colour of the sky would been dark. The colour of sky depends on the scattering the sunlight due to the atmosphere. No atmosphere means no scattering of light.

Q.8 State the difference in colours of the sun observed during sunrise/sunset and noon. Give explanation for each (C.B.S.E. 2013)

Ans. The colour of the sun observed during sunrise/sunset is reddish, while its colour observed at noon is white. At sunrise/sunset, the sun is very far away from the observer So, the sunlight travels longer distance through the light. So, more red light reaches our eye and hence sun apperas reddish.
During noon the sun is overhead and light from the sun travels less distance through air to reach our eye. In this case, scattering of all colours is very small. Hence, the sun appears white.

Q.9 A person suffering from an eye-defect uses lens of power -1D. Name the defect he is suffering from and the nature of lens used. (C.B.S.E. 2015)

Ans. He is suffering from myopia. The lens is concave lens.

Q.10 Why does sky look blue on a clear day?

OR

Why is the colour of the clear sky is blue ? (C.B.S.E. 2009)

Sol. The scattering of sunlight due to the air molecules in the atmosphere causes the sky to appear blue. Shorter wavelength (Blue colour) is scattered more as compared to longer wavelength (Red colour). The scattered blue light enters our eyes.

Q.11 What is hypermetropia or far sightedness? State the two cause of hypermetropia with the help of ray diagram, show:

(i) the eye-defect hypermetropia by using a lens.

(ii) correction of hypermetropia by using a lens. (C.B.S.E. 2008, 2009)

Sol. A person suffering from this defect can see far off objects clearly, but cannot see clearly the object situated at a distance of 25 cm or at the least distance of distinct vision.

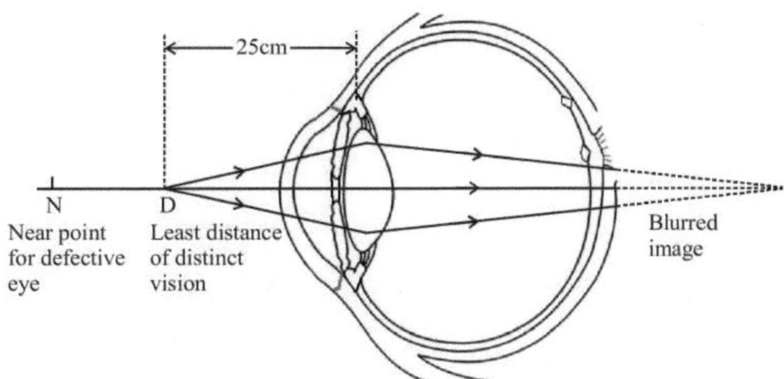

Fig. (a) Defective long sighted eye

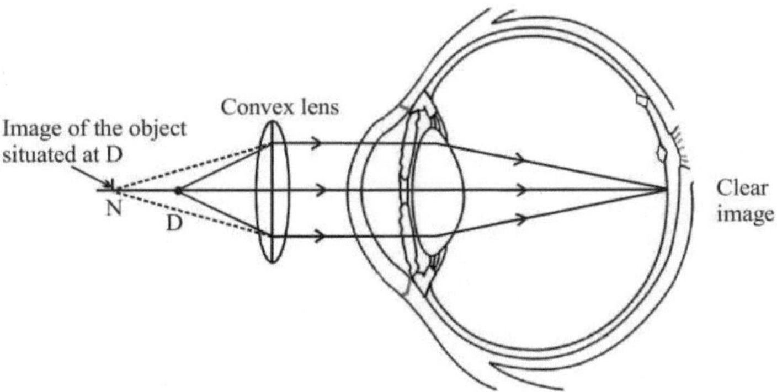

Fig. (b) Corrected lòng sighted eye

Q.12 Which type of eye defect is myopia? Describe with a neat diagram how this defect of vision can be corrected by using a suitable lens. (C.B.S.E. 2011)

Sol. A person suffering from this defect can see the nearer objects clearly but cannot see the far-off objects clearly.

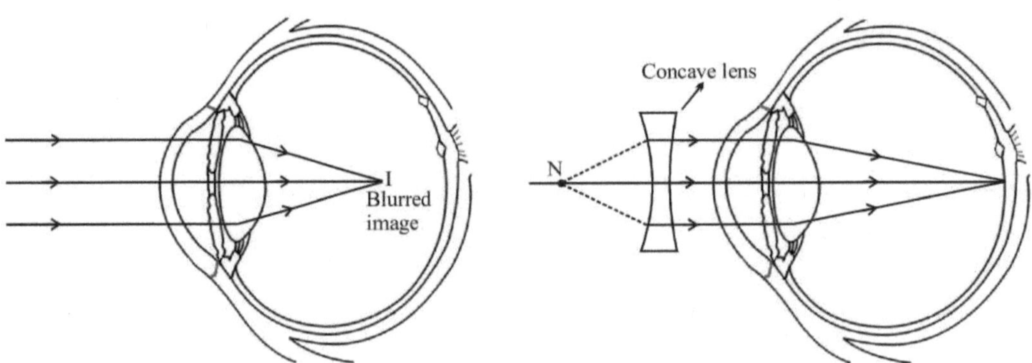

Fig. (a) Defective far sighted eye

Fig.(B) corrected far sighted eye

Q.13 In the figure given below a narrow beam of white light is shown to pass through a triangular glass prism. After passing through the prism it produces a spectrum XY on a screen.

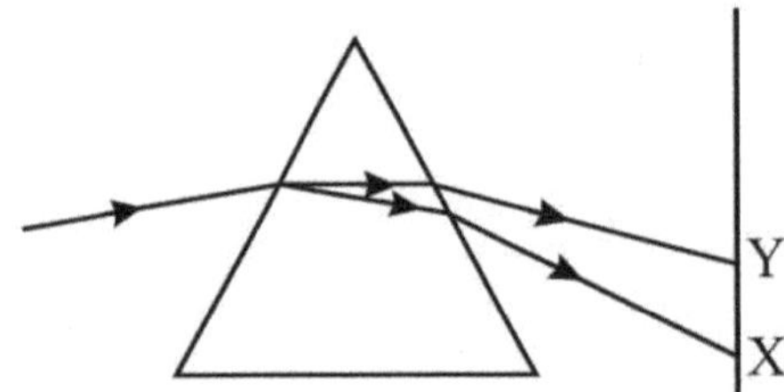

(a) State the colour seen at X and Y.

(b) Why do different colours of white light bend through different angles with respect to the incident beam of light? (C.B.S.E. 2010)

Sol. (a)

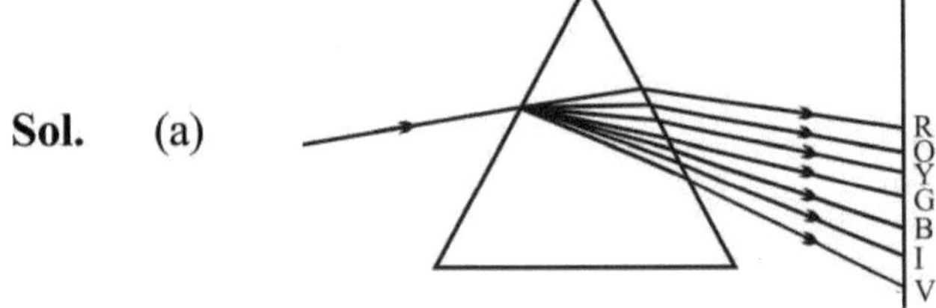

Colour seen at X is voilet

Colour seen at Y is red.

(b) Each colour has its own wavelength. The speed of light or colour depends upon the wavelength. Hence, all colours of white light are refracted by different angle.

Q.14 Draw a ray diagram to show the refraction of light through a glass prism. Mark on it (a) the incident ray, (b) the emergent ray and (c) the angle of deviation. (C.B.S.E. 2010)

Sol.

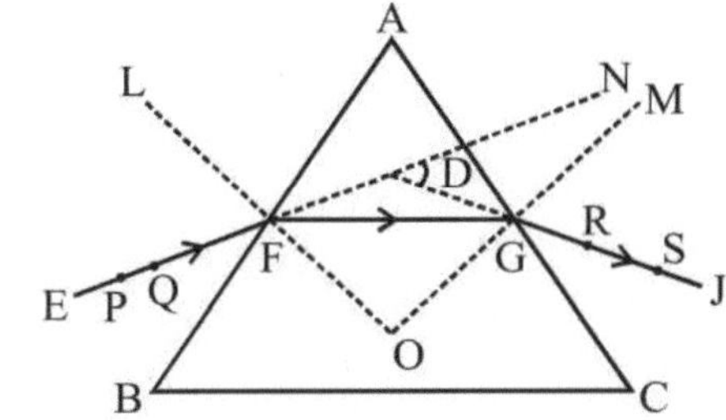

The incident ray – EF
The emergent ray – GJ
The angle of deviation – ∠D

Q.15 Draw a labelled ray diagram to illustrate the dispersion of a narrow beam of white light when it passes through a glass prism. (C.B.S.E. 2012)

Ans.

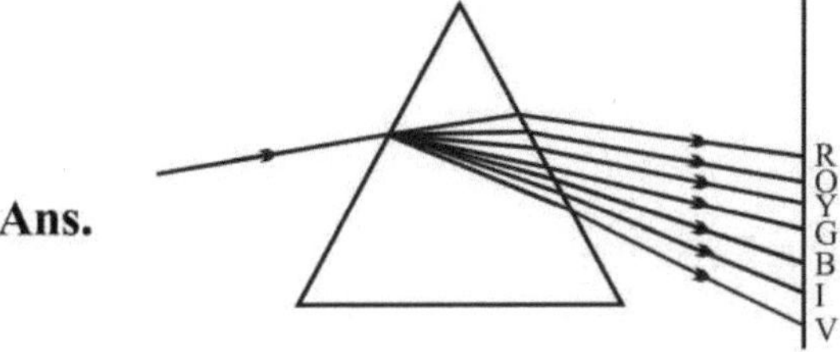

SECTION F
PREVIOUS YEAR LONG ANSWER QUESTIONS
(5 MARKS QUESTIONS)

Q.1 (a) A person can not read newspaper placed nearer than 50 cm from his eyes. Name the defect of vision he is suffering from. Show a ray diagram to illustrate this defect. List its two possible causes. Draw a ray diagram to show how this defect may be corrected using a lens of appropriate focal length.

(b) We see advertisement for eye donation on television or in newspaper. Write the importance of such advertisement. (C.B.S.E. 2013, 2015)

Sol. (a) He is suffering from hypermetropia

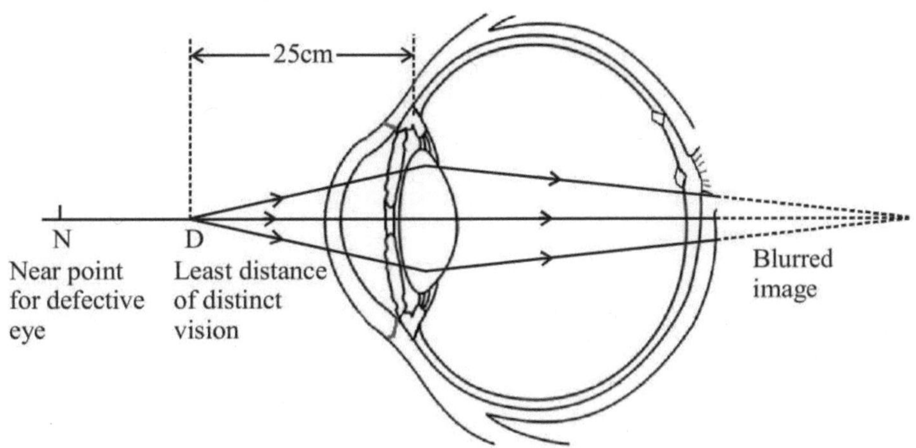

Fig. (a) Defective long sighted eye

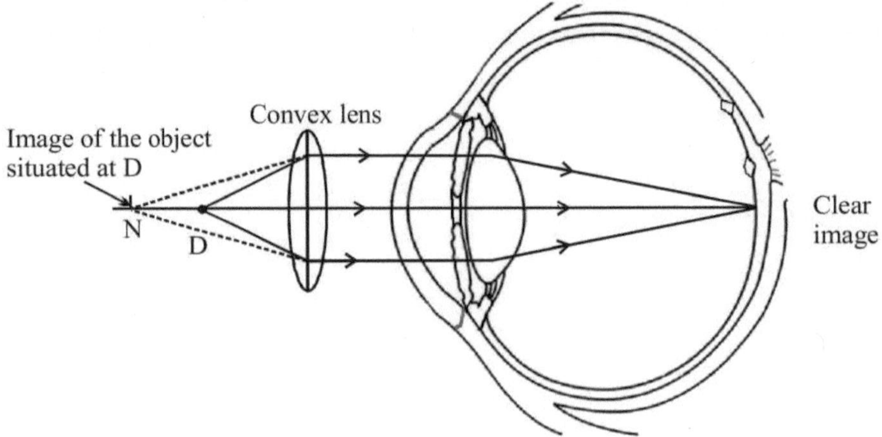

Fig. (b) Corrected long sighted eye

Causes:

1. Either the eye ball is too small or
2. The focal length of the eye lens is more

(b) Advertisement makes the common people aware about eye donation to help others. Donated eye can be used to restore vision in people who are suffering from corneal blindness. Eye donation is an act of donating one's eye after his/her death. It is an act of charity, purely for the benefit of the society and is totally voluntary.

SECTION G
PRACTICAL BASED QUESTIONS

Q.1 While performing the experiment to trace the path of a ray of light passing through a glass prism, four students marked the incident ray and the emergent ray in their diagrams in the manner shown below.

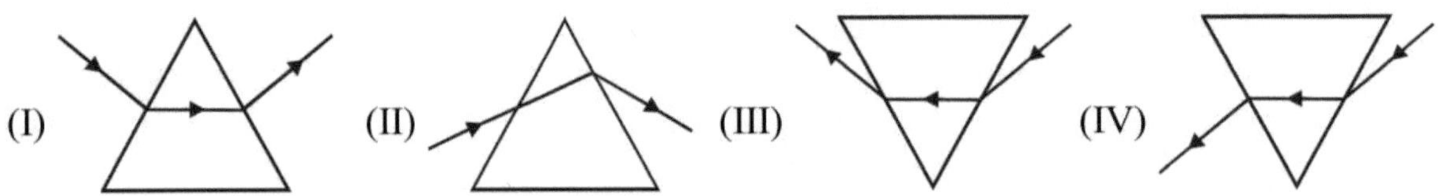

The correct path of the rays has been shown by

(A) I (B) II (C) III (D) IV

Q.2 In an experiment to trace the path of a ray of light through a glass prism for different values of angle of incidence a student would find that the emergent ray

(A) is parallel to the incident ray

(B) perpendicular to the incident ray

(C) is parallel to the reflected ray

(D) bends at an angle to the direction of incident ray

Q.3 The path of a ray of light through a glass prism is shown below :

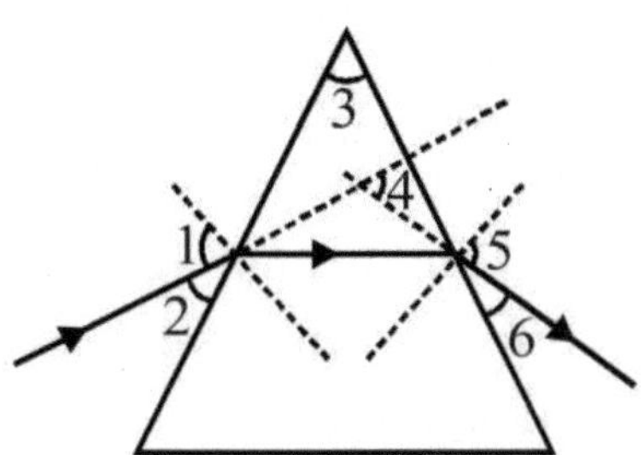

In the diagram, angle of prism, incident angle, angle of deviation and angle of emergence are represented respectively as :

(A) 1, 3, 5, 4 (B) 2, 6, 5, 3 (C) 3, 1, 4, 5 (D) 5, 4, 1, 3

Q.4 A student is observing the diagram showing the path of ray of a light passing through a glass prism. He would find that for all angles of incidence, the ray of light bends.

(A) towards the normal while entering into the prism and away from the normal while emerging out of the prism.

(B) away from the normal while entering into the prism and towards the normal while emerging out of the prism.

(C) away from the normal while entering as well as while emerging out of the prism,

(D) towards the normal while entering as well as while emerging out of the prism.

Q.5 A white light falls on a surface of a glass prism. Four students A, B, C and D recorded the sequence of colours from top to the bottom of screen. Which of the students, recorded the correct sequence ?

(A) Student A : violet, blue, green, yellow, red

(B) Student B : red, blue, green, yellow, violet

(C) Student C : red, yellow, green, blue, violet

(D) Student D : red, green, yellow, blue, violet.

Q.6 Out of red, green, blue and violet, which colour deviates the most in a glass prism ?

(A) red (B) green (C) blue (D) violet

Q.7 Out of red, green, blue and violet, which colour deviates the least in a glass prism ?

(A) red (B) green (C) blue (D) violet

Q.8 The angle between two lateral faces of a triangular glass prism is called

(A) angle of incidence (B) angle of prism

(C) angle of emergence (D) angle of refelction

SECTION H
HIGHER ORDER THINKING SKILL BASED QUESTIONS

Q.1 Seeta and Geeta are best friends and study in class X. Geeta is facing difficulty in reading the black board test from the bench in the first row in a classroom. Seeta wonders why Geeta avoids sitting in the first row. Seeta came to know that Geeta avoids milk and green vegetables. She started sharing her lunch full of green vegetables and fruits with Geeta. Geeta is now better and has started taking a 'balanced diet'.

(i) Name the eye defect Geeta is suffering from.

(ii) What values are shown by Seeta and Geeta.

Ans. (i) Hypermetropia or long sightedness

(ii) Both are good friends. Both are concerned about each other. Seeta is well aware of the importance of balanced diet. Geeta also learnt the importance of balanced diet for good health through Seeta.

Q.2 Maya and Meera are good friends and study in class X. Meera is facing difficulty in reading the black board test from the last desk. Maya came to know that Meera carries junk food in her lunch. Maya started sharing her lunch full of green vegetables and fruits. She also motivated Meera to consult a doctor and for the check up of her eyes. Meera is now better and started taking a balanced diet.

(i) Name of the eye defect Meera is suffering from.

(ii) What are two possible deformities related to her eye defect ?

(iii) What value is shown by Maya and Meera ?

Ans. (i) Myopia or short sightedness.

(ii) (a) Lens defect (increased thikness)

(b) Eyeball defect (enlarged)

(iii) concern for each other, friendship and importance of balanced diet.

Q.3 A person is able to see objects clearly only when these are lying at distance between 50 cm and 300 cm from his eye.

(i) What kind of defect of vision he is suffering from ?

(ii) What kind of lenses will be required to increase his range of vision from 25 cm to infinity ? Explain briefly.

Ans. (a) For a normal eye, the near point is at 25 cm and the far point is at infinity from the eye. The given person cannot see object clearly either closer to the eye or far away from the eye. So, he is suffering from both myopia and hypermetropia.

(b) A bi-focal lens consisting of a concave lens and convex lens of suitable focal lengths will be required to correct the defects and to increase his range of vision form 25 cm to infinity. In a bi-focal lens, upper portion is concave which corrects distant vision and lower portion is convex which corrects near vision.

Q.4 A student find the writing on the black board as blurred and unclear when sitting on the last desk in a classroom. He however, sees it clearly when sitting on the front desk at an approximate distance of 2 m from the black board.

(a) Draw ray diagrams to illustrate the formation of image of the black board writing by his eye-lens when he is seated at the (i) Last desk, (ii) front desk.

(b) Name the kind of lens that would help him to see clearly even when he is seated at the last desk. Draw a ray diagram to illustrate how this lens helps him to see clearly.

Ans. (a) (i) Formation of image of the black board writing by the eye-lens of the student sitting at the last desk is shown in figure.

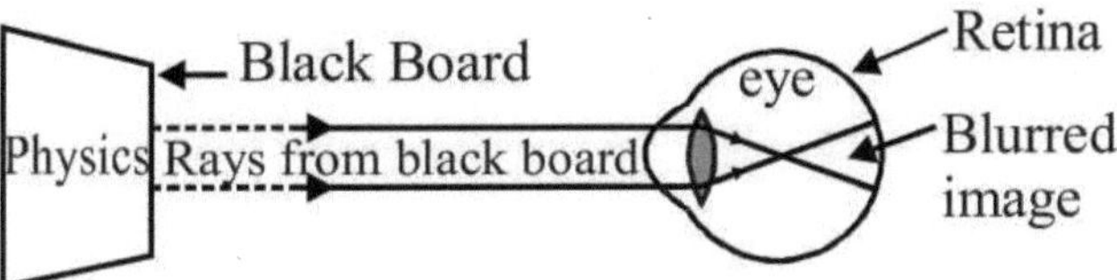

(ii) Formation of image of the black board writing by the eye-lens of the student sitting at the front-desk is shown in figure.

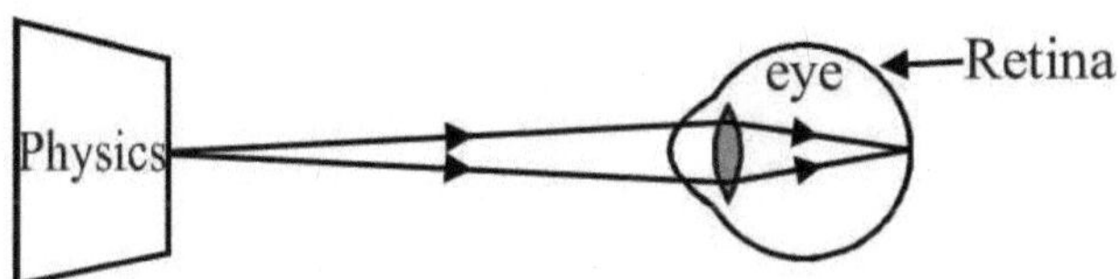

(b) Student is suffering from Myopia, so his eye defect can be corrected by using a concave lens as shown in figure.

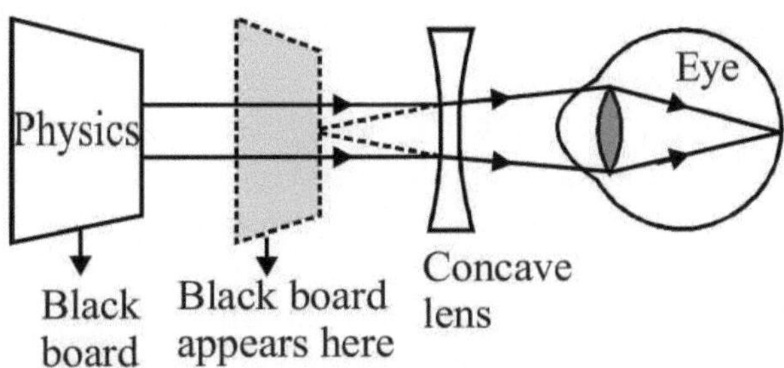

Q.5 A student finds the writing on the black board as blurred and unclear while sitting on the front desk in a classroom of a big size. He however sees it clearly while sitting on the last desk of the classroom.

(A) Draw ray diagrams to illustrate the formation of image of the black board writing by his eye-lens when he is seated at (i) the front desk, (ii) last desk.

(B) Name the defect, the eye of the student is suffering from ?

(C) Name the type of lens that would enable him to see the black board writing clearly, when seated on the front desk.

(D) Draw a ray diagram to illustrate how this lens helps him to see clearly.

Ans. (a) (i) Formation of image of black board writing by the eye-lens of the student sitting on the fornt desk is shown in figure.

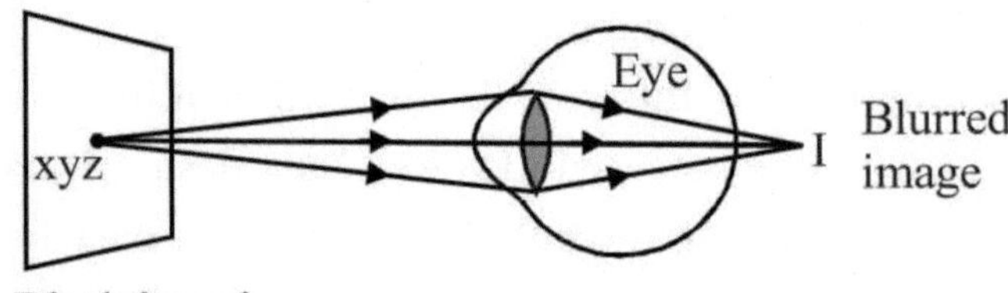

(ii) Formation of the image of the black board writing by the eye-lens of the student sitting on the last desk in shown in figure.

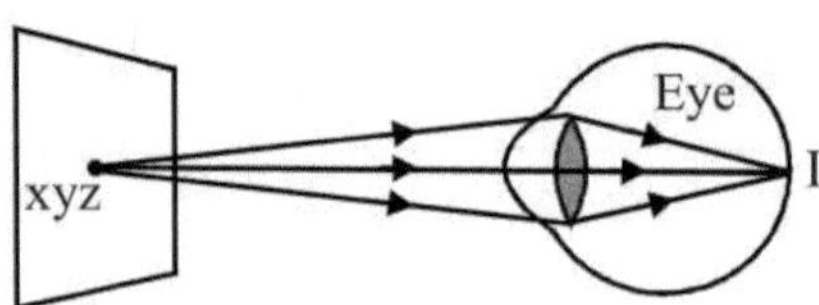

(B) Student's eye suffers from hypermetropia or long sightedness as he is able to see far off object clearly but unable to see near objects clearly.

(C) Convex lens of suitable focal length.

(D)

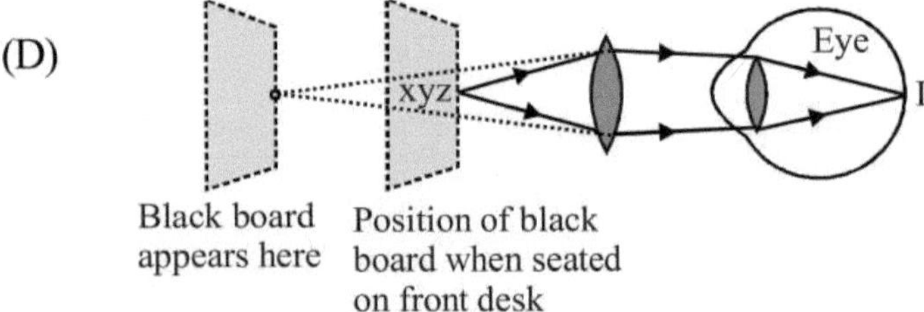

Q.6 A 14-years old student is not able to see clearly to question written on a black board placed at a distance of 5 m from him.

(a) Name the defect of vision he is suffering from.

(b) Name the type of lens used to correct this defect.

(c) State two causes of this defect.

Ans. (a) Student is suffering from Myopia or short-sightedness

(b) Concave lens of suitable focal length is used to correct this defect.

(c) It is due to (i) elongation of the eye ball, (ii) excessive curvature of the cornea.

Q.7 A beam of white light falling on a glass prism gets split up into seven colours. A student makes the following statements about the spectrum observed on the screen.

(a) The colours at position marked 3 and 5 are similar to the colour of the sky and the core of hard boiled egg respectively. Is the statement made by the student correct or incorrect? Justify

(b) Which two position correspond closely to the colour of (i) a solution of potassium permanganate? (ii) Danger or stop signal lights ?

Ans. (a) Starting form top, the colours at positions 3 and 5 are yellow and blue respectively. On the other hand, student has identified them as blue (i.e. colour of sky) and yellow (colour of the core of a hard boiled egg) respectively. Hence, the statement is incorrect.

(b) (i) Position 7 is the position of violet colour, which corresponds to the colour of a solution of potassium permanganate.

(ii) Position 1 is the position of red colour which corresponds to the colour of the danger or stop signal lights.

CONCEPT APPLICATION LEVEL - III

SECTION-A

- **Fill in the blanks**

Q.1 Telescope is used for seeing .... object at .... distance.

Q.2 The phenomenon of looming is seen in .... season.

Q.3 For correcting astigmatism we use a .... lens.

Q.4 In dispersion, different coloured lights are ....

SECTION-B

- **Multiple choice question with one correct answers**

Q.1 Twinkling of stars is visible when the stars are .
(A) near the horizon (B) overhead (C) any where (D) no definite situation.

Q.2 For an eye lens, its focal length is :
(A) Fixed (B) reducible
(C) increasable (D) both reducible & increasable.

Q.3 Eye defect at old age is called :
(A) myopia (B) hypermetropia (C) presbyopia (D) astigmatism

Q.4 Angle of deviation in a prism is the angle between .
(A) reflected and refracted rays. (B) incident of reflected rays.
(C) incident & transmitted rays (D) reflected and transmitted rays.

Q.5 According to tyndall effect, the colour or wave length of the scattered light depends upon the size of the scattering particle.
(A) False (B) Only if particles are stationary
(C) True (D) Only if the light undergoes refraction.

Q.6 To increase the angular magnification of a simple microscope, one should increase.
(A) the focal length of the lens (B) the power of the lens.
(C) the aperture of the lens (D) the object size.

Q.7 Four students studied refraction of light through a glass prism. They traced the ray of light and measured the angle of incidence $\angle i$ and angle of deviation $\angle D$ as shown in figure A, B, C and D. Which one is the correct representation.

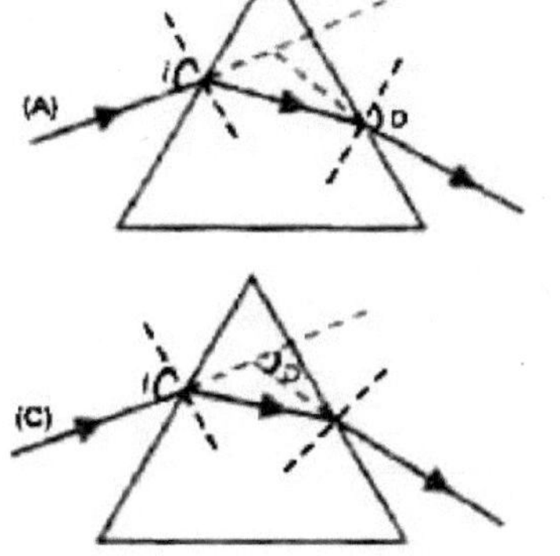

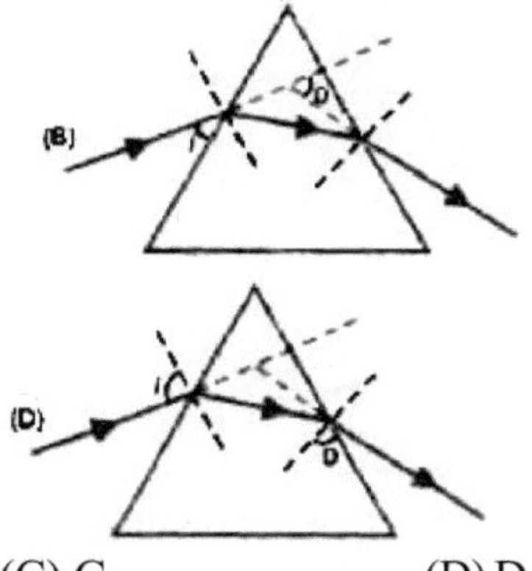

(A) A (B) B (C) C (D) D

Q.8 A student wants to have a third colour from the top corresponds to the colour of the sky after dispersion of white light through a glass prism. He placed prism ABC with BC as base as shown in figure P, Q, R and S. Which position of the prism is correct?

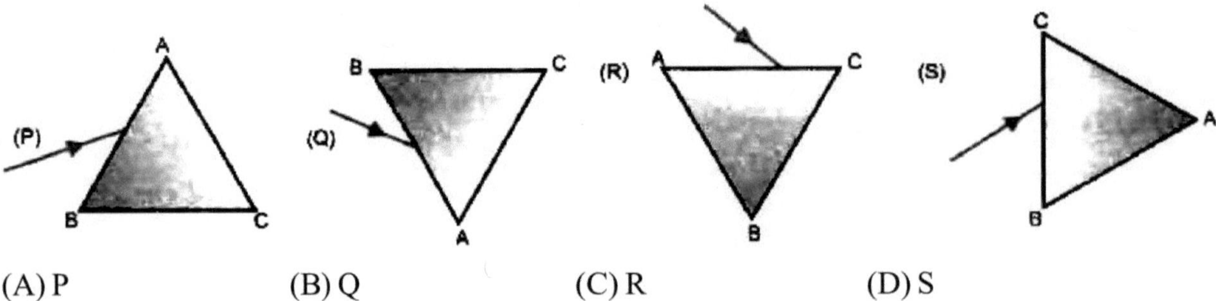

(A) P (B) Q (C) R (D) S

Q.9 Four students used two identical prism ABC (base BC) and A' B' C' (base B' C') so that a narrow beam of white light incident on prism ABC emerges out of the prism A'B'C as white light. They arranged the prisms as shown in figure P, Q, R and S. Which of the arrangements is correct?

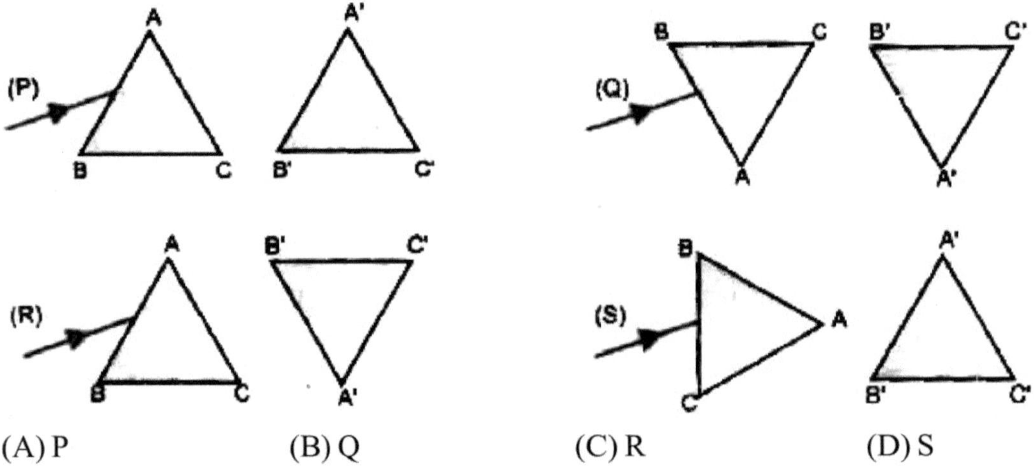

(A) P (B) Q (C) R (D) S

Q.10 Four students draw a ray diagram showing the dispersion through a glass prism. When a narrow beam of white light incident on the glass prism as shown in figure A, B, C and D. Which of the following is correct ray diagram?

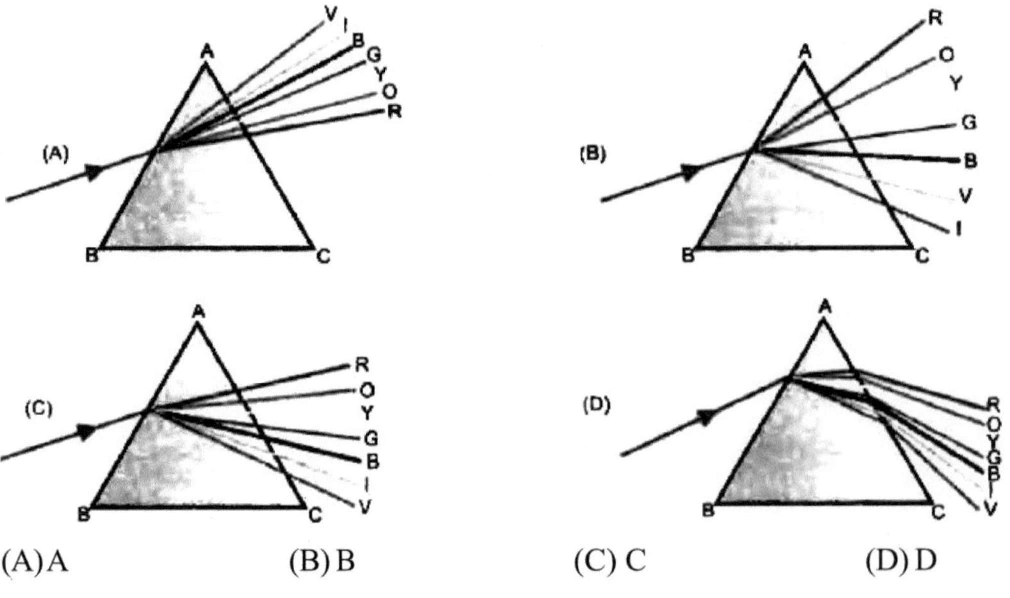

(A) A (B) B (C) C (D) D

Q.11 A student is studying the dispersion of white light through a glass prism. Which of the following positions of the prism is correct to have top colour corresponds to the colour of the solution of potassium permanganate in the spectrum obtained on the screen?

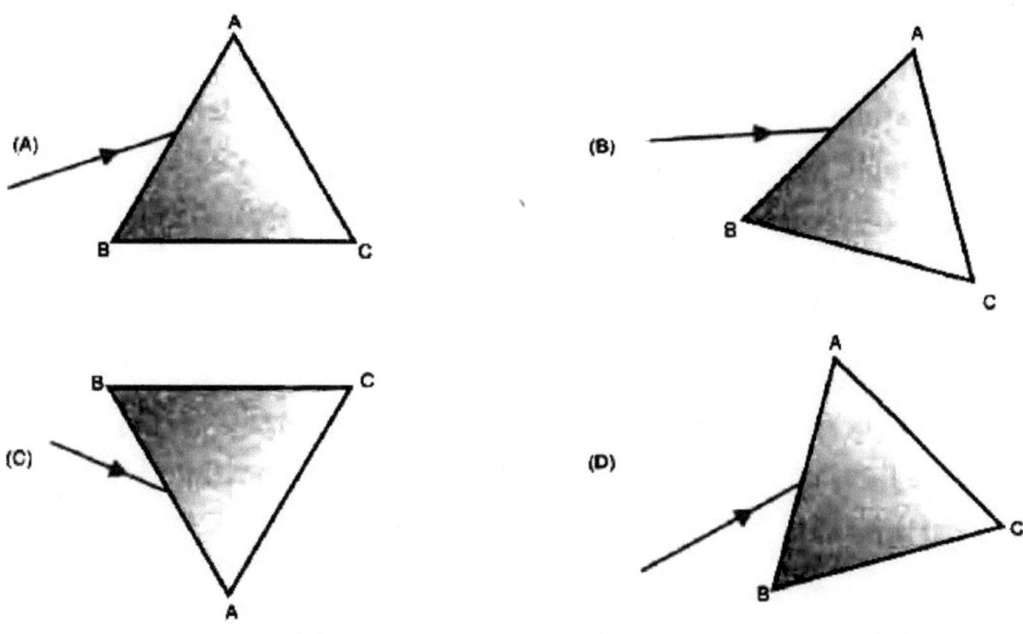

(A) A (B) B (C) C (D) D

Q.12 Near point of an eye suffering from long – sightedness is
(A) 25 cm (B) less than 25 cm
(C) greater than 25 cm (D) at infinity.

Q.13 A simple microscope consists of
(A) convex lens of large focal length (B) convex lens of small focal length
(C) concave lens of large focal length (D) concave lens of small focal length.

Q.14 Rainbow is formed due to.
(A) Reflection and dispersion of light through a water droplet
(B) refraction, reflection and dispersion of light through a water droplet
(C) only dispersion of light
(D) only refraction of light

Q.15 When we enter a dim – lit room from a bright light, we are not able to see the objects in the dim – light room for some time. This is because
(A) the iris contracts the pupil of an eye to allow less light to enter the eye in a dim – lit room
(B) the iris takes time to expand the pupil of an eye to allow more light to enter the eye in a dim – lit room
(C) eye lens is unable to make images in a dim – lit room
(D) optic nerve does not carry signals to the brain in a dim – lit room.

Q.16 The eye lens is a crystalline double convex lens made of transparent and flexible tissues. The focal length of the eye lens can be increased or decreased by.
(A) Iris (B) Retina (C) ciliary muscle (D) optic nerves

Q.17 The image distance in case of a glass lens changes, when the distance of an object from the lens increases. How ever, the image distance in the eye remains the same even when the distance of an object from the eye increases. This is because.
(A) focal length of glass lens is fixed and the focal length of eye lens changes
(B) glass lens follow lens formula but eye lens does not follow lens formula
(C) glass lens can form the image of an object placed any where but eye lens can form the image to those objects which are very close to be eye
(D) None of these

Q.18 An old man hardly sees the objects. This is because he is suffering from
(A) myopia (B) hypermetropia (C) cataract (D) astigmatism

Q.19 When a ray of light passes through a glass prism, it suffers
(A) one refraction (B) two refraction (C) three refraction (D) two reflection

Q.20 A student sitting on the last bench can read the letters written on the black board but is not able to read the letters written in his test book. Which of the following statement is correct?
(A) The near point of his eyes has receded away
(B) The near point of his eyes has come closer to him
(C) The far point of his eyes has receded away
(D) The far point of his eyes has come closer to him

Q.21 Water in deep sea is bluish in colour due to
(A) absorption of light by the sea (B) reflection of sky in water
(C) scattering of light (D) presence of plants in the sea

Q.22 The near point of a hypermetropic person is 50 cm. The focal length of a convex lens used in his spectacles should be
(A) 25 cm (B) 30 cm (C) 40 m (D) 50 cm

Q.23 The magnification of a magnifying lens of focal length 5 cm is
(A) 2 (B) 1 (C) 5 (D) 3

Q.24 For a normal eye, the near point is 25 cm from the eye lens. The distance between eye lens and retina of the eye is 2.5 cm. What is the power of the eye lens.
(A) 4 D (B) 40 D (C) 44 D (D) – 44 D

Q.25 For a normal eye, the far point is at infinity from the eye lens. The image is formed at the retina which is 2.5 cm away from the eye lens. What is the power of the eye lens?
(A) 4 D (B) 40 D (C) – 40 D (D) 44 D

Q.26 A person suffering from far – sightedness wears a spectacles having a convex lens of focal length 50 cm. What is the distance of the near point of his eye?
(A) 25 cm (B) 30 cm (C) 45 cm (D) 50 cm

Q.27 The far point of a myopic person is 140 cm in front of the eye. The focal length of the lens required to enable him to see distant objects clearly is

(A) 70 cm (B) 100 cm (C) – 140 cm (D) 140 cm

Q.28 A person of normal vision responds to the brightness of light but does not respond to the colours of light. We conclude that the retina of the eye of the person contain

(A) equal number of rod shaped and cone shaped cells

(B) more rod shaped cells but no cone shaped cells

(C) more cone shaped cells but no rod shaped cells

(D) no rod shaped cells and no cone shaped cells.

Q.29 Two boys A and B are standing at one place. After the rainfall, boy A says that he is seeing a beautiful rainbow but boy B reports that he is not observing any rainbow

(A) The back of both the boys (B) back of boy A but in front of boy B

(C) back of boy B but in front of boy A (D) Front of both the boys.

Q.30 When white light passes through a glass prism, seven colours namely red, orange, yellow, green, blue, indigo and violet are obtained on the white screen placed in front of the prism. Which of the colours correspond closely to the colour of a solution of potassium permanganate?

(A) red (B) orange (C) indigo (D) violet

SECTION-C

- **Multiple choice question with one or more than one correct answers**

Q.1 When we see an object, the image formed on the retina is :

(A) real (B) virtual (C) erect (D) inverted

Q.2 A ray of light travelling from medium 1 into medium 2. If medium 1 is optically denser than medium 2, then which of the following statements is/are correct-

(A) Speed of light is higher in medium 1 than medium 2

(B) Absolute refractive index of medium 1 is higher than medium 2

(C) A ray of light bends towards the normal when it travels from medium 1 into medium 2

(D) A ray of light bends towards the normal when it travels from medium 2 into medium 1

Q.3 Which of the following statements about Bi-focal lens is/are correct ?

(A) The upper portion consists of a convex lens.

(B) The lower part is a convex lens.

(C) The upper part is a concave lens

(D) The lower part is a concave lens

Q.4 Rainbow is produced when sunlight falls on drops of rain. Which of the physical phenomena is/are responsible for this ?

(A) Refraction (B) Reflection

(C) Total internal reflection (D) Dispersion

SECTION-D

- **Assertion & Reason**

  Instructions: In the following questions a Assertion (A) is given followed by a Reason (R). Mark your responses from the following options.

  (A) Both Assertion and Reason are true and Reason is the correct explanation of 'Assertion'
  (B) Both Assertion and Reason are true and Reason is not the correct explanation of 'Assertion'
  (C) Assertion is true but Reason is false
  (D) Assertion is false but Reason is true

Q.1 **Assertion:** Sky appear blue.

Reason: The intensity of scattered light, $I \alpha \frac{1}{\lambda^4}$

Q.2 **Assertion:** The angle of minimum deviation produced by a prism is different for different wavelengths.
Reason: $\delta = A(\mu - 1)$, where δ is the deviation produced.

Q.3 **Assertion:** A rainbow is formed in the sky on a rainy day.
Reason: Rainbow is formed due to the dispersion of sun rays, when they fall on the suspended tiny droplets of water.

Q.4 **Assertion:** The blue colour is used as danger signal
Reason: Blue colour is scattered through a small amount due to its longer wavelength than all the colour present in visible region.

SECTION-E

- **Comprehension**

  The angular size of an object is the angle that it subtends at the eye of the viewer. For small angles, the angular size in radians is $\theta = h_o/d_o$. Where h_o is the height of the object and d_o is the object distance. A spectator, seated in the left field stands, is watching a 1.9 m tall baseball player who is 75 m away. On a TV screen, located 3.0 m from a person watching the game at home, the same player has a 0.12 m image.

Q.1 The angular size of the player as seen by the spectator watching the game live.

(A) $\frac{1.9}{75} rad$ (B) $\frac{75}{1.9} rad$ (C) $\frac{0.12}{3} rad$ (D) None of these

Q.2 The angular size of the player as seen by the TV viewer.

(A) $\frac{1.9}{75} rad$ (B) $\frac{0.12}{3} rad$ (C) $\frac{75}{1.9} rad$ (D) None of these

Q.3 To whom does the player appear to be larger?
(A) The spectator watching the game live.
(B) The TV viewer
(C) The size of the player appears same to both the observer
(D) None of these

SECTION-F

- **Match the following (one to one)**

  Column-I and **column-II** contains **four** entries each. Entries of column-I are to be matched with some entries of column-II. Only One entries of column-I may have the matching with the same entries of column-II and one entry of column-II Only one matching with entries of column-I

Q.1

Column I	Column II
(A) Rayleigh scattering	(P) $i + e = A + \delta$
(B) Prism Equation	(Q) $\mu = 1/\sin c$
(C) Magnifying power	(R) $I \alpha \frac{1}{\lambda^4}$
(D) Total internal reflection	(S) $m = \left(1 + \frac{D}{f}\right)$

SECTION-G

- **Match the following (one to many)**

  Column-I and **column-II** contains **four** entries each. Entries of column-I are to be matched with some entries of column-II. One or more than one entries of column-I may have the matching with the same entries of column-II and one entry of column-II may have one or more than one matching with entries of column-I

Q.1

Column I	Column II
(A) Twinkling of stars	(P) Refraction
(B) Rainbow	(Q) Total internal reflection
(C) Tyndall effect	(R) Dispersion
(D) Advance sunrise and delayed sunset	(S) Scattering of light

SECTION-H
PREVIOUS YEAR NSO QUESTIONS

Q.1 Two equilateral prisms are arrangned as shown in figure such that a ray of white light is incident at point X. The ray of light which emerges out of the prism ___________. **[NSO 2010]**

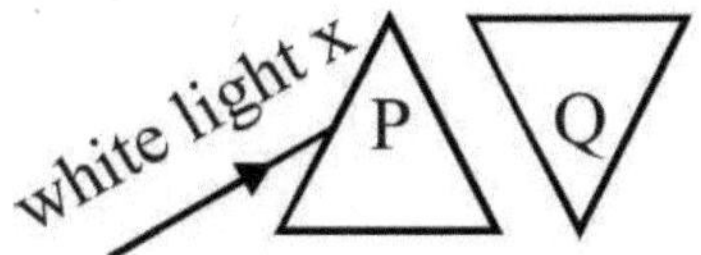

(A) Will show all the colours of spectrum (B) Will be the white light
(C) Will be orange in colour (D) Will be dull white in colour

Q.2 A long sighted person cannot see objects clearly at a distance less than 40 cm from his eyes. The power of the lens needed by him to read a paper at 25 cm is ___________ **[NSO 2010]**
(A) – 2.5 D (B) + 2.5 D (C) –6.25 D (D) +1.5D

Q.3 Read the given statements and mark the correct option. **[NSO 2010]**

Statement 1 : Fine particles in atmosphere scatter the light of shorter wavelength more.

Statement 2 : Sky appears blue.

(A) Both statement 1 and 2 are true and statement 2 is the correct explanation of statement 1.

(B) Both statement 1 and 2 are true but statement 2 is not correct explanation of statement 1.

(C) Statement 1 is true but statement 2 is false

(D) Statement 1 is false but statement 2 is true.

Q.4 An optician while testing the eyes finds the vision of a patient to be 6/12. By this he means that ______.

(A) The person can read the letters of 6 inches from a distance of 12 m. **[NSO 2011]**

(B) The person can read the letters of 12 inches from 6 m.

(C) The person can read the letters from 6 m which the normal eye can read from 12 m.

(D) The focal length of eye lens has become half that of the normal eye.

Q.5 Light is incident normally on face AB of a prism a shown in the figure. A liquid of refractive index n is placed on face AC of the prism. The prism is made of glass of refractive index 3/2. The limits of n for which total internal reflection takes placed on face AC is **[NSO 2016]**

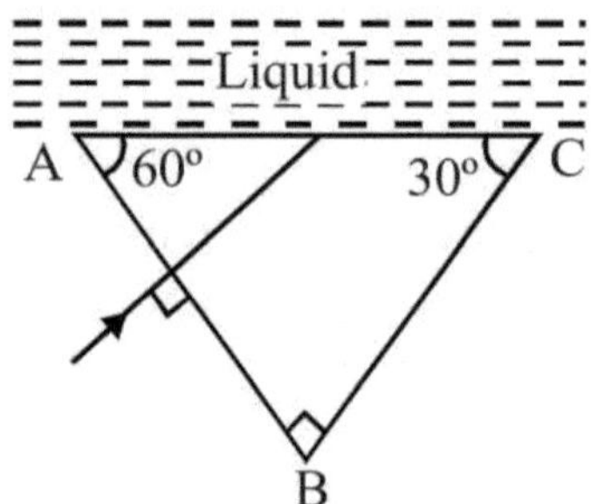

(A) $n > \frac{3\sqrt{3}}{2}$ (B) $n > \sqrt{3}$ (C) $n < \frac{3\sqrt{3}}{4}$ (D) $n < \frac{3\sqrt{3}}{8}$

Q.6 Read the given statement and select the correct option. **[NSO 2016]**

Statement 1 : A total reflection prism is used to erect the inverted image without deviation.

Statement 2 : Rays of light incident parallel to the base of prism emerge out as parallel rays.

(A) Both statements 1 and 2 are true and statement 2 is the correct explanation of statement 1.

(B) Both statements 1 and 2 are true but statement 2 is not the correct explanation of statement 1

(C) Statement1 is true and statement 2 is false

(D) Both statement 1 and 2 are false

SECTION-I
PREVIOUS YEAR NTSE QUESTIONS

Q.1 On passing white light through a glass prism. Which colour ray will deviate maximum towards its base ?

(Raj./ NTSE Stage-I/2005)

(A) Red (B) Yellow (C) Blue (D) Violet

Q.2 The image of an object form at the distance of distinct vision from the lens of a simple microscope of focal length 2.5 cm. Its magnifying power is : **(Raj./ NTSE Stage-I/2006)**
(A) 2.5 (B) 5 (C) 10 (D) 11

Q.3 White colour of the cloud is due to : **(Delhi/ NTSE Stage-I/2014)**
(A) reflection of seven colors of light (B) refraction of seven colors of light
(C) scattering of seven colors of light (D) absorption of seven colors of light

Q.4 As the thickness of the atmosphere increases colour of scattered light is found in the .... order. **(MAHARASHTRA/ NTSE Stage-I/2014)**
(A) blue, violet, yellow, red (B) violet, blue, yellow, red
(C) red, yellow, blue, violet (D) violet, blue, red, yellow

Q.5 The distance between the objective lens and the eye-piece of an astronomical telescope will be : **(Raj./ NTSE Stage-I/2014)**
(A) $\frac{f_0}{f_e}$ (B) $\frac{f_e}{f_0}$ (C) $f_0 + f_e$ (D) $f_0 - f_e$

Q.6 The twinkiling of stars is due to atmospheric : **(M.P/ NTSE Stage-I/2014)**
(A) Reflection of light (B) Dispersion of light (C) Interference of light (D) Refracton of light

Q.7 The blue colour of sky is due to : **(M.P/ NTSE Stage-I/2014)**
(A) Reflection of light (B) Dispersion of light (C) Diffraction of light (D) Scattering of light

Q.8 Convex lens is not used in : **(MAHARASHTRA/ NTSE Stage-I/2014)**
(A) simple microscope (B) spectacles
(C) telescope (D) flood lights

Q.9 The far point of a myopic person is 75 cm in front of the eye. The nature and power of the lens rquired to correct the problem, will be : **(Raj./ NTSE Stage-I/2015)**
(A) convex lens, – 1.33 D (B) concave lens, – 1.33 D
(C) concave lens, + 1.33 D (D) convex lens, + 1.33 D.

Q.10 When astronauts fly at higher altitude, the sky appears dark because : **(Maharashtra/ NTSE Stage-I/2015)**
(A) Scattering of light does not place (B) Scattering of light takes place
(C) Refraction of light takes place (D) Dispersion of light takes place.

Q.11 Which one of the following phenomena is an example of scattering of light? **(NTSE 2016 Stage 1)**
(A) Bending of rod at interface of air and water
(B) Twinkling of stars
(C) Tyndall effect
(D) Mirage in desert during summer

ANSWERS

KNOWLEDGE BASED QUESTIONS

1.	A	2.	B	3.	B	4.	B	5.	A	6.	B	7.	B
8.	D	9.	C	10.	C								

TRY YOURSELF

1. Size of pupil is inversely proportional to the intensity of the light entering our eyes.
   i.e. with increase in intensity of light, pupil size decreases and with decrease in light intersity the size of pupil increases
2. In a person, with correct eye vision, the image of an object is well focussed on the retina of his eye.
3. Focal length of lens is positive therefore, he is suffering from hypermetropia.
   Power of lens $= \dfrac{100}{f(cm)}$ $\therefore P = \dfrac{100}{50} = +2.0$ D
4. Concave lens
5. Different colours have different wavelengths. So the constituents of white light have a different angle of refraction at prism surface.
6. Violet colour light bends the most and red the least when white light passes through a prism.
7. $\delta_m = 8°28'$ 8. $i = 48.6°$
9. After the rainfall we can see the rainbow while facing away from the sun.
10. $\mu = 2$ 11. $C_d = 24°24'$

CONCEPT APPLICATION LEVEL - II

SECTION G

Q.1	C	Q.2	D	Q.3	C	Q.4	A	Q.5	C	Q.6	D	Q.7	A
Q.8	B												

CONCEPT APPLICATION LEVEL - III

SECTION-A

Q.1 Large, infinite Q.2 Winter Q.3 Cylindrical Q.4 Separated

SECTION-B

Q.1	A	Q.2	D	Q.3	C	Q.4	C	Q.5	C	Q.6	B	Q.7	C
Q.8	B	Q.9	C	Q.10	D	Q.11	C	Q.12	C	Q.13	B	Q.14	B
Q.15	B	Q.16	C	Q.17	A	Q.18	C	Q.19	B	Q.20	A	Q.21	C
Q.22	D	Q.23	C	Q.24	C	Q.25	B	Q.26	D	Q.27	C	Q.28	B
Q.29	B	Q.30	D										

SECTION-C

Q.1 A,D Q.2 B,D Q.3 B,C Q.4 A,C,D

SECTION-D

Q.1 A Q.2 A Q.3 A Q.4 D

SECTION-E

Q.1 A Q.2 B Q.3 B

SECTION-F

Q.1 (A)-(R), (B)-(P), (C)- (S), (D)-(Q)

SECTION-G

Q.1 (A)-(P), (B)-(P,Q,R), (C)-(S), (D)-(P)

SECTION-H

Q.1 B Q.2 D Q.3 B Q.4 C Q.5 C Q.6 A

SECTION-I

Q.1 D Q.2 D Q.3 C Q.4 C Q.5 C Q.6 D Q.7 D
Q.8 D Q.9 B Q.10 A Q.11 C

Printed by Libri Plureos GmbH in Hamburg,
Germany